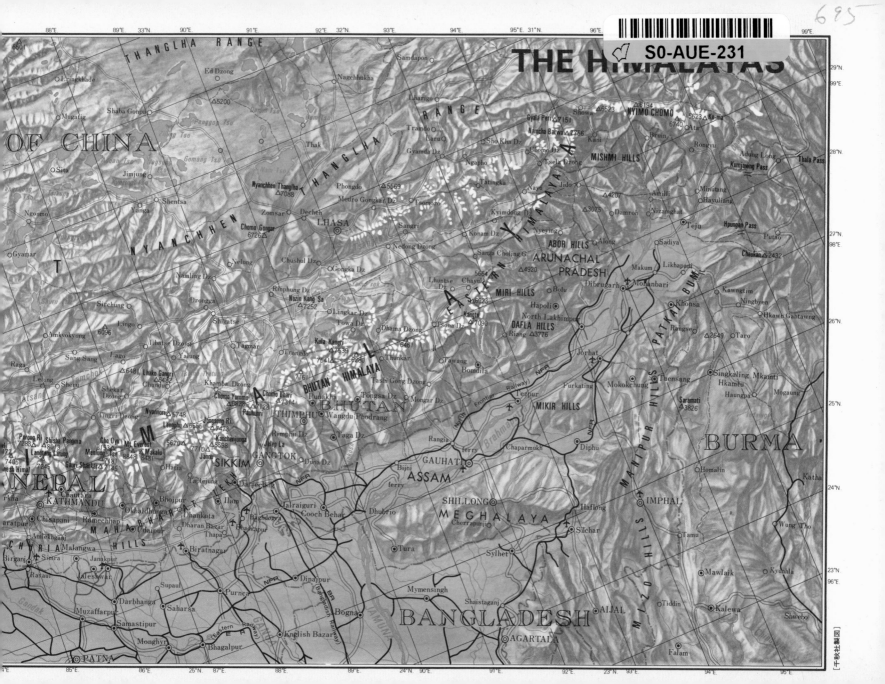

Trekking in

© Tomoya Iozawa 1980.
Published by **Yama-Kei Publishers Co., Ltd.**
1-1-33, Shiba-Daimon, Minato-ku, Tokyo, Japan.

Originally published in Japanese, in 1976,
under the title **HIMARAYA TOREKKINGU.**

Overseas sale and distribution right
reserved by **FROEBEL-KAN CO., LTD.**
3-1 Kanda Ogawamachi, Chiyoda-ku,
Tokyo, Japan. CABLE: FROEBELKAN TOKYO
TELEX: J24907 FROEBEL

Printed in Singapore

The Himalayas

Tomoya IOZAWA

Translators:
Michiko U. KORNHAUSER
David H. KORNHAUSER

Yama-Kei Publishers Co., Ltd.
Tokyo.

4

CONTENTS

1 THE HIMALAYAS AND THE SPORT OF TREKKING: BASIC INFORMATION   25

2 THE HIMALAYAS OF NEPAL   49

3 THE WESTERN HIMALAYAS 155

WHILE IN THE HIMALAYAS

Keep the mountains clean.
Consider others.
Help protect the Wild.
Avoid reckless mountaineering.

FOREWORD

Denjiro Hasegawa, a photographer, was perhaps the first one from Japan to have made long treks in the Himalayas; Garhwal to Kailash in Tibet and another one to Nanga Parbat. That was fifty years ago. Japan's first Himalayan Expedition was in 1936 to Nanda Kot in Garhwal organised by the mountaineering Club of Rikkyo University in Tokyo. However, after the Second World War, and particularly in the last two decades, Japan has become a leading nation in sending mountaineers to the Himalayas. During this period the Japanese have also trekked in the Himalayas in large numbers, and among them have been not only mountaineers and young people looking for adventure but also older persons getting away from work in search of relaxation and recreation, some seeking the Sutras of Buddhism, and many scholars and field workers. Mr. Tomoya Iozawa is probably the only one who has trekked through all parts of this beautiful range of mountains, made a full study of the area, and has finally written a book on it.

At the foothills of this Mighty Range how many cultures were born and how many flourished and how many disappeared? What magic is conjured in the minds of men merely at the mention of the word Himalayas?

There are books which deal with limited areas of the Himalayas but not one directed towards taking up the whole range which for 3,500 kilometers has scenic peaks and vistas of unparalleled beauty. Mr. Iozawa has through this book fulfilled this requirement in a most praiseworthy manner. Here the reader will find at one place a wealth of up-to-date detailed information obtained by the author by his own field studies through four detailed visits from 1970 to 1975. All descriptions are supported by excellent maps and sketches.

The book was first published in Japanese. By bringing it out in English, the publishers have brought it within reach of a much wider circle of readers. Though not a book for scholars, every reader will find in it useful, detailed and interesting facts about people and places in this wide area, and to a new visitor it offers reliable information, and for a visit, a wide choice in and around the whole of the Majestic Himalayas.

INDIAN MOUNTAINEERING FOUNDATION President

H. C. SARIN   20 Jan.1980.   NEW DELHI

∞ LEGEND

In transcribing the local names used in this volume I have attempted to follow the principle of spelling these as I heard them, whether the original language was Tibetan, Hindi, or Nepali. For the spelling of Romanized names, the official Indian Government Survey maps were consulted, along with other publications of the Indian and Nepal Governments. When these sources failed, I was sometimes forced to rely on intuition, or as these words sounded to me. As an example of the former, in a Kashmiri pamphlet the name **Pahalgam** is given, but because the official Indian Government map records this as **Pahlgam**, I chose the latter. Likewise, with **Bhairhwa** (Indian), rather than **Bhairawa** (Nepali). This may cause some confusion, but since Romanization is not always adequate, in making these interpretations, the readers' indulgence is respectfully requested.

The symbols used should offer no problem to the reader as these are commonly used in maps and atlases, regardless of culture.

The reader may share the writer's frustration over the heights of famous mountains of the Himalayas, which differ widely according to source. The figures used in TREKKING IN THE HIMALAYAS are, for the most part, taken from G.O. Dyhrenfurth, "Mountains above 7,300", BERG DER WELTE, XVII, Band 1968/69, or from maps and documents of the Survey of India and the government of Nepal.

The various prices, charges and other cash values mentioned herein, unless specifically noted otherwise, reflect the situation at the time of the most recent investigation. The reader should personally examine all subsequent commodity price fluctuations, especially those since the autumn of 1978 when there were sudden increases in the vicinity of Everest. U.S. dollar values dropped at that time to a new low of $1 to 5.00 Nepalese Rupees.

SMALL SCALE MAPS

—·—·—	Boundary, international
(contour symbol)	Contour intervals, 1000m
	Broken line shows 500m contour line
———	Railway, broad gauge
———	Railway, narrow gauge
══	Main motorable road
=	Motorable road
--------	Trail
══×══	Bridge
---×---	Pass
✈	Airport
✝	STOL field
(hatched symbol)	Large city
◎	City
⊙	Small city and Town
○	Settlement, Village
△	Mountain, Peak
•	Spot

LARGE SCALE MAPS AND ILLUSTRATIONS

═══	Motorable road
------	Trail
--×--	Pass
■	House and hut
↖ ↗	Bamboo trees (Bansu)
🌲 🌲	Coniferous trees
♀ ♀	Broad-leaved trees
⌒⌒	Scrub
⁞ⁱ ⁞ⁱ	Grass fields
(symbol)	Blocks and Boulders
(symbol)	Talus
V V	Cultivated land
⊥ ⊥	Paddy fields
⚲	Pipal trees
⚇	Banana trees
⬦	Souvenir shop
▬	Restaurant, Bar, Tea house
■	Grocery, Cereals, Vegetables
⬜	Clothes shop, Shoe store
⊞	General store, Kitchen ware shop
⊠	Work shop, (Tailor, Dressmaker Metal worker)
☐	Others

↑Winter view of **Mt. Everest** (left), and of **Nuptse**'s left shoulder (right), from **Kala Pattar** (5,630 meters).

Polygon-shaped ground, manteled with vegetation, at the edge of the **Kala Pattar** Plateau.

The essence of travel, I think, is when not only the traveller benefits, but when his very presence brings benefit, in turn, to the people of the lands being visited. It is with this thought in mind that the reader is invited to absorb as much information as possible about the fundamental character of the Himalayas and its people.

The southern slope of **Kangtega** (6,779 meters).

Sunset at **Kwangde** (6,187 meters), viewed from **Thyangboche**

Urkingmang (6,151 meters), from **Langsisa Kharuka.**

Himalayan snow pleats of **Thamserku** (6,608 meters).

Reflection of the setting sun on **Ama Dablam** (6,856 meters).

The western wall of **Annapurna**, main peak (8,091 meters).

The **Rupse Chhahara Falls** in the valley of **Kali Gandaki**.

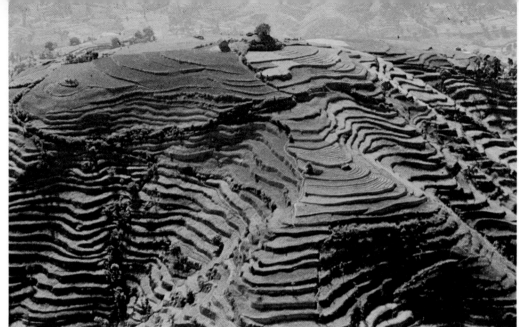

↑ Terrace cultivation in the **Mahabharat Range**.   ↓ **Koda** (millet) harvest, **Trisuli Valley**.

Plowing with a brace of oxen in the lower Kali Gandaki

Zow, a cross between the yak and cow.

Bans (Bamboo), **Kusma.**

Rhinoceros at the foot of the Himalayas

Donkey caravan approaching a rest place under a **Banyan** (pipal) **tree.**

Issoria Lathonia issaea Doubleday.

Himalayan trumpet gentian

Nettles, which cause skin-irritation

Cluster of **edelweiss**, Langtang Valley.

↑**Page 15** Cultivated land in the **Rapti** flood plain at the southern foot of the Himalayas.

P

Q

R

S

T

U

V

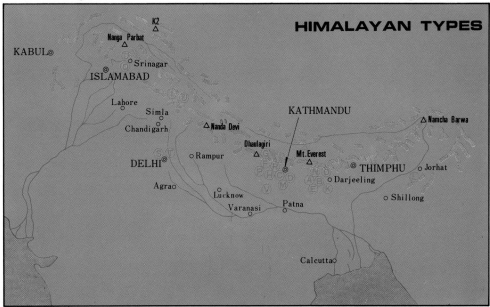

HIMALAYAN TYPES

Hipped roof house in the lower **Kali Gandaki**

Bi-colored walls and roofs made from schist, in the village of **Lumile.**

Hipped roof of thatch, with rounded corners.

House with thatched roof and bamboo walls.

Cluster of tea houses in **Kawan Dobhan.**

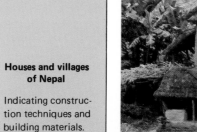

Houses and villages of Nepal

Indicating construction techniques and building materials.

Hipped roof of thatch. **Manigaon, Trisuli Gandaki**

Shingled-roof house of **Khangema.**

Thatched-roof house, in the lower **Kali Gandaki.**

Flat-roofed, stone houses in the village of **Ghasa**, middle **Kali Gandaki.**

Japanese trekking party, **Lobujye.**

Trekking by pony in the **Nainital** area.

Path, cleverly hewn out of loose areas.

Trail through the **Langtang Trough.**

AN INVITATION TO THE HIMALAYAS

We begin by making friends of the children.

The Charm of the Himalayas

Travelling in the Himalayas calls for strict reliance on the strength of one's legs, on **trekking** in the most literal sense of the term, the means by which the traveller advances over fields and into mountain wastes, along paths that have been traversed for centuries on end.

Rising above the subtropical settlements with their papaya and bananas, one sees banks of carefully terraced and tended plots which appear to reach upward into the sky. Yet higher still is a vast undergrowth of rhododendron mingled with forests of pine — the whole scene cloaked in a steaming mass of clouds and mist. And at the very top, reaching to 8,000 meters, are the stupendous mountain ridges, whose slate gray sides are adorned in places with the delicate tracery of ice and snow.

In our long trek to the Indian Plain, thick with sugar cane, we can join a party of merchants with their herd of donkeys, and as we plod downwards we are entertained by the tinkling of the bells around the necks of the animals.

The Trekking Life

Unlike life in the city, when one treks day after day, the appetite is sharpened and sleep comes easily and naturally, always ending for me in the call of the Sherpa (a mountain tribe of eastern Nepal), "Sahib, time for tea!", and I open my eyes only to be blinded by the rays of the morning sun. An enamel cup is offered by the grinning Sherpa, squatting at the entrance to the tent, his glistening white teeth seem about to jump from his sun-tanned face. The cup is filled with milky tea from which steam is rising, and suddenly the tent seems warmer. When one is trekking in the Himalayas, two meals a day — lunch and supper — are virtually the rule, as it is more important in the morning to get moving. A cup of hot tea and only the briefest snack is sufficient until lunch. As long as the sun shines, winter temperatures in the Himalayas are not extreme. Simple canvas shoes, a hat, and a woolen sport shirt with sleeves rolled to the elbow, are generally all that is necessary. When walking, the feet should come down slowly and deliberately so as to distribute the body weight evenly with each step. The trek is so long — occupying days and days — that it is useless to hurry the pace. The path, dividing at times, or merging unexpectedly, is completely devoid of route markings. Consequently, one is constantly inquiring the way of villagers or of travellers passing in the opposite direction who, in Nepal, invariably carry a large combination knife and hatchet called a **kukri**. Judging by the number of vernacular greetings we receive from passers-by, it is obvious that the local people, seeing our (Japanese) faces, have no idea that we might not understand. However, one should never ignore such greetings or feign ignorance. Rather, one should at least acquire such rudiments of language, so that if asked in Nepalese, "Where are you from?" **(Tappain kahan basunu untza?)**, one might answer, "I'm from Japan." **(Mo Japanma bastu.)** Or, if one is asked in Sherpa, "Where are you headed?" **(Kanipe oo?)**, the reply could be, "We are headed for Namche Bazar." **(Nnga Namche Bazar dain.)**

Luncheon is held from ten o'clock until noon. One should choose a scenic spot where water and firewood are available. This is the most pleasurable time of any trekking day, as one is able both to enjoy the invigorating sunshine as well as the glorious view of the snow-draped mountains. A peaceful moment might also be spent sketching the patterns formed by distant villages. The afternoon trek is necessarily slower, as one must take time to locate, before sundown, a good place to sleep and to prepare the evening meal. If one is travelling without a tent, it is necessary to negotiate quarters for the night on the second floor of a restaurant, or perhaps to beg permission to use the space under the eves of a rural cottage. Local people making trips in the Himalayas have learned to cooperate on such occasions by freely welcoming travellers into their homes, knowing that they, in turn, will be accepted when on the road. It is best, therefore, to follow local custom and to make no demands that might be deemed unusual or foreign.

1

THE HIMALAYAS AND THE SPORT OF TREKKING: BASIC INFORMATION

Carved, Lamaist prayer book

Since in Sanskrit, the language of ancient India, the word **hima** means "snow" and the word **alaya**, "dwelling-place", the word Himalaya is obviously a combination of the two concepts. Thus, when one stands on the Plain of Hindustan and gazes afar at the mountain wall looming in the distance, all coated and glistening with snow and ice, the aptness of the term, regardless of the passage of time, becomes immediately apparent.

The Himalayas lie north of the Indian subcontinent and south of the high plateau of central Asia, across whose sagging southern border they are described in a gigantic east-west arc. Bounded by **Mt. Nanga Parbat** in the west, and by **Namcha-Barwa** in the east, the main portion of this, the world's highest arcuate mountain system, stretches for 2,500 kilometers, or about the entire extent of the Japanese archipelago. Height, however, is the most distinguishing feature of the region — a fact that is amply demonstrated by simple comparison with other of the world's important highlands. Mt. Aconcagua, at 6,959 meters, for example, is the highest peak in the Americas, yet is still below 7,000 meters, while in the Himalayas there are more than 250 mountains which surpass this figure, and 14 which lie above 8,000 meters! Furthermore, since this huge assemblage is so vast in area, its individual features are extremely complex and it is therefore risky to consider any single peak as entirely representative of the whole region.

Consequently, in order to fully enjoy trekking in the Himalayas, and to comprehend the complexities, not only of what may be apparent, but of what may lie hidden from view, I feel it necessary to look into previous descriptions of the region. I will thus introduce the reader in the succeeding portions of this volume, to the nature and background of the Himalayas and its people.

NATURAL AND HUMAN CONDITIONS IN THE HIMALAYAS

PHYSICAL CONDITIONS

1. Structure

The average thickness of the earth's crust is approximately 35 kilometers, but in the Himalayan region it is roughly twice this, or between 60 and 75 kilometers. Moreover, since the underlying strata generally run laterally, while those of the Indian sub-continent to which it is attached in the south, run vertically, these two phenomena — the extraordinary thickness of the earth's crust and the disparate alignment of strata — have given rise to the theory that in ancient geological times the Indian sub-continent became detached from **Gondwanaland**, far to the south of this, and, moving northward on a convectional current in the earth's crust, collided with the stable **Angaran Bloc**, of central Asia. In the consequent upheaval, which is thought to have produced the Himalayas, the burrowing of the sub-continent under the **Angara Shield**, also elevated a vast area of oceanic sediments. This hypothesis has leaned toward substantiation because of the presence in the area of such features as 1) a three-dimensional distribution of earthquake centers, and 2) certain gravitational peculiarities. On the other hand, a discordant note is presented by the occurrence in the north of earth materials, apparently as a result of glaciation, which one would expect to find only in the south. However, scientific geological field surveys of the enormous Himalayan region are still incomplete, and it is probably too early to analyse the situation with any certainty.

The inordinate complexity of the formational processes that must have occurred when the Himalayas were formed, is indicated by the rather unnatural order of the various ranges and by the flatness of the beds of the rivers which have incised through them. Of the three major rivers of the region, for example, two follow courses which run around the mountain complex in a kind of monstrous embrace. These are the Indus in the west and the Brahmaputra in the east, both of whose origins are in the vicinity of Mt. Kailas, in the north-central portion of the region. The southern part of the highlands is divided into two portions, an eastern section, identified as the **Ganga** (Ganges) Basin, and a western, called the basin of the Sutlej, one of the headwaters of the Indus River system. From east to west, furthermore, the greatest heights of the Himalayan system have been dissected by a series of deep gorges running north and south, as a result of the erosive force of a number of streams which are generally tributary to either

of the above rivers, and which meander across the southern slopes and ultimately debouch from the south-facing front onto the plain. The Himalayas are thus divided into several drainage areas and individual mountain regions which we will now examine from north to south, according to their main geological and landscape features. The first of these, at about 5,000 meters, are the gentle heights associated with the broad, elevated plateau of Tibet, a vast and arid grassland. South of these are the Sub-Himalayas, in which the south-flowing rivers generally have their sources.

The main range, or Great Himalayas, which rises like a massive screen across the landscape, is built on the southern slope of the high plateau, and its base is at a somewhat lower elevation than that of the Tibetan highland. Immediately to the north of this, the substructure is composed of sedimentary materials from marine deposits in ancient geological times, in what was then the Tethys Sea. These strata reveal a multitude of oceanic fossils, indicating that the deposits accumulated over an inordinately long span of time, from roughly the Paleozoic era to the Tertiary period.

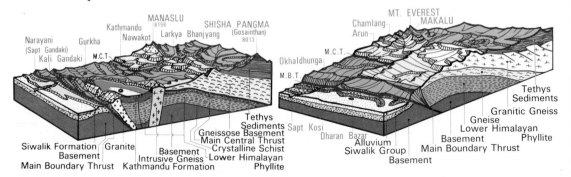

Geological Structure of the Kathmandu Area
Arita (1970).

Geological Structure of the Everest-Arun Area
Anma (1961).

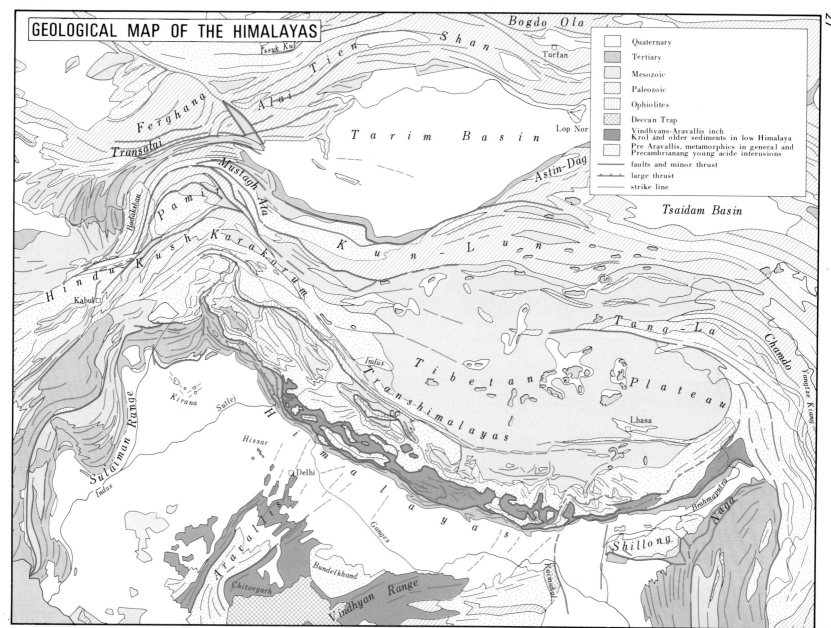

GEOLOGICAL MAP OF THE HIMALAYAS

	Quaternary
	Tertiary
	Mesozoic
	Paleozoic
	Ophiolites
	Deccan Trap
	Vindhyans-Aravallis inch Krol and older sediments in low Himalaya
	Pre Aravallis, metamorphics in general and Precambrianang young acide interusions
	faults and minor thrust
	large thrust
	strike line

Bogdo Ola

Turfan

Tien Shan

Ferghana

Alai

Tssyk Kul

Transalai

Tarim Basin

Lop Nor

Astin-Dag

Mustagh Ata

Badakshan

Pamir

Tsaidam Basin

Hindu Kush Karakorum

Kun-Luen

Kabul

Chamdo

Tang-La

Yanglize Kiang

Indus

Tibetan Plateau

Transhimalayas

Kirana

Sutlej

Lhasa

Sulaiman Range

Himalayas

Hissar

Delhi

Indus

Brahmaputra

Naga

Aravallis

Ganges

Shillong

Raimahal

Chitorgarh

Bundelkhand

Vindhyan Range

(from: Gansser, A. 1964, Geology of the Himalaya, J. Wiley and Sons Ltd.)

Granite, intruded in the Tertiary, along with schists and other metamorphics that were formed during the major tectonic activity, mentioned above and which created the Himalayas, is found in a part of the summit area and along the southern slopes. And, in opposition to the angular ridges which have been sharpened by the actions of snow and ice, there are the gentle contours of the valleys and cirques that were shaped by glaciation. The intrusion of granite here is currently thought to bear a close relationship to both the unusual height of the ridges and to the period of their formation. On the other hand, there seems little association between the shapes of the mountains and the patterns of their inner folds. However, as for such geographical features as ridges and valleys, a close look at their arrangement and direction seems to reflect the basic geological processes of bedding and joint-formation. To the south of the schists and other materials mentioned above, at about 3,000 meters, are the Sub-Himalayas, composed of transposed phyllitic sediments, formed between the Paleozoic and Mesozoic eras.

Although European scholars adhere to the theory that the Himalayas, like the Alps, are a large-scale fold (in the earth's crust), punctuated by a **nappe** structure, recent geological surveys by Japanese specialists from Hokkaido University, indicate that the primary activity in creating the present configuration was block movement as a result of thrust faulting. There are two major fault lines; the first running south of the ridge line of the Great Himalaya, and the second, further south, between the aforementioned metamorphic and phyllitic bands. It has long been realized that the rivers which cross the main ranges are antecedent streams. That is, that they were present prior to the uplift and that they subsequently have maintained a flow which has exceeded the rate of orogeny (mountain-building). The southern

limit of the Himalayas is represented by the Siwalik Hills of India and by the Churia Hills of Nepal, both of which lie just under 600 meters in elevation and are composed of gravel deposits. Between these and the Sub-Himalayas, the basins have been filled in with alluvial deposits from mountain streams, creating an environment which has been ideal for the growth of forests which have come to house a rich assortment of plants and animals.

2. Climate

Because of their height and particular topographic attitude, the Himalayas create a special high mountain climate. Furthermore, because of their very unusual height and massive scale, which occupies fully half of the troposphere in that sector of the globe and divides it into two parts, the Himalayas influence not only the gross climate of Asia and its surroundings, but also the global pattern of atmospheric circulation.

India is the heartland of the climatic phenomenon known as the **monsoon** largely because of the presence of the Himalayas, which influence the relations between the Central Asiatic Air-Mass, on the one hand, and the Indian Oceanic Air-Mass, on the other. The monsoon is characterized as a seasonal shift in the prevailing winds, whereby in summer a warm-moist wind blows onshore from the southwest, and supports the agriculture or the very livelihood of the peoples of the subcontinent; whereas, in winter, the prevailing winds, which might be northerly were it not for the earth's rotation, become north-easterly and, blowing out of northeastern Eurasia, bring dry clear weather to most of the region.

The eastern segment of the Himalayas, beyond Nepal, receives a powerful influence from the monsoon, especially in summer, while the western portion, or Punjab Himalaya, is influenced by the Westerly Winds, particularly

in winter. These bring moisture from the Atlantic Ocean and its appendages, and as these blow against the mountain barrier and major atmospheric disturbances occur, largely in the form of snow, precipitation reaches its maximum extent for the year in this season. Thus, as the western Himalayas are little influenced by the summer monsoon, while in the east, snowfall is rare in winter, there are actually three broad climatic realms here; an eastern zone, a western zone, and in-between, a central zone of transition. The central zone lies roughly between the **Garhwal** Himalayas (or Kumaun Himalayas, according to the Natural Regional Divisions of the Indian Survey Office), and the western tip of Nepal.

Although the Tibetan or northern side of the Himalayan region is generally drier and has a climate that differs from the whole, let us review the yearly progression of climatic influences, according to the Indian Government Meteorological Observatory.

While the year can be divided in two, the northeast or winter monsoon period, and the southwest period of summer, each season can also be sub-divided.

The northeast monsoon has a dry, cool period from January through February, with morning fog in the Assam area, but following this, between March and the first part of June, is the "summer" season. During the latter part of March, temperatures begin a daily ascent and by April it is already unbearably hot. Days are generally clear but skies are hazy, with a dull, tawny tinge, and visibility is poor. The period from May until June, however, is marked by frequent convectional disturbances, usually culminating in thunder storms.

The southwest monsoon can be divided into the **rainy season**, beginning in mid-June, and the **post-monsoon** season, following the latter part of September. Other than in Kashmir and Ladakh, this is the season of heavy rain and snow and, especially in the eastern sector, precipitation is liable to occur in sudden and intense downpours, which are particularly noteworthy in Assam and in the Arakan Hills of Burma.

In July and August, average temperatures are lower than those of May, but at lesser elevations in the northwestern portion of the region, where it is normally dry at that season, if the seasonal winds fail to develop with any force, since there are no clouds to obscure the sun, temperatures can reach violent extremes.

In late September, in what is known as the post-monsoon season, the rain clouds in the mountains begin to withdraw along the valley walls, and while in October, in the Bay of Bengal, tropical cyclones are apt to form, in the Himalayas, good weather with warm days, is the rule. At that time in level areas, even hot days become tolerable. Hence, by November, days are generally clear, a condition which extends into December, except that with

each passing day, temperatures drop and although this is endurable during the daylight hours, (between sunset and sunrise), the cold is intense. West of Himachal Pradesh at this season, trekking is usually impossible because of heavy snow.

Thus, the most suitable trekking seasons are: **Kashmir**, May to October; **Himachal**, September; **Uttar**, October; **Nepal**, **Darjeeling**, and **Sikkim**, October through November; **Assam**, November and March.

3. Glaciers and Glaciated Areas

Glaciers originate from accumulated snow that has not dissipated and which, as eventually it turn to ice, begins to move according to gravity. Within the ice, air-bubbles from the original snow are hermetically sealed, and though the ice is a solid, because of its extent and thickness in this case it acts as though it were a viscous substance which changes shape as gravity and internal pressures force it to flow

down a slope. Changes in the speed of movement between the interior and exterior of the glacial mass, caused by irregularities in the inclination of the valley floor, may induce the formation of gigantic cracks, or **crevasses**. Valley glaciers normally move at rates of about 30 to 60 centimeters per day, but in cases of abnormal advance **(surge)**, the rate may increase to as much as 75 **meters** per day, or, as in the outlet glacier of the Greenland Ice Sheet, to 35 meters per day. Movement, which may be sluggish in the areas of the glacial terminus or in the peripheral portions, is rapid along the central line of glacial flow.

Glaciers can occur only if, 1. there is an appropriate place where snow can accumulate, 2. where there is a sufficient supply of snow, and 3. where snow accumulation can be preserved from one year to the next. Glaciers generally have two surfaces, an **accumulation area**, where the rate of dissipation of the mass is less than that of addition, and an **ablation**

RAINFALL, ISOBARS & PREVAILING WINDS (from School Atlas, 1966, Mudrankala Mandir)

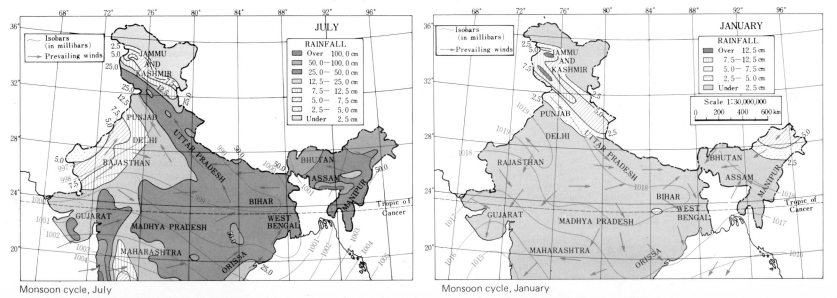

Monsoon cycle, July   Monsoon cycle, January

GLACIER FORMS
from "Illustrated Glossary of Snow and
Ice", Scott Polar Research Institute,
Special Publication Number 4,
Cambridge, 1969.

FIRN LINE

OUTLET GLACIER

ICE CAP

CIRQUE GLACIER

VALLEY GLACIER

ICE FALL

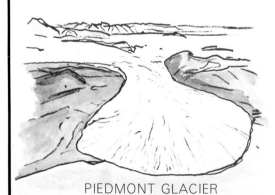

PIEDMONT GLACIER

OGIVES

GLACIATED VALLEY

area, where loss exceeds addition, the boundary between these two areas being called the **snow-line**. The subject, however, is complex (see "Mass Balance Terms", Journal of Glaciology, v. 8, No. 52, 1969, 3-7), but the following attempt at simplification is based on accepted terminology of the International Commission on Snow and Ice of the International Association of Scientific Hydrology, as published by UNESCO in 1968.

A single **balance year** is defined as "the time interval between the formation of two consecutive summer surfaces (not necessarily 365 days)" ("Mass Balance Terms", page 4), and each is divided into a **period of accumulation** and a **period of ablation**, although actually each of these is sub-divided by season. A line connecting points where, at the end of the balance year the net balance is zero, is called the **equilibrium line**.

The crevasse occurring at the head of a mountain glacier, which separates the moving snow and ice of the glacier from the relatively immobile snow and ice adhering to the headwall of the valley, known as the **bergschrund**, is readily apparent, even if located in the upper part of the glacial train. In the area of Everest during the summer rainy season when temperatures are highest, the maximum elevation for rainfall is about 5,500 to 5,600 meters, and, as this is also the time when the areas of accumulation and ablation are closest in extent, the equilibrium line will also probably tend to be somewhere around this. Thus, mild slopes at altitudes above 5,600 meters may become névé (firn) areas, where granular snow accumulates and eventually turns to ice. **Transection** glaciers are formed when glacial tongues spread from ablation areas toward lower elevations, especially where gentle slopes have developed along both sides of a ridge. But when snow and ice are trapped in a small indentation in the valley head, a **cirque glacier** is apt to form, and

when this has a large enough accumulation of ice and a broad accumulation area, its ice tongue may lop over and work its way down a river valley, in which case it is called a **valley glacier**.

In the areas around Mt. Everest, the valleys and basins are so complex that the glaciers have compound basins. Therefore, the termini of these are found at such elevations as 4,700 meters (Ngojumba Glacier), 4,920 meters (Khumbu Glacier) and 4,500 meters (Lower Barun Glacier). In each, the lower portions of their ice falls are seen to be mixed with earth materials, so that these have become "dirty glaciers", a phenomenon more common in the Himalayas than in other portions of

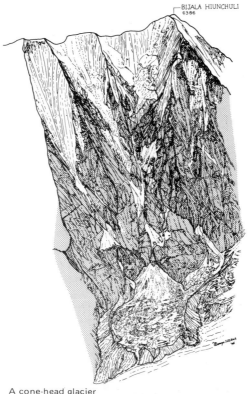

A cone-head glacier

the world's glaciated areas. The reasons for this lie apparently in the massive scale of the surrounding valleys and valley walls which feed the lower parts of the glaciers and ablation areas huge amounts of detritus. At the bottoms of the ice falls there also seems to be a kind of rotational movement, so that at the lower part of the glacier where the rate of ablation is high, earth materials may be raised and suspended in the upper (visible) portions.

One more special kind of glacier produced by the very precipitousness of the Himalayas is the so-called "**cone-head**" glacier, which is classified under **Turkestan Glaciers**, according to Professor Taro Tsujimura in the book, *Shinko Chikeigaku* (**Some New Perceptions of Geomorphology**). Here, what might normally be an accumulation area (and which is termed **pseudo-accumulation area** in such circumstances), is surrounded by bare rock walls so that the snow is not long retained but falls in great clumps to the ground where it accumulates in a conical pattern to form a glacier whose area is mostly one of ablation rather than accumulation. Such rock walls also provide a wealth of earth matter which often converts glaciers of this type into "dirty" glaciers.

At present it is still possible to study ice-age glaciation, even if snow and ice have been erased by changes in the mean temperature, thanks to the landscape which has been sculptured into one of gentle contours and which contains numerous deposits of earth materials in former ablation areas or fringing moraines, all of which reveal the glacier's work. Hence, from evidence gathered from the morphological features and the geological background of the Himalayan region, it can be estimated that at the end of the Ice Epoch, the lowest point to which glaciers moved was around 2,500 meters, and that the areal extent of the region's glaciers was approximately three times that of the present.

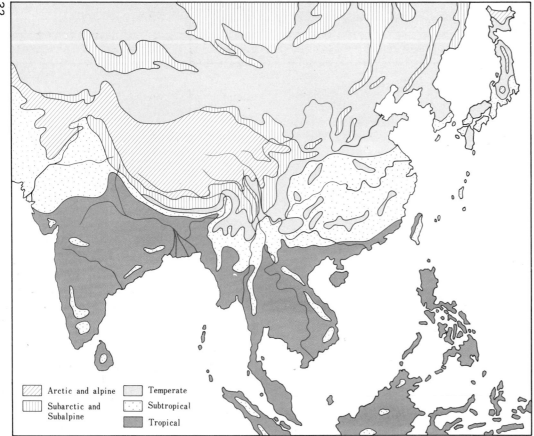

Diagram of South Asian Vegetation Types

Legend:
- Arctic and alpine
- Subarctic and Subalpine
- Temperate
- Subtropical
- Tropical

4. Flora and Fauna

As in other parts of the world, Himalayan plant associations reveal a close adherence to the climatic pattern. A general survey of the lowlands at the mountain base, reveals subtropical and semi-arid vegetation types in the **western** portion, while subtropical savanna and broadleaf evergreen (*Lignosa*) forests predominate from the center to the east. On mountain slopes, according to elevation and direction, vegetation is arranged in discrete bands, so that a perpendicular view might reveal a full, rich spectrum, from high altitude lands of snow and ice, to northerly high latitude deserts. Let us take such a view of the flora, fauna, and natural landscape, as it might be from the southern foot-hills to the towering mountains of the north.

The foot-hills region affords, in places, an opportunity, unusual in Asia, to see in virtually untarnished form, the natural environment in all its component parts. This is possible because inaccessibility has placed certain areas outside man's convenient reach. Also, such parts are often those of flood, swamp, or marsh, or are too gravel-strewn to be of much use to man for agriculture or settlement, or, more likely, are covered by almost impenetrable jungle.

A world of subtropical plant life exists up to about 1,200 meters, with the **sal** tree, dominant in both height and occurrence in a mixed forest, while along stream courses there are broad areas of long-stemmed **ditch reed**, especially where floods occur in season. In addition, there are numerous plateaus, covered with grass and gravel.

Here live such animals as the wild Asian (Indian) elephant, the one-horned rhinoceros, the tiger, leopard, cloud-leopard, the brown and Himalayan black bear, the wild boar, the blueback (bull or **nilgai**), the **axis deer (chital)**, the barking deer **(munchak)**, the hog deer, **sambar**, swamp deer, wild buffalo **(gaur)** and water buffalo, the **gibbon** or long-armed ape, the **common langur**, the *Macaca mulatta* (monkey), the **black ibis**, giant crane, the **Egyptian vulture**, a kind of **parakeet**, the gray starling, striped squirrel, muskrat, Indian python, cobra, umbrella snake and various kinds of lizards and crocodiles. In the rivers there are varieties of carp, and such local fish as the **rohu, catla,** and **mahaseer**, while in the trees there is the lovely **blue peacock**, the **swallow-tail**, and other butterflies.

After passing through sparse stands of pine that have marked the altitude zone between 1,200 and 2,000 meters, one comes to a broadleaf evergreen zone, reaching to 3,000 meters and punctuated by such species as the chestnut, oak, and camphor, rendered all the more exotic, especially in the shaded forests of the southeastern Himalayas, by the presence of such parasitic forms as orchids, Spanish and other mosses. Meanwhile, the dominance of many tall groves of rhododendron and of lower, needle-leaved vegetation that is unpalatable to animals, may suggest that other, more succulent forms were eradicated in the passage of time by the grazing of livestock. The tall rhododendron forest is further enhanced by the brilliance of its red blossoms (the national flower of Nepal), as well as by the **white magnolia**, the **purple magnolia**, and the fragrant **daphne**, from which Nepalese paper is made. Equally striking are the aforementioned swallow -tail butterflies and such others as the **four-legged monarch**, and **bright sunshine** *(Oenies)* butterflies. Small animals include the Himalayan giant bat, the *bandicota indica* (demon rat), the Himalayan bear-rat and **water rat**, while the **Great Tit** (a kind of chikadee), the **thrush**, and **gray starling**, are counted among the birds. Monkeys are of two varieties, the **rhesus** and the **common langur** (or Hanuman langur), mentioned above. Other large animals are the **lesser Panda**, as well as the already-mentioned Himalayan black bear and the snow-leopard.

After passing through a zone dominated by broadleaf-evergreen species, another zone, occupying the area roughly between 2,500 and 3,200 meters, is reached, where the following types of trees are seen; deciduous types which lose their leaves in winter, and such coniferous varieties (needle-leaved) as the Himalayan **hemlock**, and **Indian fir**, the western yew, and the **juniper**. Above this, to about 3,500 meters in the eastern sector, 4,000 meters in the western, are found stands of such moderately tall trees as the birch. And in the Darjeeling region's "Laurel Forest Zone" are found splendid examples of the towering *cryptomeria*, sent from Japan in the Meiji period (1868 ~ 1912). The **Himalayan cedar**, that one would think should be present generally, is found only in the **Hindu Kush Range**, and not at all to the east of this.

Above the median elevation zone of needle-leaved forest, one finds such butterflies as the *Parnassius hardwickei*, the *Papilio krishna* and the *Aulocera padma* (grayling), and such small animals as the **long-nosed squirrel** *(Dremomys lokriah)* and the national bird of Nepal, the **Danphe**, (the **rainbow pheasant**.)

The next highest is the **high mountain zone**, from 3,500 meters to the zone of permanent ice and snow, where grasslands predominate except that the southern slope is moist and the northern dry. Wild flowers, such as the **pink primrose**, the **purple columbine**, **gentian**, **yellow butter-cup**, and **white edelweiss** abound. Japanese will find many flowers here that will remind them of the woods at home. However, since yak, sheep, and goats have been pastured here for centuries, except for the needle-leaved varieties, most of the low vegetation has been consumed. Finally, in vast rock-strewn areas, the *Ochotona roylei* (hare), *Ochotona macrotis*, grouselike **snow partridge**, the **hedge sparrow**, the **tree pipit**, **snipe**, and the **red-billed chough** (kyomma, in sherpa).

PEOPLE AND CULTURE

1. Language and Religion

The great mountain complex is regarded as a difficult land by the people of the plains because it defies normal patterns of land-use, and because it represents a major obstacle to over-land travel. The Himalayan barrier has also hindered interchange between the peoples and cultures of Asia, as between those centered on China and on India, as well as between Asia and the so-called "west". For example, south

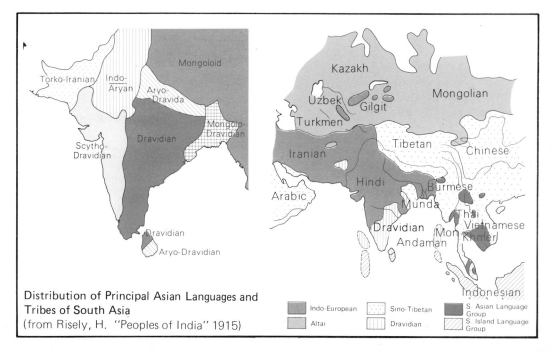

Distribution of Principal Asian Languages and Tribes of South Asia
(from Risely, H. "Peoples of India" 1915)

Indo-European | Sino-Tibetan | S. Asian Language Group
Altai | Dravidian | S. Island Language Group

of the Himalayan divide the basic stock is **Caucasoid** (Indo-Aryan), while to the north it is **Mongoloid**, as in Tibet and Burma. Language and religion have followed similar distributional patterns.

If the Himalayas can be viewed as a natural wall of defence for the Indian sub-continent against the peoples of the north, the **Sulaiman** and **Kirthar** Ranges in the west, and the **Patokai Hills** and **Arakan Yoma** in the east, are also natural ramparts — the last two being considered the most formidable of all, thanks to their generally unhealthy natural environment, made up of jungle and vast mountain reaches. On the west, on the other hand, the environment of the Khyber, Gomal, and Bolan passes, is generally arid. Hence, from ancient times, tribes have entered these from the Iranian Plateau and elsewhere, and have eventually over-run, in successive waves, the rich riverine lowlands of the Indian sub-continent.

Three important invasions to follow these routes were, [1] early hordes of Aryan nomads who swept aside all those in their path, including the urban communities that had been established in the past, as exemplified by the remains of two remarkable cities, Mohenjo-daro and Harappa, [2] the forces of Alexander of Macedon in 327 B.C., and [3] followers of Islam, who poured into northern India from the latter part of the 10th century. Consequently, the southern Himalayan region became peopled by Indo-Aryans, while farther west toward Iran, were Turko-Iranians, such as the **Baluchi** and **Pathan**. Following their initial conquest, the Aryan nomads settled and eventually fused with the indigenous population, even to the point of adopting the Hindu religion and to employing the caste system, which essentially divides the society into four functional groups. Much later, invading Islamic forces took over northern India which, by then, had become the center of another religion, the faith of Gautama, the Buddha, and Buddhism, thus displaced, never again regained its former prominence in this part of the world.

The present population of South Asia is divided generally into Indians and Pakistani, or into those — the majority — who adhere to the Hindu belief in the transmigration of the soul, and the doctrine of divine retribution, which has led them to worship such objects as oddly-shaped rock, or to have created a rich mythology, involving a variety of gods and divine legends. Ultimately, the Hindu seeks salvation of release from the work-a-day world.

The Pakistani, on the other hand, are mainly followers of Islam, which regulates the life of the individual through a series of daily duties and life-long commitments to such things as faith in Allah, according to the prophet, Mohammed (570~632 AD); and to daily prayer, according to the teachings of the Koran or sacred book; to periodic fasting, and finally, to a pilgrimage to Mecca, the holy capital of the faith.

In the Republic of India, Hindi has been declared the official language, but, according to the constitution, thirteen other languages are recognized, such as Urdu, Bengali, Assamese, Gujarati, and Kashmiri, while 250 others are also in use. Urdu is the common language of Pakistan and is, along with all those mentioned, of the Indo-European family of languages, as opposed to the Tibeto-Burman (Sino-Tibetan) family, used in the northern and eastern Himalayas.

Although the Himalayas are an obstacle for the plains-dwellers, to those living within the mountain reaches, the ranges are natural fortifications. Hence, tribal mountain peoples have often retained their individual cultures; small and independent kingdoms such as Nepal, Bhutan, and Sikkim, have managed to maintain some sovereignty and such areas as Ladakh, Spiti, and others, until recently at least, their independence.

In lower areas, south of the main ranges, live such people as the **Tharus**, a dark-skinned group and generally the population is Indo-Aryan, representing those expelled from India in ancient times by the Muslims. Higher up, such as in the Mahabharat Range, the territory is dominated by mountain tribes whose language

Pronounciation of Numbers in the Himalayas

	Examples							Numbers Heard During Research Area							Examples		
	スペイン SPANISH	フランス FRENCH	英語 ENGLISH	アラブ ARABIC	トルコ TURKISH	サンスクリット SANSKRIT	ラダック LADAKH	ヒンディ HINDI	ネパリ NEPALI	ネワール NEWAR	タカリ TAKHALI	グルン GURUNG	シェルパ SHERPA	ブータン BHUTAN	ティベット TIBET	レプチャ LEPCHA	日本 NIPPON
								(Kulu)	(Kathmandu)	(Beni)	(Marpha)	(Ghachok)	(Namche)	(Calcutta)	(口語)		(Japanese)
1	ウノ uno	アン un	ワン one	ワハド wahad	ビル bir	エカ eka	チ gChig	エク eku	エク ek	ツャウ fsan	クイ qui	グリ gri	チク chik	チ chi	チク chik	カート kāt	イチ ich / ひとつ hitotsu
2	ドス dos	ドゥー deux	トゥー two	エスンド ethndn	イキ iki	ドゥイ dwi	ニ gNyis	ドゥ du	ドゥイ dui	ニャゥ nyau	ニー ni	ニ ni	ニ ni	ニ ni	ニ nyi	ニェート nyet	ニ ni / ふたつ futatsu
3	トゥレス tres	トゥロワ trois	スリー three	サラサット thalathat	ウチ u'ch	トゥリ tri	スム gSām	ティン tin	ティン tin	ソウン soun	ソム som	スーン soon	スム sum	スム sum	スム sum	スム sum	サン san / みっつ mittsu
4	クアトロ cuatro	カトル quatre	フォー four	アルバート arbaat	ドゥルト deurt	チャトゥル chatur	bZhi	チャール char	チャール char	ビュウ pyu	プリー pri	プリー pli	シ shyi	シ shi	zhyi	ファーリ pha-li	シ shi / よっつ yottsu
5	シンコ cinco	サンク cinq	ファイヴ five	カムサート khamsat	ベシュ besh	パンチャン panchan	ンガ ℓNga	パンチ panch	パンチ panch	ンガゥ ngaw	ンガ nga	ガ gha	ンガ nga	ナー nah	ガ gna	ファニョン pha-gnon	ゴ go / いつつ itsutsu
6	セイス seis	シス six	スックス six	スィタート sittat	アルティ alti	シャーシ shash	トゥク dRůg	チェイ chei	チャー chha	クウ koo	トゥー too	トゥー thu	トゥク thuk	テュ tue	トゥ thu	ターロク tarok	ロク roku / むっつ muttsu
7	シエテ siete	セット sept	セヴン seven	サバート sabaat	イェーディ yedi	サプタン saptan	bDůn	スァート shart	サート saat	ニュウ new	ニス nis	ニー nyi	ティン dhin	デュン dun	ドゥン dun	カーキョット kă-kyak	シチ shichi / ななつ nanatsu
8	オーチョ ocho	ユイッ huit	エイト eight	サマニアト thamaniat	セキス sekiz	アシュタン ashtan	ギャ brGyad	アート ahart	アート aat	チャウ chaw	プレ pre	プレ pre	ギイ gye	ゲ ghe	ゲー gye	カーク ka-ku	ハチ hachi / やっつ yattsu
9	ヌエヴェ nueve	ヌフ neuf	ナイン nine	テッサート tessaat	ドクフ dokuf	ナヴァン navan	クウ dGů	ナウ nou	ナウ nau	グー goo	クー qoo	クゥー koo	グウ goo	グー koo	グー guh	カーキョト kă-kyôt	ク ku / ここのつ kokonotsu
10	ディエス diez	ディス dix	テン ten	アーシュラート aasherat	オン on	ダサン dasan	チュウ bChů	ダス das	ダス das	ユー yoo	チュ chu	ズューン zyu	ツチュー chhyu	チュ chu	チュー chuh	カティ kati	ジュウ jyu / とう toh

is Nepali or Pahari, and in even more elevated, snowy lands are people who speak Tibeto-Burman and whose religion is Lamaism. Such groups, from west to east, include those of Ladakh, Garhwal, Dotial, Nepal, Lepcha, Bhutan, and the entire northern region of Tibet, all of whom are of Mongoloid extraction, resembling the Japanese.

In the Lamaism of Ladakh, as it was customary in the days of the silk trade for husbands to leave home for long periods, the practise was for one woman to have many husbands. West of here, in Gilgit, however, where Islam held sway, it was the exact opposite — one husband with multiple wives. Matriarchy was practised in the Lahul District of Himachal, on the other hand, whereby a woman would be served by a number of men, as seen in the **Kulu**, an autumn festival where the only males present act as servants or guardians of the carefully groomed and bedecked females. The Gaddis (Aryans) of the northwest, to mention another extreme, are partly nomadic peoples and partly agrarian — their life style being dualistic.

Of the many tribes of Nepal, the Newars of the Kathmandu Basin were noted for establishing cities here and elsewhere, and for their skills at arts and crafts, while others, such as the Kiranti of the eastern foothills, or the Sherpa, Tamang, and Magar of the north central districts, or the Gurung and Thakali of the west-center, had a high reputation as Gurkha soldiers and, of special importance here, for their assistance to mountain-climbers.

In the area of Sikkim there are now many Nepalese but the original settlers were Lepchas and Tibetans. And, as far as Bhutan is concerned, its people are known for their rather advanced agricultural techniques, and for their adherence to Lamaism, including their faith in its priests. East of Bhutan in the Assam Himalayas, specifically in Arunachal-Pradesh, such tribes as the Dafalas, Apatanis, Abors, and

Mishmis, have supported themselves through the practise of **ladang** (**milpa** or slash-and-burn) agriculture and hunting, and are said to be feared as head-hunters.

2. History

From 2,500 to 1,500 BC, in Mohenjo-Daro and Harappa in the Indus Valley, an urban culture flourished and was marked by such artifacts as bronze-ware, ceramics, hieroglyphic writing, and personal seals. This region, however, was over-run in 1,500 BC by Aryans from the Central Asian Plateau (of southern Russia), people whose original language was akin to that of the inhabitants of India, Iran, and, in fact, of all Western Europe. The urban culture of Mohenjo-Daro was thus obliterated; the invaders simply continued their previous practises of nomadism coupled with agriculture. The most distinctive characteristics of these Indo-Aryans involved their organizing ability, especially in a military sense.

Later, the Indo-Aryans gradually merged with the native peoples and came to follow **Brahmanism**, and its doctrine of an immutable hereditary four-fold caste structure, headed by the priestly or **Brahman** caste, followed by the **Kshatrya** (warriors), the **Vaishya** (merchants and farmers), and **Sudras** (servants and laborers). From ancient times to the present, however, according to the region and the particular activity, each of these has been increasingly subdivided, so that eventually there have come to be as many as 3,000 separate functional castes. There is also an untouchable or out-caste group in any community, which would include those who have violated the caste relationships. In this system, one is allowed to marry only within the same caste.

History in India begins with the so-called Vedic Period, when the Vedas were transcribed in Sanskrit and society was noteworthy for its agrarian culture. The Aryans gradually

expanded their territory from the Punjab eastward to the flood plain of the Ganges River, supporting themselves with a Mediterranean style of agriculture centered on the raising of wheat, to which cereals and root crops were gradually added. As production increased, the surplus gave rise to the growth of an important urban culture, and as a result, a number of dynasties arose, each possessing a distinctive flavor of its own, in addition to political and military power.

In the 6th century, BC, Prince Gautama of the Saka tribe, abjured the caste system and preached a doctrine which denied the absolute and stressed impermanence, self-effacement, and adherence to the 'middle path', which eventually came to be known as **Buddhism**. Meanwhile, **Mahavira** (446-376 BC) declared that the world is composed of five elements, the soul, the substance, space, and conditions of motion and repose, and taught that to reach a state where the true self is revealed, it is necessary to discipline oneself with a regimen of physical exercise and fasting, to which end the ancient cult of **Jainism** was revived.

In the years 330-324 BC, the great expedition under Alexander III of Macedon (Alexander the Great) reached the Punjab. One century later, the Maurian king, Asoka, adopted the Buddhist faith and propagated it throughout northern India, guiding his people into a state of greater unity and affuence than had hitherto been known. But by the 4th century BC, Hinduism, which had begun earlier as Brahmanism, took on a new structure associated with two great epic poems, the **Mahabharata** and **Ramayana**, which became its scriptures, and Hinduism returned to popular favor.

The early years of the Christian era were marked in South Asia and elsewhere by the grandeur of Gandaran arts, by the exporting of Buddhism to China, the invasion of Europe by the **Huns**, the pilgrimage to India by the Chinese priest, **Fa-hsien**, and by the elaborate fashioning in stone of the Ajanta and Ellora caves.

Dividing Indian history into four stages, ancient (classical), medieval, modern, and contemporary, the 'golden age' when the culture and social order evolved and took form under **Hinduism,** is reckoned to have been during the ancient or classical stage. In reality, of course, this was also a time of struggle and turmoil, with characteristic ups-and-downs, although its prestige is hardly in dispute. Records tell, for example, of the presentation of tribute to the **Gupta**, or main dynasty of the time, by the then independent kingdoms of Nepal and Assam. Visits are also recorded by such Chinese pilgrims of the T'ang period as **Yuan Chwang,** who used the famous Silk Route for the long, over-land journey, and by **I-Ching**, who travelled by sea — both journeys occurring around the seventh century, toward the end of the Indian classical period.

At the beginning of the eighth century, the Indus River region fell under the temporary sway of the Saracen Muslims, but the society and economic structure that resulted were destroyed in the late tenth century by the Turkish Ghaznivids — also of the Muslim persuasion — who pursued here a policy of plunder and rapine from their base in Afghanistan, eventually over-running all of northwestern India. The resulting period of confusion lasted until the rise of the Mughal Dynasty in the 16th century, which brought more tolerant policies toward the followers of Hinduism in what is often termed the 'Islamic' period of medieval Indian history. Meanwhile, in 1221, the Indus River Basin was invaded by the Mongols under Genghis (Chinggis) Khan, and later events in this part of the world became known in Europe through the writings of Marco Polo of Venice, who travelled to China, Southeast Asia, and India in the years 1275-1295 AD.

In the ancient period of Nepalese history (around the 4th century AD), the **Lichchhavi Dynasty** became firmly established by king **Mana Deva**, but from the late 6th to the early 7th centuries, king **Amshuvarma** reigned, at which time he sent his daughter, the princess **Bhrikuti**, in marriage to king **Tsrong Tsong Gyampo,** of Tibet.

The medieval stage of Nepalese history was the period between the 13th and 18th centuries, when the **Malla Dynasty** prospered in the Kathmandu Basin. The rulers were generally Hindu military men who had left their homeland because of the Muslim conquest. Under their leadership, Nepal became divided into various regions, with over-all prosperity based on the activity of the **Newar** people, who profited from trade between the Plain of Hindustan to the south, and the high Plateau of Tibet, to the north — the dazzling urban culture of Kathmandu being one manifestation of such prosperity. The most prominent of these leaders was **Jayasthiti Malla**, who ruled, 1380-1394, but after about three generations the kingdom was sub-divided into three units, with local capitals at Kathmandu, Patan, and Bhadgaon, each vying with the other for power and supremacy.

The modern period of Indian history dates from May 20, 1498, when the Portuguese explorer, **Vasco da Gama**, anchored off **Kozhikode** (Calicut), and attempted the direct purchase of spices. Later, in 1500, the Portuguese build a trading port at **Cochin**, in southwestern India, but Portuguese influence was eventually superseded in South Asia by the British East India Company, which also overcame the rival and ephemeral French East India Company, while in the meantime, the Dutch East India Company was laying claim to the so-called East Indies, or latter-day Indonesia — all of whom were in quest of spices, particularly **pepper.** The weakness of the declining Mughal Dynasty had presented an attractive field for potential conquest in South Asia, to which various European nations responded by engaging the other in battle — the situation finally becoming resolved in 1757 at the **Battle of Plassey** in Bengal, when British power, under the flag of the British East India Company, crushed a rival force made up of the French and local troops, and established, once-and-for-all, the ascendency of England in South Asia.

In Nepal, the Gurkha leader, **Prithbi Narayan Shah**, taking advantage of struggles within the Malla Kingdom, by 1769, wrested control of the Kathmandu Basin, began a process of conquest and unification of the entire Nepalese mountain region, and inaugurated the **Shah Dynasty**, all of which accomplishments took about three generations. So persistent was the momentum of this expansion under the leadership of **Rana Bahadur Shah**, furthermore, that Nepalese forces pushed southward into the Garhwal area (modern Uttar Pradesh), and even further into the Plain of Hindustan, as well as northward into Tibet. It was only through a combination of Chinese and Tibetan armed resistance, in fact, that in 1792 the Nepalese were finally thrown back from **Shigatse** in Tibet, to which they had managed to penetrate. Meanwhile, in the south, Nepalese troops succeeded in subduing over 200 lowland villages before they were finally, after 1814, ousted by the British.

In 1857, an uprising of Bengali soldiers known as the 'Sepoy Mutiny', turned into a popular revolt against British suppression and among other concessions and policy changes, India was formerly recognized by the crown as an important element of the British Empire.

In 1885, in pursuance of modern reforms, the British fostered the formation of the Indian National Congress, but at the same time, the Indians were building their own (anti-British) political organization under the leadership of such stalwarts as the great **Mohandas K. (Mahatma) Gandhi**, whose aim was outright independence. The movement, however, did not reach fruition until after the Second World War, and when success was finally realized, it was piece-meal, with the Republic of India being declared an independent state (with a predominantly Hindu population) on August 15, 1947, and Pakistan (whose population is overwhelmingly Muslim), reaching independent status officially as a republic, on March 23, 1956. Later, in 1971, East Pakistan, which had been separated from West Pakistan by nearly 2,000 kilometers, became the independent nation of Bangladesh, whose population is also almost all of the Muslim faith.

Meanwhile, in February 1951, the Tibetan political administration of the Dalai Lama was dissolved by the Chinese, who declared an end to religious feudalism there, while Nepal, which had endured a dictatorship under the Rana clan since 1846, reacted to Indian independence by restoring imperial rule, in February 1951. The king, **Trubhuvan Bir Bikram Shah Dev**, who had escaped palace arrest in 1950 and fled to India, was assisted in resuming his rightful status by none other than the great Indian statesman and then Prime Minister, **Jawaharlal Nehru**.

3. Agriculture and Animal Husbandry

Patterns of agriculture and animal husbandry in the Himalayas differ according to the altitude and the extent of level land in an area. With Nepal as an example, let us take stock of the situation.

Altitude limits of settlement in the Mt. Everest Region are about 5,000 meters on the northern (Tibetan or Djarongbuk) side, and on the southern (Nepalese or Pangboche) side, these are about 3,985 meters. The inhabitants of the latter are largely Sherpas who are noted for their prowess as high-altitude porters and, of particular interest here, for their collaboration with mountain-climbers — especially as these qualities are combined with such personal traits (common among mountain people) as diligence and faithfulness.

In winter, the main activity of the Sherpas is trade, a situation facilitated by the paucity of precipitation and the tranquil movement of the glaciers, which allows relatively easy passage to Tibet. At this season also there is a lull in field work and in animal-tending, the cattle can either be left on the ground floor of a two-storied building or confined within the yard. Items of trade from Nepal include rice, hides and skings, and the zopkiyo, the hybrid calf of the yak and cow (an adult Zopkiyo is a Zow). From Tibet come ghee (clarified butter), Chinese tea, salt, and wool. From the lowlands of Nepal, yaks are purchased to transport rice, maize, salad oil, and wheat flour.

Cultivation begins about the end of January but actual sowing is done in March. At such high altitudes, the main crops are barley (planted in the spring), turnips, leafy vegetables, and white potatoes. In animal husbandry, the chief activity concerns yaks and sheep; one male member of each family being appointed to the task. When the weather warms, this individual leaves the homestead with the flock and moves to a seasonal hut in a highland grazing area, or kharka.

Those who remain—men and women alike—pursue the agricultural routine, although the more affluent farmers may hire their labor. Harvesting is begun in late August and continues into September — surpluses, over and above those required for the coming winter, being sold in Namche. The advent of a dry season in October signals the work of grass-cutting, the most onerous chore of the season in the regimen of animal husbandry. Sheep are sheered off-and-on between April and September. Grass-cutting for winter fodder is a lengthy process because it must be dried before storage. Hence, this task takes about three-days in good weather, but as much as 8-days otherwise. Most farms are also, although these are never very numerous, embellished with dogs, chickens, and goats.

Sherpa farming methods lead to the production of greater or lesser numbers of products, depending on altitude. For example, under 3,000 meters, the variety tends to increase and one finds maize, winter wheat, spinach, and garlic; while below 2,500 meters, rice and finger millet appear among the staples.

Under 2,000 meters, there are bananas, black-eyed peas, and sweet potatoes. Here, the ethnic flavor also changes from Sherpa to Magar and Kiranti, and Hinduism becomes infused into the religious pattern. In the animal realm, the water buffalo and hog grow common.

Below 1,500 meters villages become more agglomerated; roofs are of thatch and hipped. A variety of fruits is seen, including citrus types and mangoes, and among the vegetables are peanuts and the cauliflower.

Physically, the surfaces between 1,000 and 3,000 meters are marked by elaborate terracing of all the gentler slopes (aside from steep valley walls and swampy areas), all the way from the higher ridges to the middle slopelands. Since in Hinduism, the cow is sacred and cannot be eaten, these animals are put in pairs to the plow. One hypothesis, the so-called 'Laurel Forest Cultural Theory', of Nakao Sasuke, declares that all such places, from Nepal via South China to Southwest Japan, where environmental conditions — especially of climate and vegetation — are similar, there is a common association of agricultural practises and the

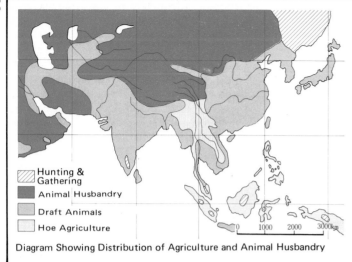

Diagram Showing Distribution of Agriculture and Animal Husbandry

Hunting & Gathering
Animal Husbandry
Draft Animals
Hoe Agriculture

0 1000 2000 3000km

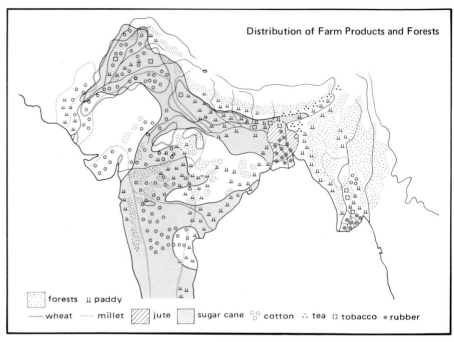

Distribution of Farm Products and Forests

forests ⊥⊥ paddy
—— wheat —— millet jute sugar cane °°° cotton ∴ tea □ tobacco • rubber

daily diet. Components of this include slash-and-burn type cultivation, the growing of taro and like root crops, the maintenance of tea gardens, mulberry groves and silk worms, and the lacquer plant. There are also certain common techniques such as 'water-bleaching' (to remove acridness in food), but the list of like products continues with tangerines, loquats, bracken, devil's tongue, and the beefsteak plant. Nakao reasons that all the cultures have drawn upon the other. There is, for example, root-crop cultivation from Southeast Asia, or the production of cereals and rice from the savanna lands, barley and wheat from Mediterranean climatic areas, and finally, soybeans and buckwheat — all becoming a single cultural milieu whenever conditions warrant.

It should be added, in conclusion, that in Northwest India, in Kashmir and Himalchal, there are semi-nomads such as the **Gaddis** and **Gujar**, who practise a form of **transhumance**, whereby the parents and male offspring tend to mount the slopes with the flock in summer in search of better pasture for the sheep, while the young married couple and their children remain behind in the ravine.

4. Mountaineering

The snow-capped Himalayas have been a familiar sight to residents of northern India since before recorded history, but this first became known in the West following the expedition of Alexander III (the Great) of ancient Macedonia, in 330-324 BC, from Persia to the Indian Punjab. It was not until the latter half of the 19th century, however, that it became generally recognized that here were assembled about 200 of the world's highest mountains.

The first trekking appears to date from about 1624 AD, when the Portugese Christian missionary, **Antonio Andrada**, with two companions, entered the Garhwal Himalayas (of Uttar Pradesh) via the Mana Pass, and travelled in the area. On the other hand, travellers from China such as **Chang Ch'en** in 139 BC, and again in 113, as a messenger along the Silk Route, ultimately to **Bactria**; or **Kumarajiva** from the 'Western Regions' to China; or **Fa-hsien** and **Sung Yün** of China, who made pilgrimages to India in the 4th century AD, all of whose travels are documented, indicate that there must have been knowledge of the Himalayas in ancient Chinese lore. Furthermore, **Yuan Chwang**, author of **Si-Yu-Ki (Great T'ang Period Records of the Western World)**, is known to have visited India, 629-645 AD, although this is much later than his predecessors.

The first modern survey of the Himalayas was made by the Indian Government's Survey Office in the 2nd half of the 19th century, but by this time some of the details of the region, such as those revealed in the botanical survey of the **Kanchenjunga** area in 1848-1849 by **J.D. Hooker**, or in the expedition of the three **Schlagenweit** brothers, from the Himalayas to central Asia, sponsored by the British East India Company, were known. Such activity, however, increased greatly with the advent of the 20th century. There were, for example, such as the Russian, **Preshewalski's**, exploration of the headwaters of the Yellow (Huang) River, the several expeditions to the Pamirs and elsewhere under the leadership of the Swedish explorer, **Sven Hedin**, the Kun Lun expedition of **Sir Aurel Stein** of Britain, and that of **Otani Kozui** of Japan, who, on three separate occasions, from 1902 to 1912, surveyed the Himalayas as far as central Asia.

Mount Everest, known previously in Tibet as Chomolungma (Recently, Jolmo Lungma, as used in the People's Republic of China) or 'Mother of the World', was not officially designated the highest mountain on earth until 1863. When viewed from afar, as from the plain to its southeast, **Makalu** in the foreground appears larger and more imposing, while from the southwest, **Gauri** Shankar, which also seems higher from that vantage point, was, in fact, long considered the highest. It was as a result of corrections and adjustments in height-readings by the Indian Government Survey Office when, in 1852, Radhanath Sikdar, a member of the agency, measured it as Peak 15, that Chomolungma became known as the world's supreme massif. And though later investigation showed that the initial reading of 8,840 meters should have been 8,848, this correction only further enhanced Everest's position. Also, since at this time (1863) the name Chomolungma was not well-known, the then director of the Indian Survey Office, Andrew Waugh, named the peak in honor of the agency's former chief, George Everest — by which it is known today, except that to the Nepalese

Government, it is Sagarmatha ('godhead').

Since the heights and locations of many high peaks of the Himalayas were originally measured from the foot of each peak by the so-called **angular survey** (indirect level survey) method, these figures would be subject to revision if levelling lines were laid and the readings were made from some more proximate location. Such a prodigious task, however, remains as an important project for the future.

The first climbing in the area is recorded as of 1883 by W. W. Graham, who ascended **Jopuno** Peak of the Sikkim Himalayas (5,935 meters), and also who trekked in the Garhwal Range. The next, in 1892, was also by a Britain, **W. M. Conway**, who conducted a scientific survey of the Karakoram Range and in doing so climbed **Pioneer Peak** (6,790 meters). Furthermore, **A. F. Mummery** attempted to climb **Nanga Parbat** in 1895 but perished in the effort, while **D. W. Freshfield** succeeded in circumambulating Mt. Kanchenjunga in 1899.

The first attempt to climb the peaks in the mountains of the 7,000 meter class occurred in 1907 by the T. Longstaff team, which tried to ascend **Mt. Trisuli** (7,120 meters) of the Garhwal Himalayas. This was followed by those of A. M. Kellas on such Sikkim mountains as **Langphu** (6,555 meters), **Mt. Sentinel, Pauhunri, Chomo Yummo**, and **Kanchengyao**. At that time, however, since the Kingdom of Nepal was following a policy of isolation, efforts were concentrated in the Garhwal, Sikkim, and Karakoram Ranges, which were relatively accessible — a situation which is almost the complete opposite to that of today.

Climbing of the various peaks of the Kanchenjunga group was done initially in 1930 and 1931 by the **Dyhrenfurth** team, while **Baltoro Kangri** (7,260 meters) and

Sia Kangri (7,315 meters) were conquered in 1934. **Mt. Nandarkot** (6,867 meters) of the Garhwal Himalayas, meanwhile, was first attempted in 1936 by the Rikkyo University Mountain Climbing Association, which managed to succeed on the first try.

Many vain attempts have been made to climb the peaks of the 8,000 meter class. For example, there were those of a German group in the Kanchenjunga area in 1929, and of Nanga Parbat in 1934, or of **Hidden Peak** by a French team in 1936, as well as such attempts on K-2 as those of 1902 by the British, of 1909 by the Italians, and of 1938 by the Americans. The first attempt on the northern flank of Mt. Everest came in 1921, when the British Royal Geological Society obtained permission from the Dalai Lama of Tibet.

After World War II there were two major changes in Himalayan climbing. The first was thanks to scientific and technological advances against such conditions as oxygen deficiency at high altitudes, temperature decline, and powerful winds, and came about through the application of such aero technics as the use of light-weight metals and plastics (high-molecular substances such as **polymers**), which allowed the development of lighter, more modern clothing, tools, and such equipment as oxygen tanks and other apparatus. The second was owing to a revision of the political climate, which saw the closing of Tibet and the opening of Nepal and hence, of new routes of access into the area.

Thus, from both the standpoint of technology and geography, the road was now open to the peaks of the 8,000 meter class, and almost immediately, the assault on the giants in this category began. In 1950, for example, a French team under **M. Herzog** succeeded in climbing **Annapurna** (8,091 meters).

The supreme moment in climbing history, however, came in 1953, when a British team directed by **J. Hunt**, with **E. Hillary** and **Tenzing Norgay Bhutia**, as climbers, ascended Mt. Everest. Following this feat, the whole nature and purpose of climbing was converted from the simple objective of achieving what others had been unable to accomplish, to the more complex goals of discovering new climbing routes and evaluating their difficulties.

Examples of these new explorations are seen in such efforts as those of a Chinese group on the northern ridge of Everest, of an American group on the western ridge, and of the British (**Bonigton**) group on the southern wall in 1975. Meanwhile, there was the assault on the southeast ridge of Makalu by the Japanese Alpine Club (JAC) expedition headed by Hara, and on this mountain's western ridge by a French team, as well as efforts by an English group on the southern wall of Annapurna. Finally, a Japanese group under Takahashi, climbed Manaslu from its western flank, and another JAC group completed the Nanda Devi twin peaks.

PLANNING AND PREPERATION FOR TREKKING

1. Danger at High Altitudes

The Himalayas are an inconcievably high range and, as such, compared to the hot and humid lowlands, provide a cool and comfortable place to make a living. Thus, from ancient times, mountain tribes like the Sherpa, have used the Himalayan environment for both agriculture and pasturage. Permanent residences are seen at heights of as much as 4,000 meters, and above this, at 5,100 meters or so, are the cottages of shepherds. Strangers, seeing that people can live normal lives here, may be persuaded that this is a perfectly safe habitat. However, although it may not be readily apparent, for those from lower altitudes, life at heights of 4,000 meters presents serious physiological problems.

At such altitudes, for example, the atmospheric pressure is only about 60 percent that of low-lying areas, the amount of oxygen is also lower, and when one considers that only a portion of the oxygen is absorbed by the lungs, the "effective" proportion is even less. The danger in human activity and to physiology at such heights stems thus from an insufficient supply of oxygen, which is often inadequate to sustain human life.

In view of the foregoing, those who anticipate trekking above 4,000 meters in the Himalayas should take steps to determine whether their physical condition is sufficiently strong for the circumstances.

Those who are apparently unsuited for high altitude travel might include sufferers from anemia, high blood-pressure, heart disease; or those with such chronic illnesses as kidney failure, asthma, and diabetes; or simply those whose physical condition is weak. However,

because research into such problems is yet inadequate, there is no definite standard to determine whether an individual is prepared for exposure to a given set of circumstances. Therefore, it is left entirely to the individual to determine beforehand what the reaction might be to high altitude conditions. Mt. Fuji, at 3,776 meters, or a height equivalent to this, is not high enough for a final test in this regard, yet if one has some weakness which might prove fatal at 4,000 meters, this ordinarily becomes apparent even at this rather moderate altitude. Experienced mountain climbers, for example, in better-than-average physical condition, who feel no discomfort when climbing in the northern Japanese Alps at 3,000 meters, may be rendered breathless and dizzy when climbing Fuji — so elusive and uncertain is the exact knowledge of one's reactions to unknown conditions.

The problems of trekking at high altitude are most acute with large groups of travellers of disparate age, physical condition, and mountain-climbing experience — particularly when there are travel time constraints. Potential trekkers should either submit themselves to a test on a peak like Mt. Fuji, or to a precise medical examination, preferably in a low-pressure, low oxygen laboratory. Only then might high altitude accidents be avoided with any certainty. Travellers also should beware of advertisements for treks which may be irresponsible in this regard. In any case, if the traveller's situation does not allow the medical or other checks mentioned above, and there is hint of risk, he should not hesitate to cancel any arrangements made.

Symptoms of high altitude sickness are liable to occur at any height, although 4,000 meters seems to be a general dividing line. Such symptoms include headache, nausea, regurgitation, breathlessness, insomnia (yet in some cases, uncontrollable sleepiness), swelling, coughing, wheezing, abnormal phlegm, exhiliration, vertigo, bewilderment, temporary stoppage of respiration, a hung-over feeling, or simply a general difficulty in breathing. There may develop feelings of hallucination, double vision, loss of a sense of direction, narrowing of the field of view, unconsciousness, coma, and, at worst, eventually death. Precautionary measures might involve such as grueling physical training, though at above 3,500 meters the schedule should be as relaxed as possible. Water should be drunk profusely and there should be a general absence of tension and worry. Individuals should train together and supervise each other closely, being especially alert for anything abnormal. If such occurs, training should be interrupted immediately without hesitation and the trainee should be returned to an altitude lower than 3,500 meters. Fitness for high altitude travel can be developed by gradual adjustment to height, by a phenomenon known as "acclimatization."

2. Various Types of Trekking

To be more specific about trekking, an individual might either join a packaged tour, or set out on his own. In the latter case, one might gather together a small expedition, with hired porters, or — as is the local custom — merely conduct a kind of individual walking trip. Summarizing these more systematically, A might be the packaged trek, B, the invididual trek with Sherpa or guide and hired porters, and C, an individual trek without a guide. In any case, accoring to regulations issued in 1976, regardless of which style of trek is chosen, when one applies for authorization the officials will expect the arrangements to be made under the tutelage of a licensed trekking concern or a travel agent.

The best example of A is the Mountain Travel organization, which handles all aspects of trekking. Clients must provide their own passage to and from Kathmandu, but otherwise the arrangements are in professional hands. The founder of this company is the famous mountaineer, Col. James Roberts, and its services are so reliable and prestigious that Sherpa guides vie with pride to be included in its roster.

One can make travel reservations with Mountain Travel through agents anywhere in the world, or simply by visiting the home office in Kathmandu. Once a reservation is made and paid for, all that is necessary for the traveller is to appear on the appointed day at a designated place, and everything for the trek will have been arranged. At such time, the client will be confronted by an assemblage which — in addition to guides and porters — will include such basic equipment as cooking utensils and food, required medical items, and the tents, which will be erected each evening at selected intervals, and spaced in such a way as to afford the maximum in comfort and privacy to the traveller, whose main responsibility thereafter is to maintain the strength of his digestive system and legs, and to proceed at a comfortable pace with rest periods as needed. One of the pleasantest aspects of an A-trek concerns the organization's responsibility to erect special tents which serve as toilets and dressing rooms, a service which is probably appreciated most by women trekkers, as these provide a measure of shelter against the curious eyes of the local people, whose attentions are particularly directed to the female members of any party. Except for such personal things as changes of clothing, cameras, and film, everything is carried by the porters. Therefore, aside from the risk of mountain sickness, trekking in the Himalayas, if done in this manner, is hardly more taxing than the general run of mountain-climbing at home.

Preferred customers of Mountain Travel are individuals or small groups of those with a broad background in mountain-climbing (perhaps in their home countries), and especially those who, regardless of past experience, hanker particularly for a trek in the Himalayas. The planning is designed to favor nature-lovers such as observers of local flora and fauna, students of human activity in an unusual setting, or those who might merely wish to revel in or to record on paper or canvas, the magnificent mountain scenery. I have had little experience with Japanese participants in such treks, but it has been my special pleasure to observe the consistently pleasant and comfortable relationships enjoyed by the clientele in this kind of tent life.

The Mountain Travel organization, in typical British fashion, takes the long-range view of such tour direction by carefully fostering and maintaining the loyalty of its guides and porters, not for the moment, but for generation after generation. The establishment of a tradition of confidence and trust is thus the quality which particularly distinguishes this concern. Trekking periods with Mountain Travel range from about one to seven weeks, and if four to five persons form a party for a one-week trek, the basic cost is about $175 each; while a 30-day trek is about $465 per person.

There are, however, at least ten such companies headquartered in Kathmandu, each conducting treks in its own way. There is even such an organization in Japan.

One drawback of the A-type trek which should be mentioned is that there is a minimum of latitude for individual initiative. One must adapt himself to the general routine of the party. This kind of trek may also be more costly.

The type-B trek, on the other hand, has the advantage of being fairly flexible in its duration and objectives, it is also more adaptable to the budgets of the participants. The key to the success of this type lies in the availability of competent Sherpa and porters, especially as it is extremely difficult to find guides who can be, at the same time, good managers, good guides, and good liaison persons with the local people.

Kathmandu-based travel agencies and trekking organizations include:

Travel Agencies (as of January 1979)

1. Third Eye Tours Pvt. Ltd., Kanti Path, Tel. 11738, P.O.Box 124.
2. Nepal Travel Agency Pvt. Ltd., Ram Shah Path, Tel. 13106.
3. Everest Travel Service, Ganga Path, Tel. 11216.
4. Himalayan Travel and Tours, Durbar Marg, Tel. 11682.
5. Yeti Travels, Durbar Marg, Tel. 11234. P.O.Box 76.
6. Natraj Tours & Travels, Ghantagar, Tel. 12014.
7. Kathmandu Travel and Tours, Ganga Path, Tel. 14446, P.O.Box 459.
8. Gorkha Travels, Durbar Marg, Tel. 13495, P.O. Box 629.
9. Shanker Tours & Travels, Lazimpat, Tel. 13494, P.O.Box 529.
10. Annapurna Tours & Travels, Ghantagar, Tel. 13940, P.O.Box 1419.
11. International Travels & Tours Pvt. Ltd., Ram Shah Path, Tel. 12635.
12. Trans-Himalayan Tours & Travels, Durbar Marg, Tel. 13871, P.O.Box 283.
13. Universal Tours & Travels, Kanti Path, Tel. 12080, P.O.Box 939.

Trekking Agencies (as of January 1979)

1. Mountain Travel, Maharajganj, Tel. 12808, P.O.Box 170.
2. Annapurna Trekking & Mountaineering Pvt. Ltd., Durbar Marg, Tel. 12736, Box 795.
3. Himalayan Trekking Pvt. Ltd., Ram Shah Path, Tel. 11808, P.O.Box 391.
4. Sherpa Trekking Service, Kopundol, Tel. 13176, P.O.Box 500.

5. The Sherpa Society, Ram Shah Path, Tel. 12412.
6. International Trekkers Pvt. Ltd., Panipokhari, Tel. 11786, Box 1273.
7. The Sherpa Cooperative Trekking Pvt. Ltd., Ram Shah Path, Tel. 11808, Box 1338.
8. Nepal Treks & Natural History, Expeditions Pvt. Ltd., Ganga Path, Tel. 14446, Box 459.
9. Trans-Himalayan Trekking Pvt. Ltd., Durbar Marg, Tel. 13854, Box 283.
10. Kanchanjunga Trekking Pvt. Ltd., Ram Shah Path, Tel. 14139.
11. Himalayan Rover Treks, Naxal, Tel. 12691, Box 1081.
12. Nepal Trekking Pvt. Ltd., Thamel Tel. 14681, Box 368.
13. Great Himalayan Adventure, Pvt. Ltd., Kanti Path, Tel. 14424, Box 1033.
14. Express Trekking (P) Ltd. Naxal, Tel. 13017.
15. Himalayan Journeys Sangril La Tours,Kantipath, Box 989.
16. Gauri Shanker Trekking Service Pvt. Ltd., Jamal, Durbar Marg, Tel. 12112, Box 881.
17. Manaslu Trekking Pvt. Ltd., Durbar Marg, Tel. 12422, Box 1519.
18. Natraj Trekking, Durbar Marg, Tel. 12014.

Again, it should be mentioned that the new regulations state that any trekking program must be compiled under the guidance of one of the above in order to enjoy the sanction of the Nepalese authorities. These agencies can also supply up-to-date information on permitted trekking areas — an important consideration, as in India and Nepal, constantly changing regulations determine which areas are accessible at any given time.

3. Trekking in India and Nepal: Some Comparisons and Contrasts

It has only been in relatively recent times that foreigners have recognized that the pleasant atmosphere that has long accompanied caravan travel at moderate elevations in Nepal, is also characteristic of the higher realms of this mountainous and long-isolated land. Attracted by the challenges of high-altitude travel, foreigners at first merely joined local expeditions, but gradually the technique of trekking was devised and what had been a practical means of travel was thus converted into a recreational activity.

In contrast, in India, which was a British colonial country for so long, trekking is imbued with an atmosphere that reflects a long-established habit of catering to a ruling class of foreign occupiers or native princes. Recently, however, in India as well, the essence of modern trekking has been recognized, and the treatment of foreigners in the future is bound to change accordingly.

The area available for trekking in India, however, is rather narrow, and there are relatively few experienced and reliable guides. On the other hand, India abounds in good recreational areas for golfing, fishing or resort living. But when it comes to long-distance walking trips, only a large, carefully-organized caravan is sufficient. Furthermore, equipment is not obtainable locally, nor is there any such custom of impromptu lodging as will be described for Nepal. At many recreational sites in India, there are, however, packs of donkeys and mules available for side trips.

4. Selection of Season and Area

The Himalayas are so high and extended that the selection of a suitable season for trekking and mountain-climbing necessarily differs according to place. For example, the section of the Himalayas from Nepal eastward, has a rainy season in summer, so mountain-climbing is best pursued in spring and autumn when it is hotter and drier. Trekking, on the other hand, may also be done in spring and summer, but the winter dry season is best.

In the Western Himalayas at high altitudes (above 2,000 meters), there is heavy snowfall in winter which interrupts all road traffic and closes all hotels, inns, and travel offices — the only sign of activity being in the **Gulmarg** ski area.

As for trekking in the state of Kashmir, June and July are the most appropriate months, while in the **Himachal Pradesh** mountains, in the vicinity of Simla, Kulu, and Manali, September is best, the time between summer and autumn.

The mountainous land at the gateway to the state of **Uttar Pradesh** is rather in-between in this regard, with a short rainy season in summer and snow in winter, so that the best times for mountain-climbing — especially when one consults the records of the past — are the periods between September and October, and May and June. Trekking here, however, since its climatological requirements differ, can be pursued virtually at any season.

The whole Eastern Himalayas can also be considered in this light. For example, since the mountains are at their liveliest in the rain, and the amount of precipitation both decreases with elevation and occurs mainly during the night-time hours, trekking is entirely possible even during the rainy season.

If the desired trekking area is located along the northern slope of the main Himalayan chain, the effect of the monsoon is minimal, so one needs to consider precipitation conditions only on the route to and from the trekking region. Mosquitoes and leeches may be a nuisance in the rainy season but such may be offset by the beauty of the flowers at this time. In all, rainy season trekking is a phase of the sport which holds many surprises, but which until the very present has been little exploited. On the other hand, the lack of access because of out-of-season airline schedules is a handicap, and in any case, the schedules that remain in effect are often unreliable.

The **Leh** area of the **Ladakh** District of northern Kashmir has been available for trekking only since the sumer of 1974. Here, since rainfall is minimal for Kashmir, trekking is possible the year round. However, summer is still the best season since one has access only through Kashmir where conditions in winter especially, are prohibitive. In the Kingdom of Bhutan (which has also become accessible recently) conditions are similar to those of Sikkim, so trekking should be done only in the period following the monsoon season.

5. Routes to the Himalayas

The route from Japan, or anywhere else, usually begins with an air journey to a point where access may be gained to the Himalayas, and it is this leg of the trip which entails the greatest expense. Any reduction in this outlay would therefore bear heavily on the cost of the entire venture. With this in mind, it would be well for the traveller to investigate, through travel agencies or the airlines themselves, whether there are discounts available for such travel. Another possibility to reduce this initial cost lies in **charter** flights, for which there are even popular organizations which publicize such travel opportunity among their members.

Access to the **Western Himalayas** can best be gained by an airline which follows the southern route between Europe and Asia, and which allows stops at such gateway cities as Bombay or Delhi, from either of which one could proceed by train, domestic airline, or even by bus.

The most convenient way to enter **Nepal**, in the **Central Himalayas**, is to fly directly to Kathmandu. Over-land routes are indicated in the general map of the Nepal Himalayas on pages 78-79. Entrance to Nepal can otherwise only be made from a Europe to Asia flight with connections to Kathmandu via Delhi, Calcutta, Rangoon, or Bangkok.

For the **Eastern Himalayas** from any of the above flights, one should arrive at Calcutta, which has air connections with both Kathmandu and **Bagdogra**, though from Calcutta one could also reach these places by train and bus. If one is ignorant of Hindi or Bengali, however, or of general conditions in India, this seemingly economical land journey can be highly uncomfortable, regardless of the rewards one might enjoy from meeting the challenge.

Connections between airlines often call for one or more night's lodging and meals, and these expenses are covered by normal tickets. Incidentally, at such times, since one is most vulnerable to price-gouging by the company, hotel, or by the attendants, it is well to be especially vigilant when such conditions arise. In any case, discount tickets often do not cover lay-over accommodations, so the traveller should be careful at the beginning to know exactly which accommodations are provided by the carrier and which are his own responsibility.

The C-type trek is less convenient than formerly because of the decline in passenger ship travel. Also since very few ships go directly to South Asia, one should be prepared to change vessels frequently. Over-land access, other than by private car, is possible by such as long-distance bus — on, for example, the London to Sydney route — or by using local buses, as needed. But in any case, one should be prepared with an International Driver's License, and with visas and permits to pass through the countries along the way.

Transportation Routes to the Foothills of the Himalayas (Local subdivisions from the Indian Government's **National Atlas**).

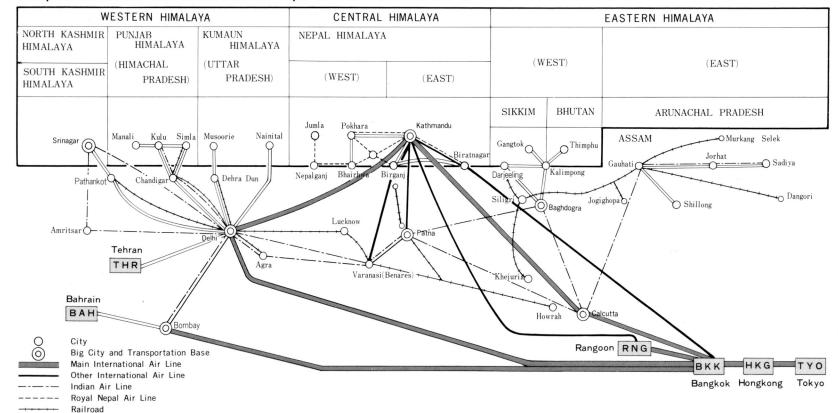

WESTERN HIMALAYA			CENTRAL HIMALAYA		EASTERN HIMALAYA	
NORTH KASHMIR HIMALAYA	PUNJAB HIMALAYA (HIMACHAL PRADESH)	KUMAUN HIMALAYA (UTTAR PRADESH)	NEPAL HIMALAYA		(WEST)	(EAST)
SOUTH KASHMIR HIMALAYA			(WEST)	(EAST)		
					SIKKIM / BHUTAN / ARUNACHAL PRADESH / ASSAM	

○ City
◎ Big City and Transportation Base
━━━ Main International Air Line
───── Other International Air Line
─·─·─ Indian Air Line
── ── Royal Nepal Air Line
+++++ Railroad
═════ Regular Bus Service

6. Compiling a Trekking Budget

The initial and possibly euphoric anticipations of the traveller are inevitably subject to the more down-to-earth processes of committing these to considerations of available time and money. To many, once the details are confronted in the light of day the whole venture may appear quite impossible. However, when one turns to the creation of an effective budget, it is surprising how attainable a Himalayan trip can become.

1) Himalayan Travel At No Cost To The Traveller

No trip has hard-and-fast rules of accomplishment. According to a letter in the MOUNTAIN NEWS, a reader complained that Himalayan travel was not for him because, in his opinion, such was the exclusive province either of those with an unusual amount of leisure time, or money, probably both; or of those for whom the conquering of unknown heights in the Himalayas was a special means of ego-gratification. However, it is even possible to visit the Himalayas without incurring any personal cost. The secret lies in the motivation of the traveller. All else is secondary.

If one is sufficiently motivated there are several ways to arrange a Himalayan trip without direct cost to the traveller. For example, one might become dedicated, and in doing so find employment which would support the undertaking. One might become the leader of a tour group, or better, the head of trekking party. More specifically, one might find a job to fit his particular talents and be sent on a Himalayan trip by his employer, as for example a newspaper man who might be asked to do a story on mountain climbing, or a photographer or artist who must make sketches, paintings, or photographs.

If this seems far-fetched, there is another, more rapid means to gain the same end by simply taking advantage of the rule which allows one person to assemble a group of 15 or more, who then become eligible (according to current regulations in India and Nepal) for discount air fares, and (of particular importance), one free passage for trips ranging from 5 to 28 days. This may take up to one year to arrange, but if carefully done, the free passage is automatically provided. The tour leader might also collect an extra amount from each of the party to cover his own exertions, even his own expenses in South Asia. It should be remembered, however, that since the main concern is to insure a safe and pleasant experience for all, certain sacrifices, including some personal expenditure, are to be expected.

2) Participation in a Group Tour

Travel agencies normally offer various kinds of group tours which involve trekking in the Himalayas, and the prices of these range from $700 to $1,200, the particulars varying from those which cover only round-trip air fare and hotel accommodations en route to the trekking site (all other expenses being borne by the individual), to those which are all-embracing except for personal expenditures on such as gifts or souvenirs. Except in countries like Bhutan where minimum costs are based on the number of days, and one must expect a total cost of at least $2,350 normal, over-all trips run around $1,000 per person, with another $400 in reserve.

3) Costs for Individual or Small-Group Trekking

For such trekking, one's funds should be divided into three parts: 1] for round-trip air fare, 2] for local accommodations, and 3] for the trek itself.

1] **Air Fares** — Round-trip, economy class tickets from Tokyo to Delhi are currently $1,115.67, with a maximum mileage privilege, whereby one can also stop off at Hong Kong, Bangkok, Kathmandu, and Calcutta, free of charge. The same flight directly from Tokyo to Kathmandu, with a one-night lay-over in Bangkok, in other words, would cost the same. Furthermore, in addition to the basic fare from the starting point to Kathmandu, one needs funds for supplementary air travel to the place nearest the actual trekking base.

There are available as well, discount air fares, designated F.I.T. and G.I.T., respectively, at $877.33 and $629.33, for a one-person, round-trip flight, but unfortunately, other attractively-priced excursion offers do not include travel between Japan and India. F.I.T. tours, however, are limited to a period of from 10 to 28 days, though one may have unlimited stop-over privileges between place of origin and destination. G.I.T. arrangements, on the other hand, cover tours of from 5 to 28 days and allow stop-overs in only 5 cities. The latter also requires parties of 15 or more, with a free ticket for the 16th. F.I.T. tours are not limited in number of persons, but only groups of 15 or more can claim a free passage.

Lay-over accommodations are provided by airlines usually if one is proceeding by the same company, although in some cases a change to another service may be allowed. Student fares are another possibility for low-cost travel but the agreement may contain complicated clauses, for which the traveller is urged not to hesitate in seeking an explanation of airline companies or travel agencies.

Those with more time than funds have always been partial to sea travel, but unfortunately such is largely a thing of the past. Today, passenger ships are often as expensive as airplanes, and many freighters no longer accept passengers.

However, some may still desire passage by ship, and for this a brokerage firm which usually handles freight may be able to provide some clues.

Within India, air travel is relatively inexpensive, although the cheapest means is still train or long-distance bus. Overland travel in Nepal is so limited by local conditions that one would do well to inquire at an embassy or consulate as to available accommodations. In any case, for anything other than air travel, one should be prepared to exercise the utmost in patience and determination.

Overland access to South Asia from Europe is possible by rail, bus and private camper. Among these, there is, for example, the aforementioned regular round-trip bus service between London and Sydney, via Delhi and Kathmandu — timetables and scheduled arrivals usually being posted at hotel counters in Kathmandu, especially at the Hotel Blue Star (Telephone 12379) and the Camp Hotel (Phone 13145). Some travel groups are also interested in recruiting new members for this service. However, whatever bus route one chooses, the fares are customarily posted along with the schedules.

2] Expenses for Local Accommodations

Since the details of accommodations in hotels and inns in the Himalayan foot-hills are given later, the following will cover this subject generally, both for A-grade facilities (better-than-average) and B-grade (of somewhat lower standing than the guide-book listings).

A-grade hotels in India, for example, charge $10 to $30 for a single room, $18—45 for a twin; while B-grade places are $2—7 for a single,

$5—10 for a twin in Indian-style hotels, and only $1 in Government-run hostelries. United States dollars are required by law in Delhi for hotel expenses. Otherwise, local currency may be used, but the change will be returned in Rupees, which convert at rates usually unfavorable to the traveller, making it expedient to carry sufficient change to cover such contingencies.

A-grade hotels in Nepal, Western-style, charge $5—24 for a single room, $10—35 for a twin. B-grade lodgings and guest houses (without meals) are only $2—4 single, $3—6, twin. And if one can tolerate dormitory-style sleeping, bed charges are but 40¢ a night. With meals and miscellaneous expenses, daily living costs are in the neighborhood of $35 in India for A-grade, $9 for B; while in Nepal, $30 for A-grade, $7 for B. One is wise, of course, to carry more than the minimum amount.

3] **Trekking Expenses** a] for preparation, b] for expenses en route, c] for gratuities.

a] Equipment and Supplies — since but 20 kg are allowed per person on economy air tickets, it is often well to acquire equipment and supplies locally. $150 should be enough for a period of 20 days.

b] En Route Expenses, including upkeep for porters and guides, run around $1 per day per person for such things as firewood and bus fares. Multiply the number of trekking days by the number of people in the party, to arrive at an estimate of total expenses.

c] Gratuities run from $1.50—$2.00 per person for guides, $1—$1.50 for porters.

Other expenses might be for tobacco and other personal needs, but in very cold areas or where there is snow and ice, porters and guides must be provided with suitable clothing and equipment. This should be included in the contract, which should be carefully explained to all concerned, witnessed, and signed, before the trek is undertaken.

Price List in a local Selected Shop, Namche Bazar
November 30, 1972

Goods	(Sherpa)	Amount	Price in Nepal Rupees
potatoes	(Riki)	1 pathi	4:00
rice	(Da)	1 pathi	29:00
flour	(Maida)	1 pathi	14:00
noodles	(Tokpa)	1 pack	5:00
sugar	(Chini)	1 pathi	40:00
condensed milk	(Duht)	130 oz in can	8:00
beer, canned	(beer)	1 can 225 g	16:00
		large can	22:00
tomato juice		large can	20:00
cheese	(Somar)	medium can	18:00
biscuits, (Monaco)		1 pack	6:00
instant coffee (Nescafé)		small can 50 g	10:00
canned sardines	(Nya)	small flat can 160 g	6:00
cigarettes (Asa)		20 pieces	1:00
peanut butter		400 g	12:00
tea		small pack	8:00
oil	(Khanatel)	one bottle	2:00
matches	(Checta)	12 boxes, small	3:00
soap	(Sabun)	100 g	2:00
candles		12	7:00
toilet paper		1 roll	6:00
trekking boots		one pair	100:00
tennis shoes		one pair	20:00
wool socks		one pair	20:00
down jackets		1	250:00
kerosene		1 bottle	4:00
tibetan caps		1	15:00

(1 pathi ≒ 4 kg)

4] **Gross Estimates**

In the writer's personal experience, a single individual trek of 10 days to two weeks, calls for about $300 per person, and for a party of 3 or 4, $170 per person; while an individual trek of 20 days with porter and guide calls for a minimum of $400. The list shown herein reveals the details of prices for certain basic items, and if this seems out-of-date, it is usually possible, by pricing sample items, to apply any price changes across the board. One additional expense is that for accident insurance, a prerequisite for any trek. A reserve fund of about $675 per person, as stated, is probably sufficient.

One should also be ready with application forms for visa extension and authorization to trek, and with extra funds to cover climbing fees. Extra funds are also needed to permit some latitude in dealing with trekking agencies.

7. Clothing and Equipment

As a rule, one's gear should be as small and light as possible. For example, from my own experience on leaving Japan between fall and winter, I carried:

1) Clothing and Bag

a. Hat — a golf cap is a good choice, or at least one with a visor.

b. Jacket — as it is well often to carry heavy articles on one's person, it is convenient to have a jacket with many pockets.

c. Trousers — long pants of stout material are recommended.

d. Shoes — any weight mountain boots are good, but especially ones that are well-broken in and comfortable.

e. Underwear — this should be as lightweight as possible.

f. Shirts — long-sleeved with large pockets. Sleeves can be rolled up in warm weather.

g. Socks — these should be thick.

h. Bag or Rucksack — strong enough for essential items, yet small enough to be admitted as hand-luggage on an airplane.

2) Hand Luggage

a. Cameras, books, film, foreign-made articles — should all be registered with customs before departing the home country, or you may be charged when you return.

    b. Umbrella — superfluous perhaps in a dry season but essential. This should be large enough to protect both the user and his ruck-sak.

    c. Passport, Immunization Record, and Air Tickets — should all be carried at all times, along with **traveller's checks** and **insurance policies.** Also, the serial numbers of cameras, lenses, and other equipment; the numbers and denominations of traveller's checks, amounts and kinds of currency, and accident or health insurance policy numbers, should be written in a small notebook and carried.

    d. Time-pieces, pencils, and notebooks, altimeter, and compass, personal medical sup-plies and pharmaceutical items, should be con-sidered.

    3) Baggage (20 kg limit, to be checked through on ticket). All should be chosen with care as to weight, size, and strength. These might include:

    a. **Unobtainable Locally in South Asia**

1] Rucksack — One that is roomy, strong, light-weight (see above).

2] Padded Clothing — Needed at higher elevations; unnecessary otherwise.

3] Film — Reduce the bulk by removing all unnecessary wrapping.

4] Head-lamp, sketchbook, and field note-book — if required.

5] Scale — for weighing luggage for air travel.

6] Underwear — both winter and summer types.

7] Knitted hat or cap — convenient for high altitudes.

8] Shirts — half-sleeve type of linen or cotton.

    b. **Possibly Obtainable Locally**

1] Sleeping Bag — I recommend one that is feather-padded and weighs approxi-

mately 1.2 kg.

2] Handkerchiefs, kleenex*, artist's brushes and writing implements.
    * = see next section.

3] Emergency pharmaceutical goods (for such as superficial skin injuries, stomach and intestinal up set, colds or influenza).

4] Socks (see above).

5] Sweaters — thick yarn knit is preferrable.

6] Sport Shirts — long-sleeved, wool, are best.

7] Cosmetic Items.

    c. **Easily Obtainable Locally** (see paragraph 4., below)

Tobacco can be purchased at duty-free shops upon leaving the homeland or elsewhere, but regulations differ by nation as to how much the traveller may import.

    4) Items Required Directly for Trekking — All these are available locally except for klee-nex, slide fasteners (zippers), and a ladle, if necessary. Disposable tissue is produced rather universally but is often of poor quality or in inconvenient form. Regular kleenex should either be brought in or obtained in the larger cities or at tourist sites. Locally-obtain-able items might include:

    a. Shoes — light canvas, mountain-climb-ing shoes and sandals.

    b. Knives — these can be any style, in-cluding the local **Kukri,** but the traveller should remember that knives now cannot be carried into an airplane.

    c. Cookware — A pressure cooker is par-ticularly useful, also a frying pan and cover, a rolling pin and pastry board, a tea kettle, and a thermos flask (such as those made in China).

    d. Towels, soap, detergent, cleanser, and toilet articles.

    e. Matches, tobacco, needles and thread, spare buttons, shoe laces, paper, and ball-point pens.

8. Customs and Manners

The old saying, "When in Rome . . .", is a wise slogan for Nepal and India. The traveller would do well in this regard to read diaries and the records of the personal experiences of others.

For example, in South Asia the attitude toward money is quite different from that in Japan or perhaps other cultures, and it is of special importance to the traveller to be ac-quainted with this particular local custom. For one thing, paper money that is considered damaged is not accepted by local banks in South Asia, when such currency would be per-fectly acceptable at home. For another, in Indian banks it is the custom to punch a hole in the (white) area near the watermark of a bill so that these can then be strung together. Nobody would complain about such deface-ment, yet the slightest irregularity along the borders of the note could render it utterly valueless. Therefore, when one receives money at a bank or post office, or change at a store, it is imperative to insure that not only the amount is correct but that the bills are physical-ly undamaged according to custom. An even more important aspect is that failure to ob-serve these particulars in the eyes of the local people, is a mark not only of a person who is careless with money, but who is generally loose and untrustworthy as well. In addition, when one exchanges money, or while watching another who is counting his change, the transac-tion is accompanied by a kind or ritual whereby the counting and confirmation should be loud and obvious, and from which the attentions of both parties should never stray until all is for-mally concluded.

There is special importance in India attached to the use of small change, which always should be carried for tips. If this is not done, there is a tendency to squander one's currency. Moreover, many establishments will refuse the larger denominations of paper money, even for the purchase of required food. The traveller without sufficient small change, in other words, faces the risk of going hungry. Furthermore, one always seems to use more small change than is received in return. Therefore, when exchanging currency at the airport on arrival in South Asia, it is well to take some extra time and effort to obtain a good supply of coins.

In Japan and other nations, it is common both to see cameras being toted and freely used. However, in South Asia this is rarely the case. And when occasionally a camera is seen, there is much more importance attached to the picture-taking. At home in Japan and elsewhere, there are few places where photography is prohibited (except perhaps near United States military bases), but in South Asia one is not allowed to take photographs around such as airports or from airplanes, or of soldiers or military places, railroads and railway operations, bridges, irrigation networks and dams. Consequently, those who snap pictures indiscriminately are considered peculiar at best, and otherwise are apt to be suspected of espionage.

Therefore, if one is seriously intent upon photography in South Asia, it is best to be prepared with official letters of explanation from such as directors of tour agencies, ambassadors or consular officials.

Our Faithful Porter, the Yak

2

THE HIMALAYAS OF NEPAL

Children of Jomosom

Of the 14 peaks in the world higher than 8,000 meters, 9 lie in the Himalayas of Nepal. This section of the giant massif is in the center and sags southward from the basic arcuate chain. Actually, it encompasses two countries, the Kingdom of Nepal, and the Tibetan Autonomous Region of the Chinese Peoples' Republic. In Nepal, this part of the Himalayas has been divi--ded into three parts by the erosive force of three rivers, whose deeply incised valleys form routes of access from South Asia to Tibet. These are the **Kosi** in the east, the **Gandaki** in the center, and the **Karnali** in the west.

Each of these segments is distinguished by its own spectacular valleys, its verdant basins and, of course, its towering peaks, and all are pleasant trekking areas. Moreover, virtually all are open to trekkers — the only restricted areas being along the borders with other nations.

Since trekking has been practised in Nepal from the most ancient times, this deep heritage has helped to perpetuate until the present, a warmth of association between traveller and resident which is so often lacking in our modern society. The traveller should attempt to emulate this spirit at all times in order that such tradition is preserved. Modern trekkers thus have a responsibility not only to maintain a proud tradition but also to insure the healthy future of the activity, the nature of which embodies the very kinds of mutual respect between individuals and a magnificent geographical setting which, as the habitat of civilized human beings, one might hope would be characteristic of the future world. Here, one is confronted by two possible means of existence, one where money is the only reward, and one based on reciprocal thoughtfulness and esteem for the rights of others, where kindness is often a reward unto itself.

(Panorama labels, left to right:) API-SAIPAL GROUP — GURLA MANDHATA-HUMLA GROUP — DHAULAGIRI HIMAL — ANNAPURNA HIMAL — MANASLU GROUP — KANJIROBA HIMAL

Api 7132 · Gurla Mandhata 7728 · Saipal 7031 · Kailas 6714 · Kanjiroba Himal 6883 · Kanjelaruwa 6612 · Hiunchuli Patan 5916 · Jumla · Putha Hiunchuli 7246 · Churen Himal 7371 · Gurja Himal 7193 · D-IV 7661 · D-II 7751 · Dhaulagiri-I 8167 · Nilgiri 7061 · Tilitso 7132 · A-South 7219 · Annapurna-I 8091 · A-III 7555 · A-IV · Machhapuchhare 6993 · A-II · Kanglu 7937 · Kanglu 7009 · Manaslu 8156 · Pk.29 7835 · Baudh · Gurl

Surkhet · Dhorpatan · Baglung · Pokhara 762 · Butwal

Mountain Groups of the Nepal Himalayas and Their Famous Components

The Segments of the Himalayas of Nepal and Their Main Massifs

The distance between the Terai Plain at 200 meters above sea level, and the Plateau of Tibet, at 5,000, is only 50 to 150 kilometers, yet within this narrow area, bounded on north and south, respectively, by the Inner-Himalayas and the Mahabharat Range, and lying in three gigantic east-west arcs, are the Main or Great Himalayas, the highest part of the entire Himalayan system. South of this, between the Great Himalayas and the Mahabharat Range, is a mid-altitude land, including the Kathmandu Valley and the Pokhara Basin, the two most densely-populated portions of Nepal. Further south, between the discontinuous, east-west running Mahabharat and the Churia Hills, a lower but similarly elongate, parallel system, lies a basin-like lowland, called the Inner Terai.

As previously mentioned, three rivers, the Karnali, Gandaki, and Kosi, all tributaries of the Ganges, have eroded from north to south through these high chains, segmenting Nepal into three discreet realms. Secondary branch streams of these rivers have dissected these realms still further, and in the following, in text, pictures, and other illustrations, these subregions, together with their principal settlement areas and highland features, will be discussed.

Gurla Mandhata=Humla Group

Gurla Mandhata	7728
Nalkankar	6635
Takpu H.	6400
Snow Peak	6000
Takhu H.	6629

Api=Nampa Group

Api	7132
Nampa	6754
6700 Pk.	
N1 6700Pk.	
Rakshya Urai	6630

Saipal Group

Saipal	7031
6922 Peak	
6684 Peak	

Changla=Kubi Kangri Group

Tsanpo Ri	6574
Changla H.	6715
6715 Himal	
Kubi Kangri I	6856
II (west)	6640
III (extreme east)	6562
IV (east)	6448
V (extreme west)	6438

Kanjiroba Himal

Kanjiroba Main S. Peak	6883
Kanjiroba Main N. Peak	6861
Kande Hiunchuli	6627
Kanjelarwa	6621
Tso Karpo Kang	6556
Hanging Glacier Peak	6500
Kang Chunne	6443
Lha Shamma	6412
Bijala Hiunchuli	6386
Kang Nuntong	6248

Hiunchuri Patan Group

Hiunchuri Patan	5916
North Peak	5857
South Peak	5840
5557 Peak	
5226 Peak	
5395 Peak	

Dhaulagiri Himal

Dhaulagiri I	8167
II	7751
III	7715
IV	7661
V	7618
VI	7268
Churen Himal	7371
Putha Hiunchuli	7246
Gurja Himal	7193
Gama Pk.	7108
Tukche Pk.	6920

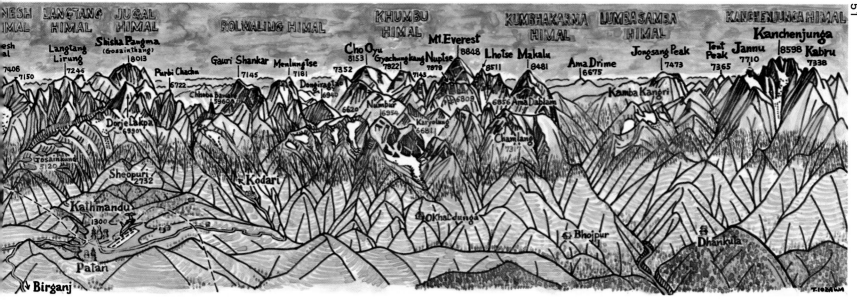

Annapurna Himal

Annapurna I	8091
II	7937
III	7555
IV	7525
Gangapurna	7454
Annapurna-South	7219
Tilitso Peak	7132
Nilgiri North Peak	7061

Manaslu Group

Manaslu	8156
Himal Chuli	7893
Dakura (Pk.29)	7835
Himlun Himal	7125
(Ratna Chuli)	
Kang Gulu	7009
Cheo Himal	6812
Baudha Pk.	6672

Ganesh Himal

Ganesh Himal I	7405
II (Lapsang Karbo)	7150
III	7130
IV (Pabil)	7102
V	6950
VI (Lamput)	6480
VII	6350
Paldol	5928
Chamal	7177
Tabsar	6100

Langtang=Jugal Himal

Shisha Pangma	8013
(Gosainthan)	
Phola Gangchen	7661
Langtang Lirung	7246
Langthang Ri	7239
Porong Ri	7284
Gang Benchen	7211
Big White Pk.	7083
(Lenpo Gang)	
Dorje Lakpa	6990
Kyungka Ri	6979
Shalbachum	6918
Phurbi Chyachu	6722

Chhoba Bamare Group

Chhoba Bamare	5970
Lapche Kang	
Lapisha Gang	
Kukur Raja Danda	

Rolwaling Himal

Menlungtse	7181
Gauri Shankar	7145
Pigferago Shar	6718
Ghengkur	6801
Takargo	6782
Hakun (Lundartsbugo)	6765
Chobutse	6660

Khumbu Himal

Mt. Everest	8848
(Chomolungma, or	
Sagarmatha)	
Lhotse	8511
Lhotse Shar	8383
Cho Oyu	8153
Gyachun Kang	7922
Nuptse	7879
Changtse	7553
Cho Ausi	7352
Chamlang	7313
Pumo Ri	7145
Numbur	6954
Dongiragtao	6940
Chumbu	6853
Peak 43	6769
Kangtega	6809
Panaiotoupa	6696
Karyolung	6681
Thamserkn	6623

Khumbhakarna Himal

Makalu	8481
Chomo Lengzo	7790
Peak 6	6739
Peak 3	6477

Lumba Samba Himal

Tsetse Kang	6800
Omboh Himal I—IV	
Ama Drime	6675
Lunbasamba Peak	5670
Kamba Kangri (Three	
Sisters) I—III	

Sharphu=Ohnmi Kangri Group

Ohnmi Kangri	7028
Sharphu I	7070
Sharphu II	
Tsajirun	6960
Pandra	6850
Nupchu	6690
Shao Kang	
Lashar I	6930
Lashar II	6860

Kanchenjunga Himal

Kanchenjunga	8598
South Peak	8476
Yalung Kang	8420
Kambachen	7902
Jannu	7710
Jongsang Peak	7473
Dome Kang	7442
Tent Peak	7365
Twins	7350
Talung Peak	7349
Kabru N. Peak	7353

FAMOUS MOUNTAINS OF THE NEPAL HIMALAYAS (under 8,000 meters)

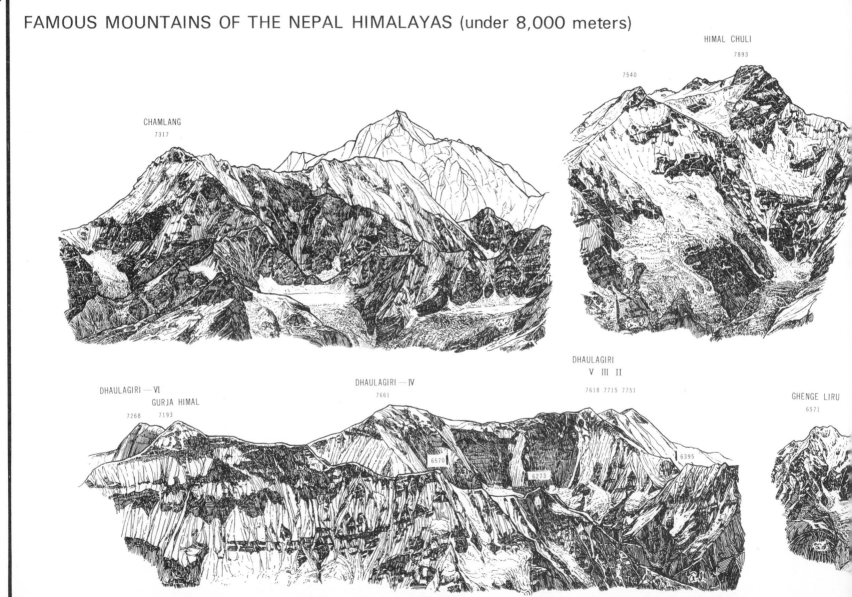

HIMAL CHULI
7893

7540

CHAMLANG
7317

DHAULAGIRI
V III II
7618 7715 7751

DHAULAGIRI — IV
7661

GHENGE LIRU
6571

DHAULAGIRI — VI
GURJA HIMAL
7268   7193

6570

6273

6395

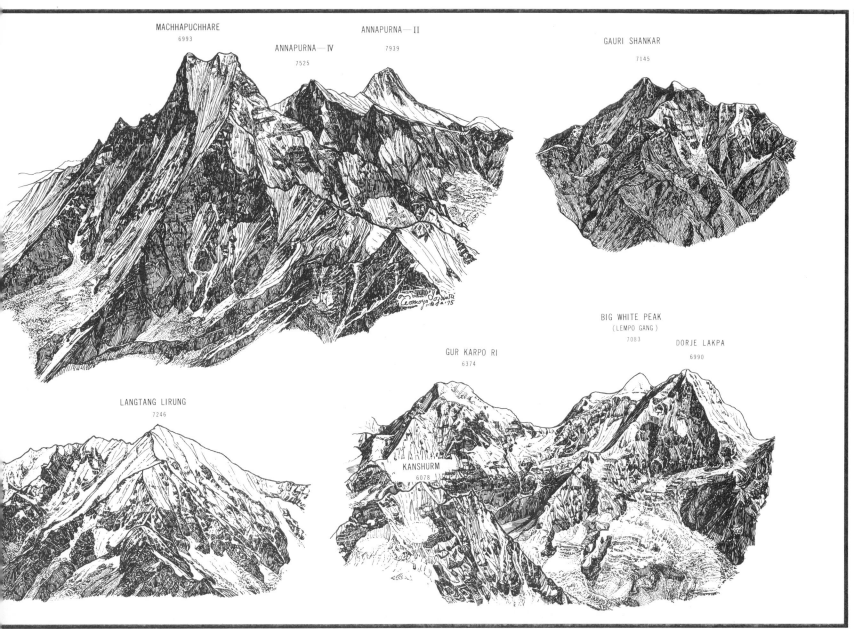

MACHHAPUCHHARE
6993

ANNAPURNA — IV
7525

ANNAPURNA — II
7939

GAURI SHANKAR
7145

BIG WHITE PEAK
(LEMPO GANG)
7083

DORJE LAKPA
6990

GUR KARPO RI
6374

KANSHURM
6078

LANGTANG LIRUNG
7246

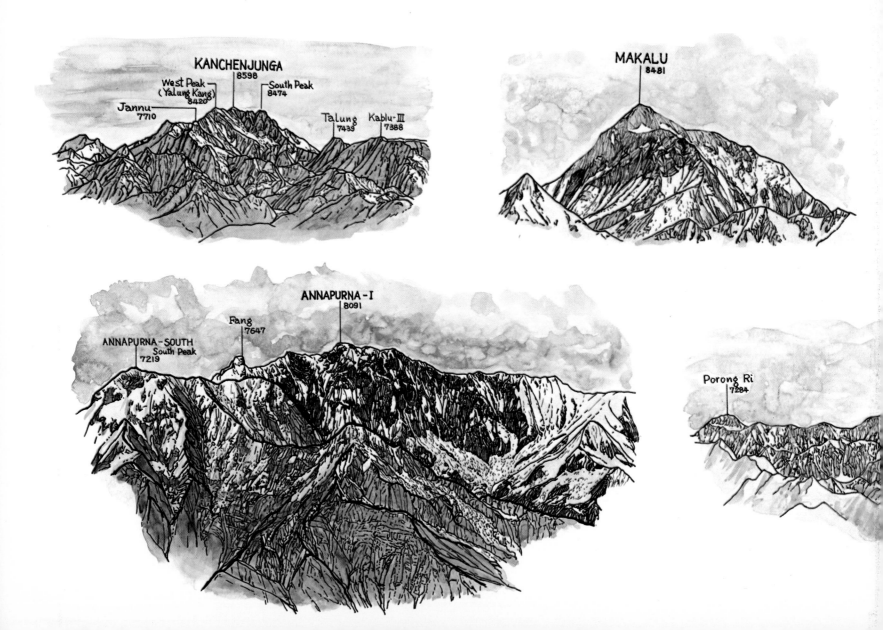

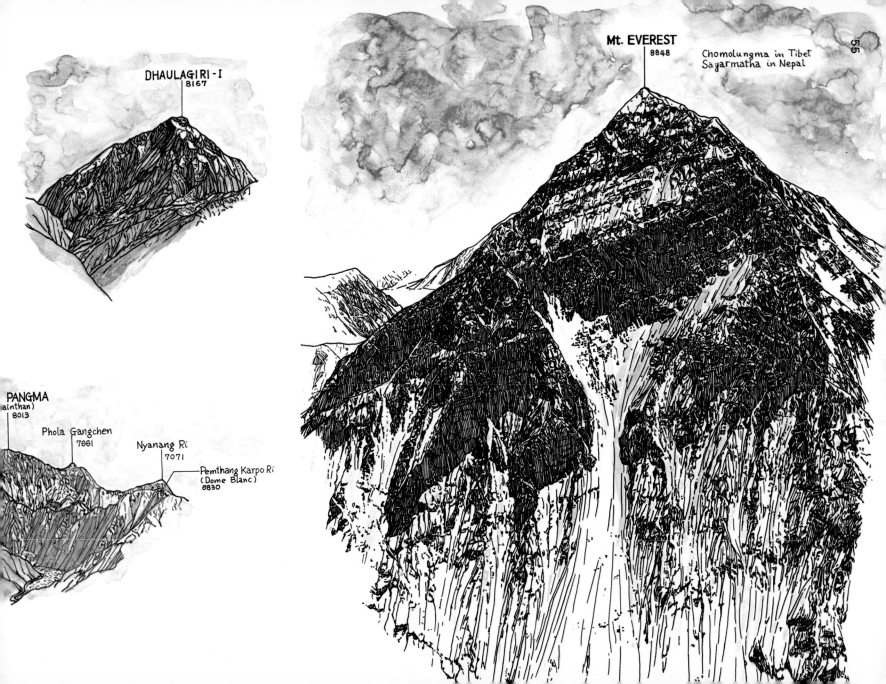

DHAULAGIRI-I
8167

Mt. EVEREST
8848

Chomolungma in Tibet
Sagarmatha in Nepal

PANGMA
(ainthan)
8013

Phola Gangchen
7661

Nyanang Ri
7071

Pemthang Karpo Ri
(Dome Blanc)
6830

This city, the capital of the Kingdom of Nepal, with a population of about 250,000, was founded in approximately 720 AD, in the reign of king Guna Kama Deva, of the Lichchhavi Dynasty. And, although there is scant archeological evidence, it is rather apparent that since Medieval times, Kathmandu has been a place of importance as a city-state, together with its two neighboring suburbs, Patan to the southeast and Bhadgaon to the east. Kathmandu, for example, still exhibits remnants of ancient brick ramparts, within which are crowded the four to five-story brick buildings of the present, each enclosing an inner court, so that the effect from the air is that of a honey comb. Between these structures is a labyrinthian maze of narrow streets, but outside the ramparts is the more modern world of spacious Western-style houses and buildings, giving the city an inner, ancient core, and an outer modern periphery. Kathmandu is thus a place where the visitor can savor to the fullest the most pleasurable aspects of such a trip, from the archaic Buddhist and Hindu temples, to the seemingly Medieval crowds at the local bazars. It is from this point, as the true gateway to the Himalayan region, that the trek will begin.

1. Arrival at Kathmandu

When the hills of the Mahabharat Range, with their cloak of broadleaf forest, which has thus far seemed so distant against the towering, snow-covered Himalayan peaks, begins to approach more rapidly, one should prepare for another sudden change of scene, to the lush paddy lands of the basin known as the Vale of Kathmandu. Circling for the approach to the airport, at 1,300 meters above sea level, one can look down upon various tiled roofs of the white Buddhist structures and other buildings.

Upon arrival, one should immediately submit the disembarkation card (filled out before landing), together with the Immunization form and passport containing the visa for Nepal (or if this is still to be procured, it can be obtained at the time). Officials will then stamp the visa with an entry permit and provide a **Foreign Exchange Transaction Form** from the Nepal Rastra Bank. Passports, certificates, and other forms are then returned to the traveller who proceeds to **customs**. Here, a porter should be instructed to bring all checked and hand baggage for examination to the least-crowded customs inspector. Cameras, tape recorders, and the like, should be declared at this time to insure that these will not be sold while you are in the country. Otherwise, after so stating, all else can usually be considered exempt, and if nothing seems unusual to the inspector the luggage will be marked with chalk and the incident ended. It should be remarked, however, that frequently such items as incidental gifts, or even such things as might be considered daily necessities at home, may at such times be questioned or subjected to additional duty.

Following the customs inspection, one moves to the money exchange booth and submits the form noted above, on which is written the amounts to be converted. The form is then authorized and returned, as it must be surrendered upon departing Nepal. One should allow about 15 Rupees (Rs) for a taxi, 50 Paisa (Ps) to 1 Rs for porters, 20 Rs for food and drink — all told about 100 Rs, which should be in 10, 5 and 1 Rupee bills, with coins in denominations of 25 and 50 Paisa. The smallest coin is 5 Paisa and is similar to the Japanese ¥1 or the American 1¢. At this time, one should be sure to confirm the exchange rate by examining the notation on the back of the Foreign Exchange Transaction form that has been authorized and returned. One should also confirm that the bills are undamaged — as noted in the foregoing — and if so there should be no hesitation about refusing these and demanding other currency. When all is confirmed, all forms and other documents in order and the luggage gathered and checked, the traveller is ready to depart the airport. At such moments, however, since it is common for an item of luggage to be overlooked, one should be particularly wary.

Although some may be interested in finding lodging by simply exploring on foot the various possibilities, hotel or other accommodations can be arranged by telex through airlines before departing the home country or at the information booth in the Kathmandu airport.

Departure from the airport lobby is usually the signal for one to be surrounded by a swarm of children and other insistant supplicants from hotels and inns, who implore the traveller to surrender his luggage and be guided to one place or another. It is necessary then to disperse the pesky children by firmly declaring a lack of change for tips, and by proceeding purposefully to a legitimately waiting taxi, preferrably one with a meter that has fixed charges. Luggage, at this point, should be handled personally, or if this is impracticable, a porter should be engaged at the customs area to accompany the traveller to a taxi.

If metered taxis are unavailable, one should learn the exact fare to his destination before entering the vehicle. According to a recent visit, the fare from the airport to center city was between 12 and 15 Rs. One should also memorize the taxi number, as when difficulties arise over charges and the authorities become involved, such evidence is needed.

One may now feel he has finally arrived in Kathmandu. However, there can be no relaxation until accommodations are fully secured and the traveller is in his room. Only then can luggage be opened. Another important matter is the arrangement for the trek, and this should be attended to at once, before any sight-seeing. However, in doing so, one is bound to become acquainted with many other aspects of the scene.

2. Life and Living

At the bottom of the Kathmandu Basin, slightly to the southwest, is the city of Kathmandu. In ancient times the name **Nepal** applied only to this area, and even as recently as 15 or 16 years ago a foreign party heard local hill people referring without distinction to the nation and its present capital. The use of the term valley **bottom** in describing the urban site is appropriate as it is here that several rivers and streams come together to form the Bagmati River, whose direction undergoes a radical shift to the south at this point, after which it flows via the Chobar and Katuwaldaha valleys southward, eventually to the Terai Plain in the southern part of the country. The city of Kathmandu lies in the first quadrant of a loop described by the Bagmati River entering from the east, where it takes on the Vishnumati River from the north and makes its radical turn southward toward the Terai Plain. The old city occupies an extremely narrow rectangle measuring only about 1 kilometer from east to west and 2 kilometers from north to south. On the eastern margins is a green area which, from north to south, houses the royal palace, the water reservoir, the Ratna Park, army headquarters and drill area, and the national stadium. Northeast of this green belt are large Western-style mansions, foreign embassies and other public buildings, including the administrative offices of His Majesty's Government of Nepal. Lining the old roads through and around this area are the local bazars and the typical houses and buildings of the region.

The old city is actually built on a series of terraces rising from a flood plain formed by two rivers, the highest portions representing the surfaces that have most stubbornly resisted the degrading effects of centuries of riverine erosion through the basic sedimentary material which underlies the entire site.

As stated, the old city is extremely cluttered, with four to five-story tile-roofed, brick buildings, each encircling a closed court, whose decorated wooden windows lend a picturesque air. The ground floor of these buildings is usually a shop, the upper floors being used for residences or business offices, although the fourth and fifth floors of these vertical tenements have frequently been converted into apartments, which are rented. In its present vigor and vitality as a center for commerce, trade, and the arts, the city of Kathmandu still reflects the activity of the Newari people, an urban ethnic group which since medieval times, has provided the basic cultural element.

While trekking may be the principal objective of the expedition, the life of Kathmandu can only be properly appreciated if one's schedule allows sufficient leisure to browse among its various wonders. And since much time is needed for such essentials as obtaining visa clearances and extensions, procuring Sherpa guides and porters, acquiring equipment and provisions — not to mention sightseeing and general shopping, one should plan on a minimum of four days for all this, exclusive of week-ends and holidays. As can be seen in the accompanying list, hotel and inn accommo-

	Name	Number of Beds	Single Rate	Twin Rate	Other	Phone
①	Hotel Soaltee Oberoi	218	$30.00	$42.00	Bed only	11211
②	Hotel De L'Annapurna	196	$24.00	$36.00	Bed only	11711
③	Hotel Shankar	270	$24.00	$34.00	Bed only	11973
④	Hotel Blue Star	95	$14.00	$22.00	Bed only	12379
⑤	Hotel Crystal	105	$15.40	$22.00	Bed and Breakfast	13611
⑥	Hotel Panorama	70	$4.82	$8.03	Bed only	11502
⑦	Hotel Green	18	$4.00	$7.50	Bed only	11961
⑧	Hotel Mount Makalu	62	$7.25	$10.50	Bed and Breakfast	13955
⑨	Hotel Paras	35	$3.50	$6.00	Bed and Breakfast	11233
⑩	Hotel the Nook	54	$7.00	$11.00	Bed only	13627
⑪	Hotel Manaslu	54	$6.00	$10.50	Bed and Breakfast	13471
⑫	The Camp Hotel	45	$3.00	$5.00	Bed and Breakfast	13115
⑬	Hotel K. T.	32	$2.45	$4.45	Bed and Breakfast	14417
⑭	Kathmandu Guest House	82	$1.50~4.50	$2.00~5.00	Bed only	13628
⑮	Taragaon Hotel Pvtltd. (Hotel Village) Bunglows	—	$10.50	$17.50	Bed only	15409
⑯	Hotel Malla	150	$23.00	$35.00	Bed only	15320
⑰	Hotel Yellow Pagoda	53	$14.14	$22.09	Bed and Breakfast	15492
⑱	Hotel Leo					11252
⑲	Hotel Lali Guras	30	$5.22	$15.66	Bed only	13304
⑳	Hotel Sugat					14929
㉑	Hotel Lhotse					15474
㉒	Hotel Valley View					13687
㉓	Hotel Woodlands	102	$12.00	$18.00	Bed only	12683
㉔	Hotel Yak & Yeti	110	$31.00	$42.00~72.00	Bed only	13317
㉕	Hotel Everest International	166 rooms	under construction	(open 1979)		14960

Hotels and Lodges in Kathmandu (1978)

□ Building
▣ Hotel and Lodge
▨ old town area
□ new town area

dations vary widely in quality and price, but in this regard, the traveller, rather than simply searching for an adequate room, would do well to be especially on the lookout for a place with toilet and bathing facilities which are properly supplied with water.

Among the hotels listed in the chart, numbers 1, 2, 4, 5 and 13, proudly boast such amenities as air-conditioning, but naturally these come at a price. If one's visit is so bent on trekking that the stay in Kathmandu can only be brief, of course it may be expedient to cater as much as possible to one's tastes, regardless of the expense. But if the schedule will allow and the stay can be more leisurely, it is diverting to have less imposing lodgings, from which one can explore the neighborhood to seek out small eating places which might take particular delight in the preparation of local delicacies.

Restaurants in Kathmandu have expanded recently in number and in the sophistication of their offerings. On the other hand, there is an unusually high turn-over among these places, so that on any given visit, one is apt to find a complete revision of names and ownerships. It may thus be impractical to attempt an introduction to certain establishments, but since such considerations are so important when one is on the road, the following is offered as a tentative guide.

Since hotel dining rooms are easily available to the visitor, these provide a good base, especially for those with little or no experience on the "outside". Set meals offered in the less expensive hotel dining rooms, moreover, are often attractive and satisfying fare. In those of the Hotel Soaltee Oberoi (No. 1) and the Hotel de L'Annapurna (No. 2), furthermore, although these are unquestionably first-class, in the tourist season, even with reservations, the visitor cannot expect very prompt service. The dining room (called **The Other Room**) of the

Hotel Crystal (No. 5) in the business section of the old city, is particularly noteworthy. Such of their items as the hamburger steak platter, which arrives sizzling hot and steaming on its iron plate, directly from the oven, are both reasonable and delicious. Since menus, however, frequently list items whose designations are intended to be humorous or witty, the traveller may be hard-pressed to make the proper interpretation. For Indian food, the venerable **Indira,** on New Road, can be especially recommended. Since some items are served exclusively at dinner, the traveller can be guided to some extent in his selections, by noticing what others are eating. In this way, the uninitiated can quickly be introduced to favorite local dishes.

For Chinese food, the **Tong Fong Cafe,** near the Yellow Pagoda Hotel (No. 17), is a good example of a genuine Chinese restaurant.

Japanese meals are to be had at the **Kushi Fuji,** close to the northern side of the Hotel de L'Annapurna. Slightly farther north, on the ground floor, is the RaRa, which has good **udon** and **oden.**

For Tibetan food, the **Utse,** near the Kathmandu Guest House (No. 14), is inexpensive.

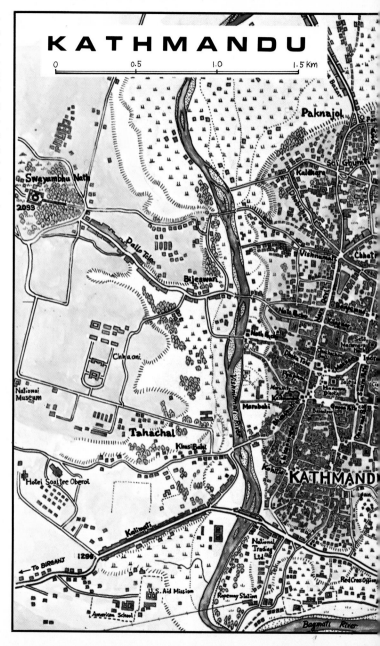

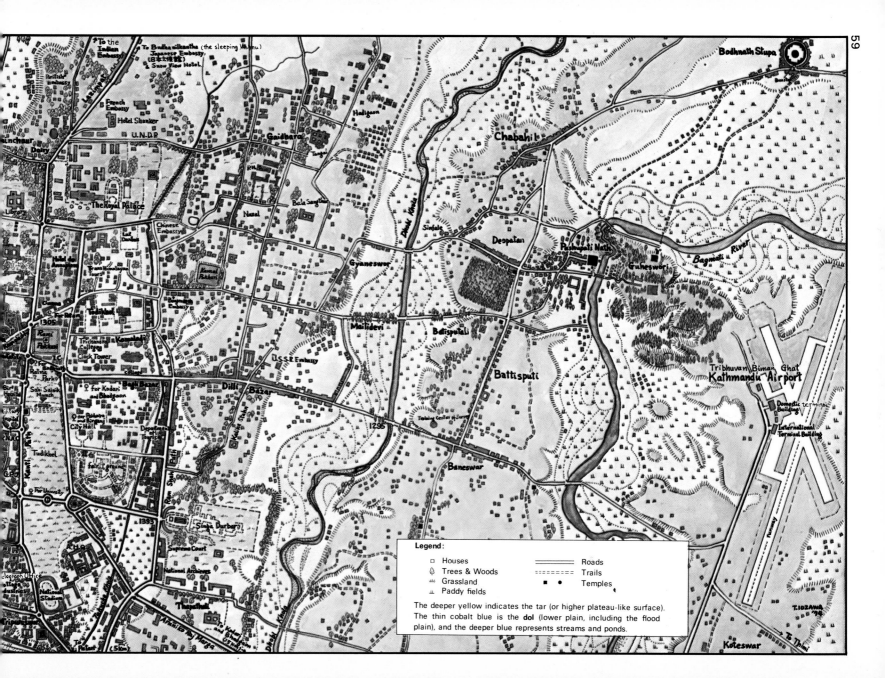

Bodhnath Stupa

To the Indian Embassy

To Budhanilkantha (the sleeping Vishnu)
Japanese Embassy
日本大使館
Snow View Hotel

British Embassy

Laxmipath

French Embassy

Hotel Shanker

U.N.D.P.

Gaidhara

Haligaon

Chabahil

Deopatan

Pashupati Nath

Dhobi Khola

Bagmati River

The Royal Palace

Library

Chinese Embassy

Simfale

Guheswori

Gyaneswor

Naxal

Bala Sangbu

Kamal Pokhari

Trans Himalayan Tours

Hotel de Annapurna

Burmese Embassy

Mailidevi

Balisputali

Battisputi

Tribhuvan Biman Ghat
Kathmandu Airport

1305

Rani Pokhri

Trichandra College
Clock Tower

Kamaladi

U.S.S.R. Embassy

Ratna Park

Bir Hospital

Tripureswor

Sahi Sainik Munch

for Kodari and Bhadgaon

Bagh Bazar

Dilli Bazar

Domestic Terminal Building

International Terminal Building

for Kodari and Bongmai

Department of Tourism

City Hall

1295

Training Center of Jorpati

Tudikhel

fair ground

Kanti Path

Baneswar

1393

Singha Durbara

Supreme Court

National Archives

Telegraph Office

National Stadium

Dhobi Khola

Thapathali

Arniko Raj Marga

To Kodari and Bhadgaon via Bagmati

Koteswar

To Thimi

T. IOZAWA '74

Shops and Goods, Kathmandu Bazar

SIGHTSEEING IN KATHMANDU:

3. Bazars and Historical Ruins

The city of Kathmandu is thought to have grown out of the expansion of the bazars and inns associated with a main thoroughfare which, from west to east, crosses the Vishnumati River (the main tributary of the Bagmati) and heads northeast by the Old Royal Palace to Asan, a prominent traffic node. And if such establishments were significant historically in generating an urban milieu, they remain so today as the driving force behind the city's vitality and **raison d'être**. Here is the embodiment of a scene already described, in which the cries of salespeople intermingle with a cacophony of sounds, from the horns of passing cars, pedicabs, and miscellaneous vehicles, or the lowing and bleating of wandering bands of cattle and sheep, to the general clamor of waves of people moving endlessly by. Here, also noted in the foregoing, are the narrow streets flanked by multi-storied buildings, whose age-darkened, picturesquely-carved windows and window-sills bring a note of calm to an otherwise raucous scene. As I once heard remarked by an American visitor, the sensation aroused by this display of Oriental verve is like a journey through a time tunnel into the atmosphere of the city life of ancient Europe.

The broad street which turns to the west at the Royal Nepal Airlines (RNAC) office and which contains a variety of western-style stores and shops, is known as Juddha or New Road. As in the sketch, the entrance to this street is marked by a large white gate which is also the point of entry through the brick wall surrounding the old castle town. If we pass through the gate and amble down Juddha Road to the dead-end, then turn toward the broad square around the Old Royal Palace, we can thus proceed to the bazar.

As for the Old Royal Palace, an earthquake in 1934 knocked one of its towers awry, as can be seen from its present tilted condition. Indeed, as this area, along with Japan, is located

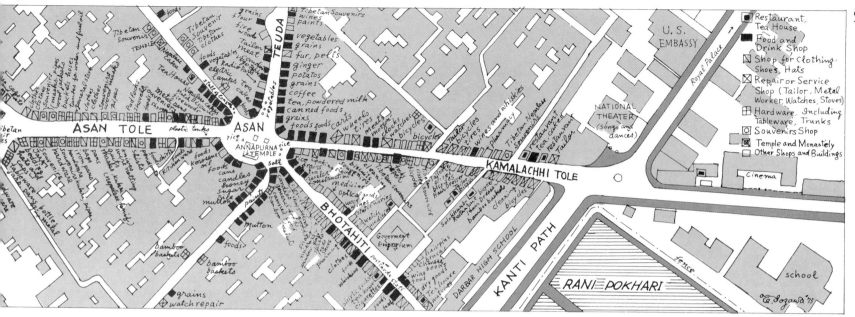

Legend:
- ▨ Restaurant, Tea House
- ■ Food and Drink Shop
- ⊠ Shop for Clothing, Shoes, Hats
- ⊠ Repair or Service Shop (Tailor, Metal Worker, Watches, Stoves)
- ⊞ Hardware, Including Tableware, Trunks
- ⊙ Souvenirs Shop
- ▨ Temple and Monastery
- □ Other Shops and Buildings

Map labels include: TEUDA, ASAN TOLE, ASAN, ANNAPURNA TEMPLE, BHOTAHITI, KAMALACHHI TOLE, KANTI PATH, RANI POKHARI, DARBAR HIGH SCHOOL, NATIONAL THEATER (Songs and dances), U.S. EMBASSY, Royal Palace, Cinema, school

E. Jozawa '75

within one of the world's most active tectonic zones, one wonders how the buildings surrounding the bazar, which seem generally to be of simple brick construction, have for so many years managed to escape complete destruction.

On the right, beyond the aforementioned open space, is a building identified by white Corinthian pillars, and on the left, the Kumari Bahal (**Kumari Mandel**, or Resident Temple of the Living Virgin). This is followed by another open space where there are other religious structures, from a building in the pagoda style, to Buddhist stupas. Another turn to the left reveals a tall, three-storied wooden temple called the **Kasthmandap** which, in 1596, was constructed from a single giant tree, and from whose name the present designation of **Kathmandu** is believed to have been derived. By circling around to the right at this point, one can now enter into the **Hanuman Dhoka,**

The corner of Juddha Sadak
14 APR. '73 E. Jozawa

or the gate where, by paying admission, one is allowed to enter the Old Royal Palace grounds. The open space just traversed is encircled by a succession of Buddhist statues and contains a large tower, around which moves a constant throng of worshippers. At the base of the pillars supporting the roof of this tower, statues of

men and women, in a protective stance, are intertwined to guard against the possibility that the Thunder Goddess within might accidentally tumble from her perch.

On the north side of the Old Royal Palace is the **Taleju** temple, whose gate is opened once a year — a magnificent structure built around an imposing tower. North of this are the stalls marking the entrance to the Kathmandu Bazar, which then runs on, interrupted only by nodes formed by the arrival of various tributary streets and lanes. On the northwest corner of the first such node, called **Indrachok**, on the second floor of a building, is the **Akash Bhairab**, a Hindu temple, and hereabouts are many stalls selling cloth of various kinds, notably reddish or mustard-colored materials for the making of the Indian **sari**. Surrounding the following node, close to the **Machhendra Nath** (temple), are stalls selling hardware, as well as others

カトマンドゥの旧王宮. *G.Ogura* *10 APR '73*

pers and tap the bells hanging at each corner of the building. Behind this are stores selling sugar, oil, and candles, and large outlets for various comestibles, making this a vital area in the quest for provisions for the trek. Running east from Asan is another street, **Bhotahiti**, with shops and stalls dealing in books, also pharmacies and taverns, and continuing along the **Kamalacchi Tole** (an extension of the Asan Tole, above), is a group of stalls offering bicycles, kerosene stoves, paper goods, bamboo articles, and watches. Northwest of Asan, along the **Teuda Tole**, aside from the usual foods, the wares displayed include furs, radio parts, and firewood.

After browsing in the bazar, it is often fascinating to stroll about historical and other places of special interest in the suburbs. On a prominent height in the western outskirts, for example, the **Swayambhu Temple (Nath)** is noteworthy especially for its large-eyed golden stupa, as well as for a ritual of Buddhist chants, held daily at three o'clock in the afternoon. This site also affords excellent views of the entire basin. Other special temples around Kathmandu include the **Pashupati**, east of the city, and directly north, the white stupa of **Boddhanath**. The road which leads from the Japanese Embassy northward to the foot-hills can be used to visit the **Budhanilkantha**, a temple where a reclining deity sleeps comfortably on the waters of a pond. One can also, of course, participate in a professional tour in a regularly-scheduled microbus run by one of the

dealing in clothing materials. In the evening, the temples of this area generally hold musical and hymn-recitation sessions, which makes it an attractive destination for tourists. Aside from taverns and pharmacies, however, most of the stalls are closed down by eight o'clock, although the temples and tea houses remain busy until later.

The Machhendra Temple, noted above, holds an interesting ceremony once a year in April, whereby a large float is constructed and then, throughout one whole day is hauled to a temple of the same title in the nearby town of Patan. Continuing on from this node are a succession of souvenir stalls featuring **Kukri** knives, Rama and other Hindu masks, and dolls.

The next node, the aforementioned **Asan**, is at the center of the entire tumult, perhaps because of the presence of numerous stalls and stores dealing in food and foodstuffs. On the southeast, one can see the **Annapurna** Temple, a small structure, where worshippers weave around clockwise between the strolling shop-

Durbar Square in Kathmandu
0925
14 April '73
G.Ogura

Kathmandu-based travel agencies. These tours are convenient as they quickly cover such of the sights described in the following as the suburban communities of Patan and Bhadgaon, the Himalaya Lookout Station, and a temple with a bizarre ritual marked by the beheading

of a sheep.

4. Kathmandu Valley

The Kathmandu Basin, which commands the Kingdom of Nepal, and which is surrounded on all sides by the rugged and majestic Nepal Himalayas, is the most extensive area of level land in the entire mountain realm. The breadth of its agricultural domains and wealth of its harvests are accountable for the maintenance here of high population densities, and for pro-

viding the impetus for the artistic technology and commercial bearing of the Newari people. The flat portions of the basin are essentially on two levels, the lower being known as the **Dol**, which contains flood plains converted into paddy fields, and the river beds themselves, and appearing from afar like huge grooves in the landscape. The **Tar**, or higher surface, is made

up of the tiered terraces alluded to in the foregoing. These terraces or beds contain two or three levels of ground-water, and reach heights (from sea level) of from 1,250 to 1,400 meters; the city of Kathmandu, as mentioned, having an average elevation of 1,300 meters. Therefore, although Kathmandu is located at about 27°N. latitude and should have a regular subtropical climate, the average temperature recorded for the month of June is only 27°C, and for January, 7°C, making a somewhat more comfortable regime than might be expected at that latitude. Monthly precipitation during the May to September rainy season averages from 100 to 300 mm, and in the October to April dry season, from 15 to 45 mm. Wind direction is from north or east in the rainy season, and from west or northwest in the dry season.

The northern portion of the basin is composed of archaic granite, while the southern is made up of sedimentary material overlain by quaternary deposits which reach depths of 380 meters at their thickest. According to relatively recent surveys, both the above features have been modified by a gigantic fault, which has dissected the basin from one side to the other. As previously described, the rivers from the surrounding mountains have gathered together at a point to the south of Kathmandu, from whence a single valley wends its way southward in the typical pattern of a centralized river system.

According to the National Census of Nepal of 1952 ～ 1954, the population of the nation was 9,756,000 at that time, making the present estimate around 11,000,000, and since the Kathmandu Basin then had a population of about 470,000 persons, it should now have in the vicinity of 530,000, of which around 250,000 would be residents of the city itself, giving the capital about half the population of the entire basin. Furthermore, along with Kathmandu there are such other urban places in the basin as the aforementioned cities of Bhadgaon (Bhaktapur), with a population of about 90,000, and Patan (Lalitpur), with 150,000 (which were formerly rival city-states of Kathmandu), and such smaller cities as Thimi, Kirtipur, Sankhu, and Khokana. Thus, it is obvious that roughly 90 percent of the basin's population are city-dwellers.

Prominent Scenic Look-outs In The Surrounding Mountains

1) **Kakani**, 2,066 meters (6,778 feet) — along the bus route to **Trisuli** where the bus passes over Mt. Kakani, northwest of Kathmandu. From here are splendid views of such peaks as Manaslu, Himal Chuli, and Ganesh Himal. The distance from Kathmandu is only 32 kilometers.

2) **Nagarkot**, 2,166 meters (7,106 feet) — follow the winding road from Bhadgaon northeast through a forest, richly populated with various species of local vegetation, to the summit of Nagarkot. From here, Dorje Lakpa, Purbi Cachu of the Jugal Group, and a broad mountain scene all the way to Mt. Everest, can be seen. The site is but 35 kilometers from the capital.

3) **Dhulikhel**, 1,585 meters (5,200 feet) — located on the Kodari Highway, an excellent bus road linking the Kathmandu Basin with Lhasa, the capital of Tibet, at a point where the road leaves the basin. Views are similar to those of Nagarkot, above.

4) **Daman**, 2,300 meters (7,546 feet) — situated where the Tribhuvan highway south to India reaches a summit as it crosses the Mahabharat Range. Though fairly distant from Kathmandu, this best of all the lookouts affords a sweeping view of the Himalayan peaks, from Dhaulagiri to Everest.

Other Famous Lookouts

Budhanilkantha (the Sleeping Vishnu) — Proceed by bus from the Shaheed Gate, via the Japanese Embassy, northward to Bansbari and walk along the dirt road for an additional 4 kilometers to the open area around the **Budhanilkantha** (see reference in Part 3, above). Here, within a protective fence, is a pond on which a bronze figure of a deity, reclining on a bed of snakes, seems to float serenely on the water.

Godavari — after passing through Patan and Harisiddhi and continuing south-southeast for about 13 kilometers, the southernmost extent of the basin is reached. At the dead-end formed by the mountain wall is the Royal Botanical Garden, which features displays of wild orchids.

Chovar — follow the road to Tribhuvan University and continue southward to the Bagmati River, where the basin is blocked by a mountain wall. Here, the river has eroded through the basic paleozoic materials and, according to legend, a valley was created for the benefit of his fellow-men, by Manjusri, a disciple of Buddha. The **Adhinath** (temple) is nearby.

Dakshin Kali — here, the Hindu goddess, **Kali,** is celebrated each Tuesday and Saturday in a ceremony where chickens and sheep are beheaded and offered in sacrifice.

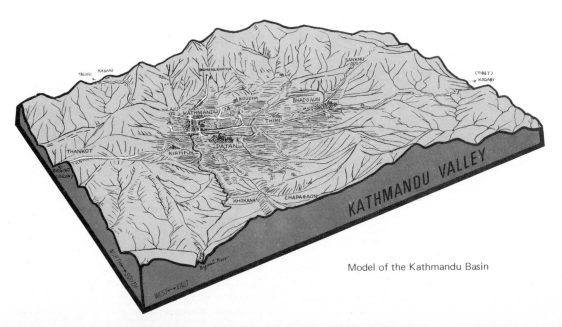

Model of the Kathmandu Basin

KATHMANDU 浮上

13th JAN. '72
R. Ozawa

1: Morning in Kathmandu
2: Vegetable Market, Kathmandu
3: Statue of Vishnu Reposing On A Bed of Snakes
4: Ratna Park Intersection
5: Candle Festival On A Spring Night

← Page 65 and 66

The Kathmandu Surface

There was once a time, we are told, when the Kathmandu Valley was a glistening lake whose shores were constantly washed by golden waves. Here, Manjusri descended from the heavens and, after examining a broad area round-about, was inspired to convert **Chovar** as the most idyllic spot into a rich land for the benefit of human-kind. Smiting the earth with his sword, the lake waters flowed gently away and a fertile basin was born. Seeing a hill appear, Manjusri cried out in Sanskrit, 'Swayambhu!' ('My Own Land!').

カトゥマンドゥ の 庶民生活

12th JAN
1972

T. Izawa

Saturday, Market Day In The Namche Bazar

Rock salt and textiles are brought from the north by Tibetans, while rice and tangerines are provided from the south by the Rai, Limbu, and Tamang tribes—all of whom conduct their dealings in Nepalese paper money.

← Page 68

Rear Windows, Kathmandu

Confined to my inn with a cold on New Years Day, 1971, from the back window of the building I sketched these houses which, as described, are of brick, usually 5-stories in height, and contain an inner court-yard. Some are converted vertically, all five floors being used by a single family, while others are divided conventionally into lateral apartments. Water is available only on the ground floor but since cooking occurs on the fifth, the labor entailed is prodigious. The roofs are used for laundry. Toilets are few and far-between. The back alleyways in the inner maze of lanes are often filled with trash and refuse. Why should food be prepared on the 5th floor? Because there are no chimneys.

Westward of Lower Tame on a steep slope, standing like a fortress, is this lamasery.

On The Road From Namche

← Settlement, Namche Bazar, in the glaciated valley.

The Road Between Namche and Thyangboche

Ice Pinnacle of the Khumbu Glacier →

The scene from Kala Pattar provides no such views of the ice falls of the Khumbu Glacier. One has to climb the strata covering the surface to eventually obtain the view of the pinnacle shown in this photograph.

1: Water-Carrier in Patan
2: Woman Dyeing Cloth in Bhadgaon
3: Doing Laundry, Bhadgaon

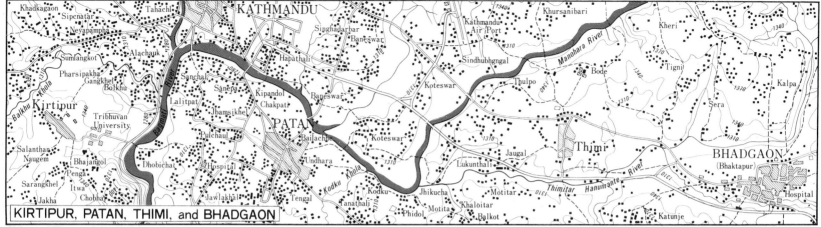

KIRTIPUR, PATAN, THIMI, and BHADGAON

Cities and Towns of the Kathmandu Valley

5. Towns of the Kathmandu Valley

As noted, the Kathmandu Basin, in addition to the capital, contains the secondary cities of Patan and Bhadgaon and a number of smaller cities, such as the aforementioned Thimi, Kirtipur, Sankhu, and Khokana. Other small cities are Bungamati, Chapagaon, Bodagaon, Thankot, Balaju, Dharmathali, and Tokha. While the city of Khatmandu changes constantly with each new generation, the smaller cities, more or less in inverse proportion to their sizes, are altered less in appearance and ways of life, and if one has a few days to spare for visits to such places, the rewards are often highly gratifying.

Although each city and town has its own particular history, there is a common and familiar pattern to the town structure. First, these settlements were all originally built by the Newari people, and as such, each is punctuated by temples and shrines which reflect the common dedication to the union of religion and life. These structures are usually seen within a compound, either as the nuclei of cities or as more isolated enclaves in the outskirts. In the former case, Boudha is an almost ideal example, although Kirtipur, with its temples celebrating the god, Bag Bhairab, or the city of Bungamati, with its temple of Machhendrath, or even Kathmandu, Patan, and Bhadgaon, with their religious edifices, could also be included. In the latter case, Chapagaon, with its Vajra Varahi temple in the suburbs, or Sankhu, which has the Vajrajogini, are also good examples.

Other standard features of these cities include elaborate water reservoirs, painstakingly maintained over the years, and normally located in pairs with a road in-between, and the much-mentioned three or more-storied houses of sun or kiln-dried brick with baked tile roofs — the average height of towns being rather uniform but differing slightly according to the town. The older streets are either of cobblestone or brick, and are laid out in a design that suggests the grid pattern. And, that these appear as castle-towns is reflective of their long struggle to thwart the attempts of the Gurkhas to subdue the entire Kathmandu Basin.

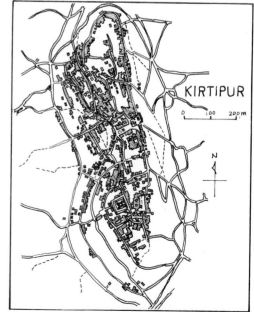

KIRTIPUR

0   100   200 m

Kirtipur Town Plan

Newari Wood Carver, Patan

Thimi, A Pottery Town

A — Mask Shop in the Eastern Outskirts of Thimi

The Nyatapola Temple, Bhadgaon

The Ganesh Statue, Patan; Golden Gate, Bhadgaon; Stone Temple Statue, Kirtipu

Back Alley, Bhadgaon, In The Medieval Style

6. Patan, Bhadgaon, and Others

I) Patan (Lalitpur)

Patan, the second city of Nepal, was built by King Vira Deva in the year 299 AD, and though its present population is only 150,000 it is thought to be older than Kathmandu. It is also the center of the Buddhist faith of this region.

Being, in addition, the focal point of Newari arts and crafts, Patan has many shops offering Buddhist statuary and antiques. However, as mentioned, as the permission of the National Museum is required to export such things, one should be cautious in these purchases.

Buses for Patan leave Kathmandu from a terminus in front of the National Theater at the northwest corner of the Rani Pokhari Pond, an extension of the bazar. Every fifteen minutes one leaves here and, after crossing the Bagmati River and climbing a hill, finally arrives at the Patan Dhoka, the gate into the ancient fort, from where one proceeds on foot. Upon entering the gate, with Patan College on the left, one would do well to continue as far as the Asoka movie theater and, where the pavement ends, turn right into Khache Tole and, ultimately, right again as far as the plaza in front of the Royal Palace.

Interesting sights associated with the plaza include the Krishna Mandir Temple, the head of the Yoganarendra column, the statue of King Malla, and facing these, the Taleju Temple, the Palace, and the museums. From here, a ten-minute walk to the southeast brings you, on the right, to an imposing building housing the Mahaboudha Temple, originally built in the 14th century, partly of Indian-style terra cotta which, because of its essentially brick construction, fell victim to the earthquake of 1934, and has since been rebuilt. South of this is the ancient Buddhist temple, Rudna Varna Mahavihar. Also, by walking south-southwest from

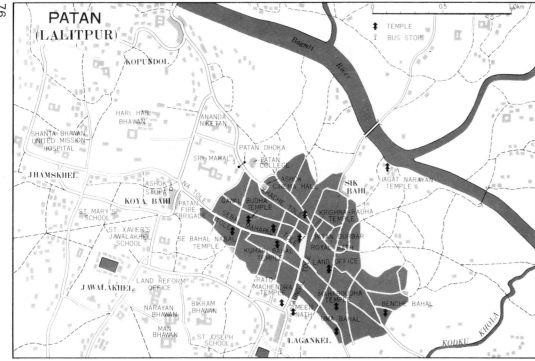

76

PATAN (LALITPUR)

TEMPLE
BUS STOP

KOPUNDOL

HARI HAR BHAWAN

ANANDA NIKETAN

SHANTA BHAWAN UNITED MISSION HOSPITAL

PATAN DHOKA

PATAN COLLEGE

SRI MAHAL

JHAMSKHEL

ASHOK STUPA

KOYA BAHI

NA TOLE

PATAN FIRE BRIGADE

ASHOK CINEMA HALL

SIK BAHI

JAGAT NARAYAN TEMPLE

ST. MARY'S SCHOOL

ST. XAVIER'S JAWALAKHEL SCHOOL

GAWAL BUDHA TEMPLE

MHACHE TOLE

KRISHNA RADHA TEMPLE

SEBA TOLE

MAHAPAL

SE BAHAL NABAL TEMPLE

KUMARI BAHAL TEMPLE

PATAN DURBAR

ROYAL BATH

LAND OFFICE

JAWALAKHEL

LAND REFORM OFFICE

RATO MACHENDRA TEMPLE

NARAYAN BHAWAN

BIKRAM BHAWAN

MAN BHAWAN

MEEN NATH

MAHABOUDHA TEMPLE

UMA BAHAL

BENCHE BAHAL

ST. JOSEPH SCHOOL

LAGANKEL

KODKU KHOLA

Bagmati River

the Palace, on the west side of the street is the Rato Machhendra Nath, to which as noted, a float is hauled each April. Opposite this is the Meen Nath, together with the famous Hiranya Varna Mahavihar, a three-storied, golden pagoda, as well as the five-storied pagoda of the **Kumbheswar** Temple.

At Jawalakhel, south of Patan, are Tibetan camps where such of their folk products as carpets are obtainable. West of this is a zoo, noted for the red, Lesser Panda, and if one continues further to the west across a suspension bridge over the Bagmati River, around by Kirtipur, and back to Kathmandu, a comfortable one-day journey can be concluded.

2) Bhadgaon (Bhaktapur)

The third largest city of the basin, Bhadgaon, has an official population of around 90,000, but in area, is larger than Patan. Also, since compared to Kathmandu and Patan it has changed less in recent years, the city is said to have been placed under protective legislation designed, for historical reasons, to preserve the urban cultural landscape. The city was originally established in 889 by King Ananda Deva.

Moreover, as regular trolley-bus service has recently been established from Kathmandu, this form of access can be added to the mico-bus service and the longer-distance buses destined for Kodari. Transportation to and from Bhadgaon has thus grown increasingly more convenient. The departure point for Bhadgaon-

bound trolley buses is located south of the National Stadium. Regular buses leave from **Bus Square,** east of Ratna Park. In addition, one can request full or half-day sight-seeing tours of travel agents, or rent a bicycle from one of the rental agencies and make a personal tour.

The best route is to take the highway running south of Singhadurbar (an eastern suburb of Kathmandu) and proceed eastward through the new governmental office area until you reach the western fringe of Bhadgaon, then turn on to an old road and enter the city. The urban site is actually located on a series of level terraces that rise to the north of the Hanumante River, and though there is a valley leading in from the north, Bhadgaon occupies a higher position along a ridge of adjacent hills extending from Nagarkot in the northeast. The old road leads on to become a kind of hill trail through a pine forest, where the traveller is beguiled by the pleasant atmosphere created by the murmuring of the wind through the trees.

Patan

When the topmost level is reached and the government and military installations are pass-

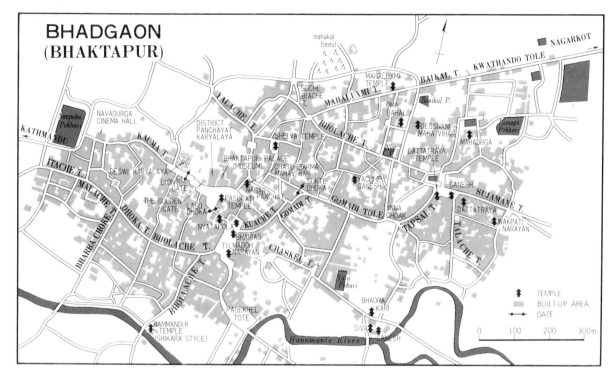

BHADGAON
(BHAKTAPUR)

The gate of Thimi

ed, beyond these, on the left, is an embankment and finally, the bus terminus. At this point, by entering an ancient-appearing, grass-covered gate, you are afforded a view of the waters of the Bhadgaon Siddha Pokari reservoir, built by a ruler in the 17th century.

By circling half-way around this pond and proceeding along the northern edge of the city, you ultimately come to a plaza in front of the old Palace. Another route leads directly down the slope to the south to the principal thoroughfare through the city—a kind of W-shaped shopping street running roughly east and west. However, the following pertains mainly to the former route to the old Royal Palace.

This structure is immediately impressive for its wooden windows, whose decorative carving, while familiar enough, reaches a new height in this exquisite example attributed to King Yaksha Malla, under whom it was constructed in 1427 — the guilded gate being added later, in 1756. Adjacent, are museums of art and antiquity where Buddhist figures and other sculpture are displayed. The road to the south from the palace also leads to a decorous five-storied pagoda set on a high stone foundation and known as the Nyatapola Temple, the finest example of its kind in the basin. Thirty-six meters high, it narrows toward the top in the local style.

3) Thimi

Thimi is fundamentally a pottery town and most of its citizens are of that particular caste. Earthenware water jugs, crocks, ornaments, and so on, are specialties.

4) Kirtipur

The city of Kirtipur lies atop an elevated piedmont table-land, and the views of the landscape roundabout are excellent.

From the city center, a narrow, saddle shaped area containing a temple and a reservoir, if one proceeds northwest to the temple at the highest point in the local relief, there is a clear view of Mt. **Gosainthan** (Shisha Pangma).

THE NEPAL HIMALAYAS

◎ Entrance point of Nepal for foreigeners

0   25   50   75   100km

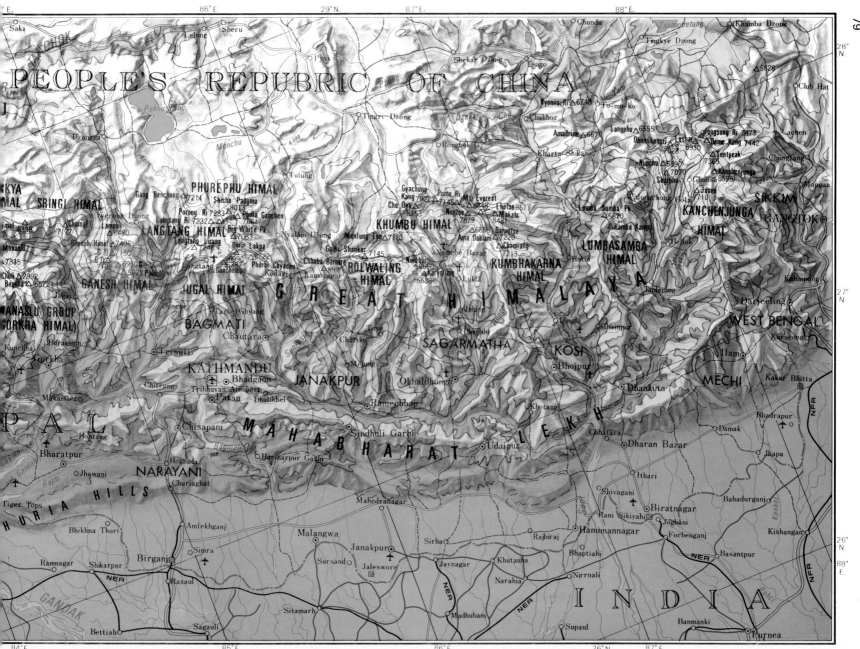

TREKKING IN THE HIMALAYAS OF NEPAL

1. Applying for Visa Extension and Trekking Permits

If visas are obtained at Embassies in foreign countries, one is permitted to remain in Nepal for four weeks subsequent to the date of entry, but if one applies after entering the country, the period of stay is only one week. Therefore, if one intends to trek for one month or more,

visa extensions are necessary. Furthermore, since visas permit visits only to Kathmandu, Kaski, Pokhara, Chitwon, and Lumbini, special trekking permits are needed for all other destinations.

Thus, not only the visa-extension application must be submitted, but, at the same time, any trekking permit applications for places other than the approved few. Application forms for both, according to the regulation of April 16,

Trekking Courses	Terms (days)	Maximum Elevations (in meters)	Danger of Altitude ×warning ○safe	Glacier Walk ○need △may do	Local Food ○easy to get ×hard to get	Gross Estimate (in U.S. Dollars)
1 EVEREST B.C. KALA PATTAR Foot hills of Mt. Everest	on foot only 35 use airplane 15	5,600	×	○	○ but expensive	700~850 500
2 GOKYO COURSE Foot hills of Mt. Everest	on foot only 30 use airplane 10	5,400	×	△	○ but expensive	600~700 410
3 IMJA KHOLA Foot hills of Mt. Everest	on foot only 30 use airplane 10	4,800~5,500	×	△	○ but expensive	600~700 410
4 ROLWALING KHOLA To Namche Bazar via Tesi Lapcha	use bus and airplane approximate 20	5,750	×	○	×	530~850
5 HELAMBU North of Kathmandu	8~10	3,000~3,600	○		○	250~300
6 GOSAINKUND Glacial Lakes, A Hindu Holy Place	10~15	4,600	×		×	330~400
7 LANGTANG VALLEY	12~15	4,000	×	△	○	350~420
8 FOOT HILLS OF GANESH HIMAL	10~15	4,200	×		×	350~420
9 BURI GANDAKI VALLEY The Manaslu Group	20~25	3,300~5,200	×	△	○	600~700
10 MARSYANDI VALLEY AND MANAN	20~25	3,600~5,200	×	△	○	600~700
11 FOOT HILLS OF MACHHAPUCHHARE	3~7	1,600~3,600	○		○	150~200
12 ANNAPURNA SANCTUARY	10~15	4,000	×	△	○ the inner part is hard	240~420 (bus) (airplane)
13 KALI GANDAKI VALLEY	14~18	2,700	○		○	300~380
14 JOMOSOM TO TILITSO LAKE Via Muktinath	20~25	5,400	×	○	×	350~400
15 DOWN STREAM OF KALI GANDAKI	14	2,500	○		○	300~350
16 JUMLA TO POKHARA	use airplane to Jumla 21~25	4,200	×		×	500~630
17 RARA LAKE FROM JUMLA	use airplane to Jumla and back 10~14	3,700	○		×	400~500

1976, are to be obtained through travel and trekking agencies that are approved by the Nepal Mountaineering Association and when completed, should be submitted together with photographs and fares. Charges for visa extensions are 10 Rs for each week, plus 1 Rs; for trekking permits, 16 Rs for one week, 31 Rs for two, 46 Rs for three, and 61 Rs for four. For visa extensions, it is also, necessary to convert $5.00 per day per person, which transaction will be noted in the Foreign Exchange Transaction Form, previously mentioned. Visa extensions are limited to one month and are renewable up to three times. Trekking permits are obtainable either for east or west Nepal, but not for both in a single application.

Specific towns, villages and check points along scheduled trekking courses should be noted, by name, in the trekking application, along with the intended length of stay in each, up to one month.

2. Trekking Preparation

The traveller must, by now, have procured his entire retinue, including guides, porters, provisions, and equipment.

The Indian Government Ordinance Survey Office has prepared large-scale maps for many parts of Nepal, but at the same time the use of these is restricted. It is only natural to assume, also, that any large nation will have compiled a comprehensive series of detailed maps, based on satellite imagery, remote sensing, or aerial survey. Unfortunately, however, these are generally unavailable as well. Therefore, in order to accomplish a successful trek without such detailed and accurate aids, one must either have intimate knowledge of the trekking course and all destinations, or have at his disposal, capable, knowledgeable guides. Travel agencies specializing in trekking can usually provide appropriate personnel — normally Tibetans or members of the Sherpa tribe — or one might seek advice from foreigners who have already had such experiences. While in Kathmandu, one might even be solicited by guides who are out of work at the moment. However, as noted, such arrangements should have been properly concluded long before the trek begins, with a third party as witness, and preferably with all stipulations legally stated and agreed to by all concerned. These should include such predeparture items as basic salaries, transportation expenses, holiday allowances, and the cost of required provisions and equipment.

Once the guide is hired, one should proceed to such other matters involving his assistance as the employing (aside from the matter of their wages) of porters, who will thereafter be under his direction. On the subject of provisions, the daily food budget should be gone over carefully with the guide, and his opinions

Mountains and Peaks The Courses (Elevations in meters)	Other themes of the courses
Mt EVEREST (Sagarmatha) 8848, LHOTSE 8511, MAKALU 8481, CHO OYU 8153, Nuptse 7879, Pumori 7145, Ama Dablam 6856, Taweche 6542, Kangtega 6685.	Sherpa life, lama monastery, alpine flora, bird watching, glaciers, Abominable Snowman.
Mt EVEREST 8848, LHOTSE 8511, MAKALU 8481, CHO OYU 8151, Gyachung Kang 7922, Nuptse 7879, Taweche 6542, Cholatse 6440, Kajo Ri (Gyajo Ri) 6186.	Sherpa life, lama monastery, alpine flora, bird watching, glaciers, Abominable Snowman.
LHOTSE 8511, LHOTSE SHAR 8383, MAKALU 8481, Nuptse 7879, Pk 38 7589, Chamlang 7310, Baruntse 7220, Ama Dablam 6856.	Sherpa life, lama monastery, alpine flora, bird watching, glaciers, Abominable, Snowman.
CHO OYU 8153, Chhoba Bamare 5970, Gauri Shankar 7145, Ghegkur 6801, Dongiragutao 6940, Takargo 6793, Chobutse 6689, Hakun (Lundartsbugo or Kang Nachugo) 6735.	U Shaped valleys, moranic lakes, ice falls, fiirn basins, Sherpa life, bird watching.
Lengpo Gang (Big White Peak) 7083, Dorje Lakpa 6990, Phurbi Chyachu 6722, Urkinmang 6151, Pongen Dopku 5930, Naya Kanga 5846.	Sherpa life, alpine flora, glacial lakes, bird watching.
Ganesh Himal 7406, Ganesh-II (Lapsang Karbo) 7150, Ganesh-IV (Pabil) 7102, Langtang Lirung (Ganchhen Ledrub) 7246, Chimisedang Lekh 5822, Naya Kanga 5846.	glacial lakes, alpine flora, Hindu religious events, Sherpa life, bird watching.
Ganesh Himal 7406, Langtang Lirung (Ganchhen Ledrub) 7246, Naya Kanga 5846, Ganchempo 6387, Urkinmang 6151, Lanshia Ri 6145, Kimshun 6745, Shalbachum 6918, Pemthang Karpo Ri (Dome Blanc) 6830.	valley glaciers, hangig glaciers, U shaped valleys plateau glaciers, Taman life, alpine flora.
Ganesh Himal 7406, Langtang Lirung 7246, Ganesh-II (Lapsang Karbo) 7150, Ganesh-IV (Pabil) 7102, Paldol 5928, Himal Chuli 7893, Pk. 29 7835, MANASLU 8156, Annapurna-II 7937.	alpine flora, bird watching, Taman and Sherpa life.
MANASLU 8156, Himal Chuli 7893, Pk. 29 7835, Baudha 6672, Ganesh-II 7150, Ganesh-IV (Pabil) 7102, Ganesh-II 7130, Sringi Himal (Chamar) 7177.	folklore of the Tamang and Bhote (Tibetan)
Himal chuli 7893, Pk. 29 7835, MANASLU 8156, Lamjung Himal 6983, Kang Guru 7010, Annapurna-II 7937, Annapurna-IV 7525, Annapurna-III 7555, Gangarna 7454, Tilitso Peak 7134, Pisang Peak 6091.	folklore and life of the Gurung and Bhote (Tibetan), landscape change from cold desert to tropical forest.
ANNAPURNA-I 8091, Annapurna-South 7219, Gangapurna 7454, Annapurna-III 7555, Machhapuchhare 6993, Annapurna-IV 7525, Annapurna-II 7937, Lamjung Himal 6983, MANASLU 8156, Pk. 29 7835, Himal Chuli 7893.	Gurung life, deep gorges, alpine flora, bird watching.
ANNAPURNA-I 8091, Roc noir 7485, Glacier dome 7193, Gangapurna 7454, Annapurna-III 7555, Machhapuchhare 6993, Fang 7647, Annapurna-South 7219, Hiunchuli 6441, DHAULAGIRI-I 8167.	glaciers, glaciated landforms, alpine flora, bird watching, the Gurung life.
DHAULAGIRI-I 8167, ANNAPURNA-I 8091, Nilgiri North Pk. 7061, Nilgiri South Pk. 6839, Tukuche Peak 7134, Tilitso Peak 7134. Tukuche Peak 6920,	landscape and culture change from dry cold desert to wet tropical forest, canyons and gorges of the Kali Gandaki, hot springs, alpine flora, bird watching.
DHAULAGIRI-I 8167, ANNAPURNA-I 8091, Nilgiri North Pk. 7061, Tukuche Peak 6920, Tilitso Peak 7134, Glacier dome 7193, Gangapurna 7454, Gundang 6584.	cold desert, glacial lakes, lonicera steppe vegetation, alpine flora, bird watching, Hindu holy places, Bhote (Tibetan) life, Thakali life.
DHAULAGIRI-I 8167, Nilgiri South Pk. 6839, Gurja Himal 7193, Dhaulagiri VI 7268, Dhaulagiri IV 7661, ANNAPURNA-I 8091.	Magar life, changes of vegetation from temperate forest to subtropical and tropical forest, bird watching, local bazars.
DHAULAGIRI-I 8167, ANNAPURNA-I 8091, Gurja Himal 7193, Churen Himal 7371, Putha Hiunchuli 7246, Kagmara Lekh-V 5887, Triangle Peak 5864, Guthumba 5806, Bijora Hiunchuli 6386, Kande Hiunchuli 6627.	sub-arid landscape and the local life of western Nep Nepal, bird watching, alpine flora.
Kande Hiunchuli 6627, Chankheli Lekh 4753, Changla Himal 6715, Saipal 7031.	Rara lake (2,980m), local bazars, old capitals of western Nepal.

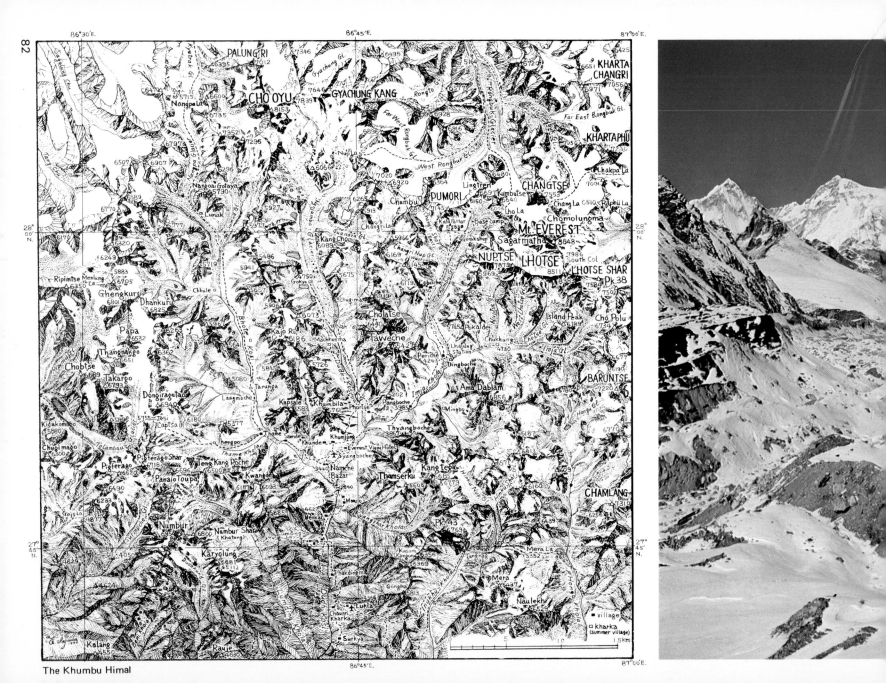

The Khumbu Himal

The Mountain and Upper Portion of the Ngojumba Glacier are known as Cho Oyu (8,153 meters)

and advice noted. If the agreement provides his food, for example, to avoid difficulty later, it might be well to ascertain whether he is an adequate cook, and whether he himself might have a prodigious appetite. As a general rule, one should carry far more provisions than might be required in daily living at home. One way to reduce the number of porters needed is to depend more on local food supplies. But if this is an objective, it is well to acquire as soon as possible, a tolerance for such fare.

As for equipment, although ground-sheets are always useful, if the trek is to be in a mainly uninhabited area, the requirements may differ from those of a more ordinary one where lodging in houses might eliminate the need to carry tents. Sleeping bags and down-padded clothing are indispensable, but such as ice axes, climbing irons, and rope, are generally unnecessary.

3. Selection of the Trekking Course

There are various points of view as to how the trekking course should be chosen. For example, if one wishes to survey a particular mountain, it is necessary to consider the time of year when viewing conditions are optimal, whether the course selected will provide such views, how much time is available, and whether the objective can be accomplished within the established budget. Even those who may think that any Himalayan experience is worthwhile, have different interests and tastes. And since one has already gone to an extraordinary amount of trouble and expense to plan such a trip, the ultimate goal should be to visit a place that represents not only the fulfillment of an ambition, but one which offers the traveller at least some guarantee of safety and well-being. Some may wish to examine at first hand, formerly isolated mountain peoples whose culture is a product of many generations. Others may prefer to observe the ecological cycles of local

plants and animals and to compare these with what may exist under similar climatic and other environmental circumstances at home. Still others may be interested in the Lama, Hindu, or other religions, in order to note in their original settings, the conditions of prominent faiths that have been exported to other parts of the world. Finally, there may be some who merely wish to bask in the glory of the mountain scenery, to enjoy the local liquors and the group singing of such as Tibetan folk-songs. Therefore, in plotting a trek, one should try to allow in the scheduling, sufficient latitude for the exercise of individual preferences.

Since the trekking under discussion here is to be entirely at altitudes of more than 4,000 meters, the most important consideration is, as repeatedly stated, the vital matter of high altitude sickness. And if one has the slightest personal doubt after reading about this in the foregoing sections, the whole plan should be abandoned. Another important consideration concerns the choice of the proper season, and how much time will be required. The basic plan should therefore try to cover, in the most reasonable and efficient fashion, all these factors, according to the particular circumstances.

The success of any plan depends not only on the aptitudes of the parties involved, but also in no small measure, on sheer luck.

The attached list of courses is thus presented as an attempt to assist in these processes, and the potential trekker is implored to study it carefully and completely.

TREKKING IN THE FOOTHILLS OF MOUNT EVEREST

This course, which allows intimate views of the world's highest mountain, despite the ready availability of other trekking courses which may be both easier and safer, is the most popular of all.

As mentioned many times, one should be constantly aware of the dangers lurking at high altitude, and even if everything has progressed satisfactorily, one should always be on guard against a sudden change of fortune. For example, plans to alter the schedule and at a moment's notice, shift to a safer altitude, should be built into any trekking program.

1. Planning and Preparation

In applying for trekking permission, one should be certain that such places as the following are included in the plan: Namche Bazar, Everest Base Camp, Thame, and Gokyo, and if the trek is to be entirely on foot, one should also include Jiri, Junbesi, and Chaunri Khaka. In addition, although this will be discussed later, if an excursion to the south is desired, the names of such large communities as Okhaldhunga, Bhojpur, Dhankuta, Dharan Bazar, and Biratnagar, should be accurately noted.

Since this course is one of the standard itineraries, not only of Mountain Travel but of smaller agencies, regular and otherwise, a request for the experience would be greeted with no surprise. On the road, it is often amusing to encounter in huts along the way such items, unobtainable in Kathmandu and apparently discarded by previous groups, as dried vegetables and canned confections, which have somehow found their way to the shelves of way-side shops. These things, however, appear quite by chance, so one cannot depend on such a system of supply. Furthermore, recent price rises for such miscellaneous items may reflect a tendency for the local people to become somewhat jaded from their experiences with travellers who are, all too often, willing to pay any price for a desired commodity. On the other hand, at the Namche Bazar market, held each Saturday, one can obtain such staples as rice, tangerines, potatoes (white and sweet), and eggs. Kerosene, lamp oil, tissue, and socks, are also available at virtually any ordinary shop.

Condiments, sugar, vegetables, bouillon cubes, thick candles, jerry cans for kerosene, thermos flasks, pots and pans, dishes, utensils, and special batteries, must be procured in Kathmandu. Film, note-taking equipment, and the like, as noted in the foregoing, had better be imported from home.

As for money, not only is it necessary to convert currency into Nepal Rupees, but one should be sure to receive new bills, and to have a good supply of notes in such small denominations as 10, 5, and 1. Vinyl and cloth bags for carrying supplies should be purchased at the Kathmandu Bazar, along with back packs (panniers) to be carried by the porters.

For miscellaneous air transportation to the trekking base, this can be scheduled at such places as the RNAC office, the Everest View Hotel, Trans-Himalayan Tours, or other travel agencies, but one should be sure that the return passage is reserved as well. Although the cost of such travel for the Sherpa or guide is customarily borne by the foreign trekker (**sahib**), according to a tacit agreement, such tickets are sold at a discount. Since flight baggage charges are in addition to the basic fare, one must decide whether to transport needed items or to try to purchase these in Namche at inflated prices. Porters can normally be hired locally at the trekking base. For fuel, firewood is obtainable locally, and there is always the traditional dried yak dung. Also, in these highlands, the charge for firewood includes delivery, so it is possible to have a fire even during winter at **Gorakshep** (on the Khumbu Glacier).

2. Namche Bazar

Namche is the commercial hub of the Khumbu District, and is located on the shoulder of a plateau at the Y-shaped confluence of the Dudh Kosi, the principal river system of the region, with the Bhote Kosi, its chief western tributary. The plateau appears to have been planed off at this point by a massive ice sheet which moved by during the glacial epoch, depositing in its wake on the plateau, some gigantic rocks transported from Mt. Khumbila (5,761 meters), which rises majestically in the north.

Khumbila is the legendary home of the guardian goddess of the Khumbu District, whose presence seems to be manifested in the atmosphere of two villages, Khunde and Khumjung, both situated at the base of the plateau, almost as though they were being peacefully nurtured at her bosom. In contrast, Namche is located in a depression on the southern face of the plateau, and since the slope falls off sharply on the down-hill side of the town, the whole setting appears to be teetering on the brink. The depression is a kind of narrow, cirque-like feature containing a flat portion at the bottom and facing south, toward the sun. On the other hand, since the winds constantly sweep through the site, there is an atmosphere of insecurity, to which the townspeople have responded virtually in one breath, as though they were members of a single and uncommonly harmonious family.

Since the elevation is 3,440 meters, if one plans to fly directly to Syangboche, east of the town, it would be well to schedule a stay of at least two days in Namche, in order to adjust to the altitude change.

The road which winds its way up from below, suddenly reaches a point where, on the left, is a huge boulder commanding the entire panorama of the town. Each Saturday at this point on the highway, an out-door market is held by an assortment of people from a variety of places, who may live as much as 5 to 10 days travel from one-another. They gather here each week to sell such things as rice, eggs, tangerines, grain, peanuts, sweet potatoes, (American) corn, butter, sugar, ginger, black tea, and wool, all of which has been transported here on their backs. Since these folk are wearing their local costumes, those from the lowlands of the south are apparent by their huddled postures as they attempt to ward off the chill, while traders from northern parts can be recognized by their shapeless, padded, seemingly shabby garments.

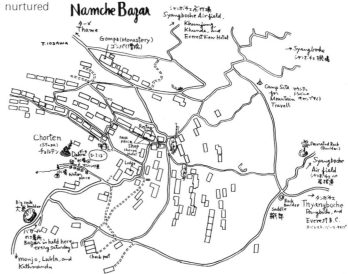

EVEREST VIEW HOTEL
3 DEC. '72 A. Ozawa

A one-hour climb from Namche Bazar brings you to the **Syangboche** air field, which is connected by a ridge to the Everest View Hotel, located on the next highest slope. The tall coniferous forests that one might see elsewhere in a subalpine zone at 1,500 to 2,300 meters, are found here at 3,850 meters. Those who arrive by plane should walk slowly and take extra-deep breaths.

A Pastoral Hut in Pibre

Entering the second-from-the-bottom of six pastoral huts made of piled-up stone, I was served the following meal.

The main course, a Sherpa specialty, was **rikru**, consisting of flour (**kru**) and white potatoes (**riki**), the latter of which were grated on a flat stone which glistened with embedded crystals. Flour was then added and the molded patties were baked on a hot stone griddle. The hot patties were then coated with butter and sauce of chile pepper, garlic, and cheese.

This is a time of feverish activity for the merchants, most of whom have walked all night, taking little more time for rest than occasional catnaps. Villages along the routes customarily have tea houses or rest shelters where foot travellers can recoup their energies, and even in open country, here and there, such shelters may be maintained. Thus, by moving deliberately from one sheltered place to the next, these intrepid traders have travelled night and day to Namche in order to tend their shops and stalls.

At the bottom of the depression is a stupa-like figure, called a **Chorten**, near which, at contrasting heights, are two springs which seem always to be surrounded by clusters of housewives and women of various sorts, engaged in animated chatting and gossip. And, along the road between the springs, are five huts containing mill-wheels, to which people have attached **sutras**, in the manner of **mani-wheels** (stone, Buddhist prayer wheels), so that as these revolve, the 'gee-gee' sounds suggest that the sutras are mechanically recited for the benefit of human-kind.

The road which leads from the area of the giant boulder and the Saturday bazar, passing above the two springs and by two or three inns (including the International Footrest), finally reaches the town center where, as it turns to the right, are more inns and a retail store. Lodging in the village can be had either at the inns or the restaurants, where it is also possible

Lukla air field and the east peak of **Kwangde**

The Village of Thame →

The houses of Thame are arranged along the left border of a flattish area surrounded by moraines. Here, women can be seen, each with a water jug on her back, gathered around either of the **chhypung** (springs), located in both the upper and lower parts of the village. The white precipice of **Ten Kang Poche** appears close and towering.

to hire Sherpa and porters. Furthermore, these are convenient places to inquire about such things, even if they themselves have no vacancies. And, if one has a friend here, or the friend of a friend, such people can easily be solicited to help provide lodging.

Slightly up the hill from the giant boulder is a Government check-point where one should be sure to present the trekking permit, passport, and the detailed itinerary, so that such things as arrival and departure times can be recorded in the official records.

3. From Namche to Thame

At a point south of the plateau mentioned above, the Dudh Kosi gathers all the secondary streams of the Khumbu District and together these then flow southward. The Bhote Kosi, noted above as the principal western tributary, flows to this confluence from Tibet, so, as its (Tibetan) name suggests, if one follows the river to its source in the Nangpa Glacier, and climbs its gently sloping surface to the summit where it meets the Kyaprak Glacier from the north, then descends the latter, the route followed provides a relatively easy passage to the village of Kyaprak in Tibet.

Furthermore, judging by the frequency of their accounts of the ascent over the **Nangpa La** (pass), the trip to Kyaprak seems a rather common one to the residents of the Khumbu District. Generally, it is said to take four days from Thame to Kyaprak, but rumor has it that,

88

by hurrying, it can be done in three.

Foreigners, however, being officially barred from Tibet, would find their permission to visit Namche inadequate to cover them beyond Thamo, the check-point to the northwest of the village. The farthest north that one is allowed to visit is the village of **Thame,** where there is a fork in the Bhote Valley and an important passage westward to the **Tesi Laptsa** (pass and summit), which leads to the Rolwaling Valley.

This latter pass, moreover, since it is perched on the eastern side of a talus slope in a region of snow and ice, is famous as a site of fatal accidents.

Lower Thame is situated on a terrace in the valley floor and is surrounded by moraines from the glacial epoch — the terrace apparently having been formed by an ice sheet moving from the vicinity of Tesi Laptsa, in the west. Upper Thame, on the other hand, is on the west

bank of the main stream (of the Bhote Kosi), and is located on morainal and glacio-fluvial deposits of the Langmoche Glacier. The residents of both Upper and Lower Thame are naturally of the Sherpa tribe, but their original culture is slowly becoming diluted by influences from outside, brought in by mountain-climbers.

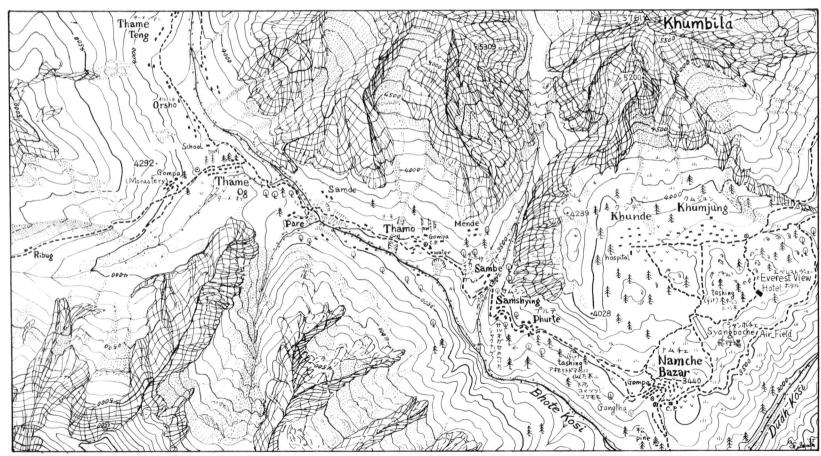

Diagram of the Trekking Course to Thame

4. The Gokyo Course

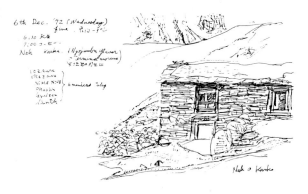

The most awe-inspiring ice feature of the Khumbu District is the Ngojumba Glacier which flows from two points of origin on the southern slopes, respectively, of Mt. **Cho Oyu** (8,153 meters) and Mt. **Gyachungkang** (7,922 meters). Several lakes have formed along the glacier's western border, their outlets apparently having been blocked by its lateral moraines, and Gokyo is located near the third lake, counting from downstream. It is identifiable by the presence nearby of several pastoral huts.

The destination of this course is a hill lying to the northwest of Gokyo, between the huts and the next lake upstream. From here, the panorama, not only of the two peaks mentioned above but of a host of summits in the 8,000 meter class, including Everest, Lhotse, and Makalu, which rise like immense saw-teeth from the glacial ridges and crags, is truly superb! The Gokyo Course should take about one week, round-trip, from Namche, but it may be even more interesting, according to invididual predilection, to extend this to ten-days or so, in order to explore additional look-outs and trails.

The largest and most prosperous village of the area is **Khumjung**, which lies in the shadow of the hill Shangboche, at the foot of Mt. Khumbila. Near the village are fields, partition-

ed by stone-walls, which confine the yak and cattle to certain fields for grazing, and keep them out of others which may contain agricultural products. The course now follows a trail which has been most cleverly laid out across the rocky slope east of the village. By weaving its way around rocks and boulders, it finally emerges on the eastern slope of Mt. Khumbila. Crossing this slope, where one might catch sight of an occasional mountain goat, the trail slowly descends to, and crosses, the Dudh Kosi, where one should ascend the left-bank and head downstream to the plateau which is covered by a canopy of birch forest and a kind of Spanish moss. This scene, familiar enough in other high-latitude lands, is rather unique here for its back-drop of snow pleats — a striking sight especially in the sun — set against an even higher background in the towering walls of the distant Himalayas.

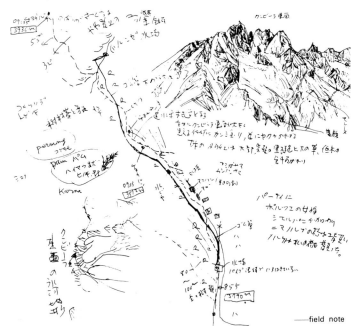

—field note

The first day one should aim to lodge over-night at Portse, a peaceful village on the plateau, where negotiations can be made to rent a pastoral hut farther upstream, and for the delivery there of fire-wood. The second day's journey might end at a hut in **Nah**, on the terminal moraine of the Ngojumba Glacier. It should be remembered, however, that at these altitudes, one should expend less than 70 percent of the energy that might normally be required for such distances — the extra proportion being used to overcome the differences in atmospheric pressure. Therefore, by lodging overnight at intervals, one should plan to reach **Gokyo** within two or three days.

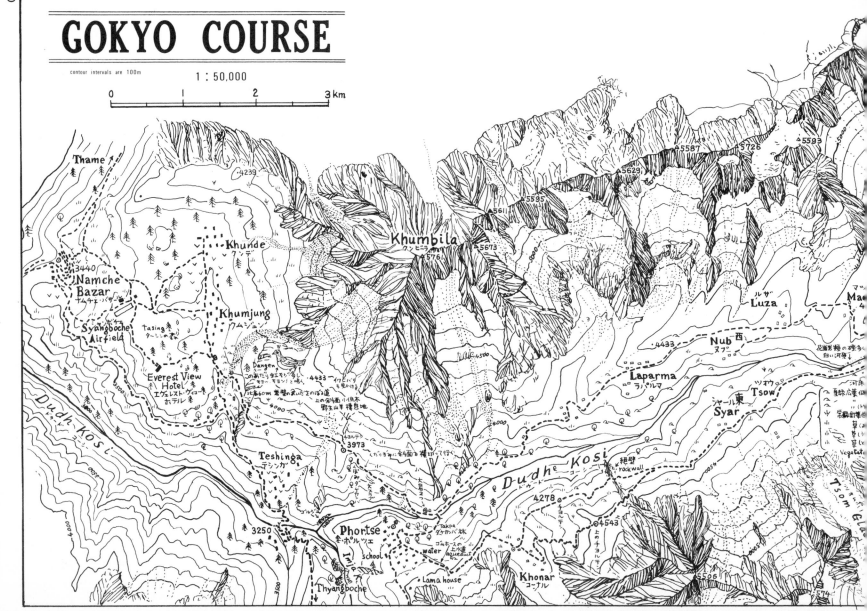

GOKYO COURSE

contour intervals are 100m

1 : 50,000

0   1   2   3 km

Thame

△4239

Khunde
クンデ

Namche
Bazar
ナムチェ・バザール
3440

Syangboche
Airfield
シャンボチェ

Khumjung
クムジュン

Everest View
Hotel
エヴェレスト・ヴィュー
ホテル

Khumbila
クンビラ
△5673
△5761

△5611

△5595

△5623

△5587

△5726

△5593

Luza
ルザ

Ma
Ma

Nub 西
ヌブ

·4433

Laparma
ラパルマ

Tsow
ツォウ

Syar 東
シャール

Dangen
·4433

·3973

Teshinga
テシンガ

3250

Phortse
ポルツェ

school

water aqueduct

Lama house

Thyangboche
チャンボチェ

Takpa
ダケカンバ林

Khonar
コーナル

Dudh Kosi

Dudh Kosi
ドゥード・コーシ

△5506

△4278

·4543

rock wall
岩壁

△5574

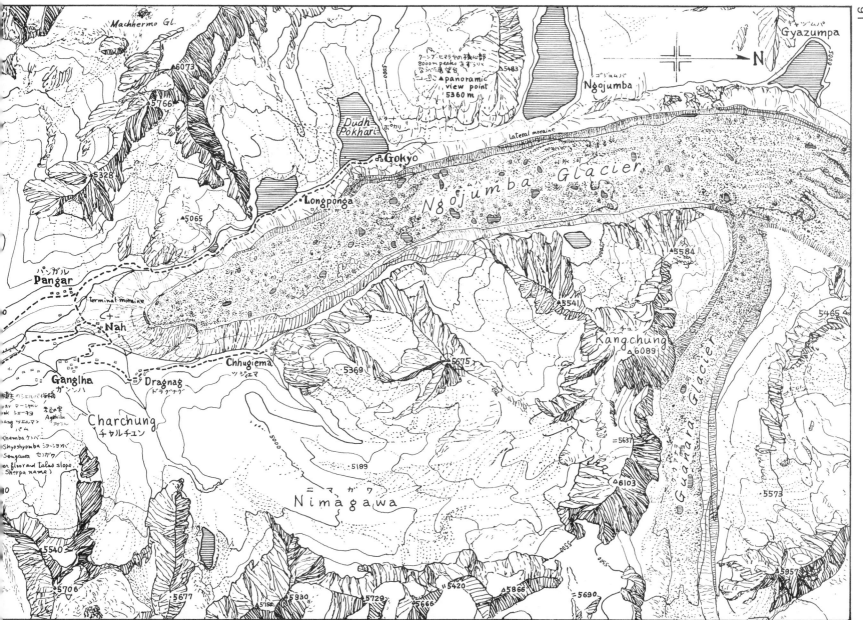

Machhermo Gl.

△6073

△5766

Gyazumpa

クーンブ・ヒマラヤの核心部
8000m peaksをまねうり
など大展望台
□ ▲panoramic
view point
5360 m

△5483

Ngojumba

Dudh-
Pokhari

▲Gokyo

Longponga

Ngojumba Glacier

lateral moraine

△5584

△5328

△5065

パンガル
Pangar

terminal moraine

△5541

△5465

Nah

Chhugiema
ツジエマ

5369

△5675

Kangchung
△6089

Gyanara Glacier

Ganglha
ガンハ

Dragnag
ドラグナグ

再生のシェルパ俗称例
...... マーシャレ
ok ...... 茶色の字
...... Agohlu
...... アゴル
ang ツエマン
.... ハム
khenaba ケンバ
Shyoshyomba ショーシヨガ
Sengawa センガワ
floor and Talas slope.
Sherpa name)

Charchung
チャルチュン

△5631

Nimagawa
ニ マ ガ ワ

5189

△6103

△5573

△5540

△5957

△5706

5677

5930

5729

5420

△5866

5690

5666

△5152

△5158

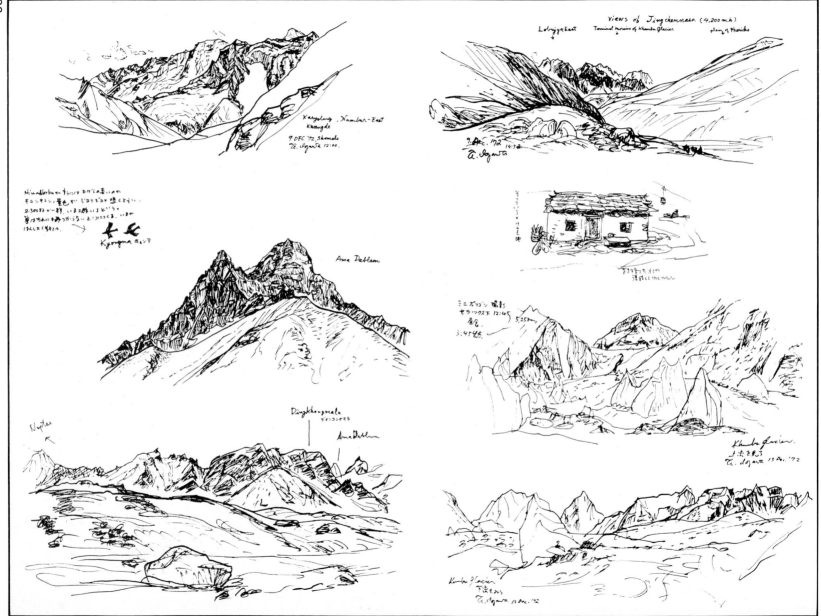

Views of Jingchennada (4,200 m h)

Lobujya East   Terminal moraine of Khumbu Glacier   plain of Phariche

Kanjalung , Nambur-East
Kwangde

9 DEC '72 Shomale
Ā. Aogaufa 12:00.

9. Dec. '72 14:52
Ā. Aogaufa

Ama Dablam

Dingkhongmala
ディンコンガマラ

Ama Dablam

Nuptse

Khumbu Glacier.

Ti. Aogaufa 13 Dec. '72

Khumbu Glacier

Ti. Aogaufa 13 Dec. '72

From field-note sketches.

5. The Everest Base Camp Course, and Kala Pattar

Two of the most pleasurable experiences in Himalayan trekking are either to ascend to the foot of the world's highest peak where, under the Ice Fall of the Khumbu Glacier, mountain-climbers normally establish their base camp; or to climb the 5,600 meters to Kala Pattar, which lies beneath the peak called Pumo Ri, and gaze beyond at the southwest wall of Everest, which looms above Nuptse, at 7,879 meters, in the foreground. It should be remembered, however, that since these courses are all at altitudes where the oxygen is only about half that of the lowlands, a normal walking pace will probably produce an intense constriction of the lungs and a desperate gasping for breath. The surrounding panorama of ice and rock stands out in such unimaginable clarity, on the other hand, that one's ability to judge distance, especially after long residence in the sullied atmosphere at lower elevations, is entirely confounded. Ordinary perceptions of landscape features tend to lose their perspective, so that the whole distant milieu of peaks and ridges becomes, in effect, one huge backdrop — a kind of shallow screen where near and far are indistinguishable. One can no longer say, for example, when looking at the western slope of Mt. Nuptse, just where the Ice Fall of the Khumbu Glacier is located. Nor is it possible with any certainty to judge whether there is any depth at all to the moraine of the southern glacier of Cholatse.

A truly comfortable trip is possible only if one's normal walking pace is reduced to about half, so that the first day one proceeds from Namche to Thyangboche, the second to Pangboche, the third to Pheriche, the fourth to Thukla, the fifth to Lobujye, and sixth to Gorakshep.

At Night In a Hut at Lobujye

Leaving the hut in the middle of the night when the moon is a bit larger than half, the sky, which otherwise might be dark and laden with stars, is pale blue, so that the white massifs in the backgroung seem to stand very close. The air is extremely calm, but from beneath the Lobujye Glacier, shown on the left, water is quietly trickling out of the ground, and when I scratch my head, the noise in my ears appears to echo against the stillness of the night sky.

14 Dec. '72

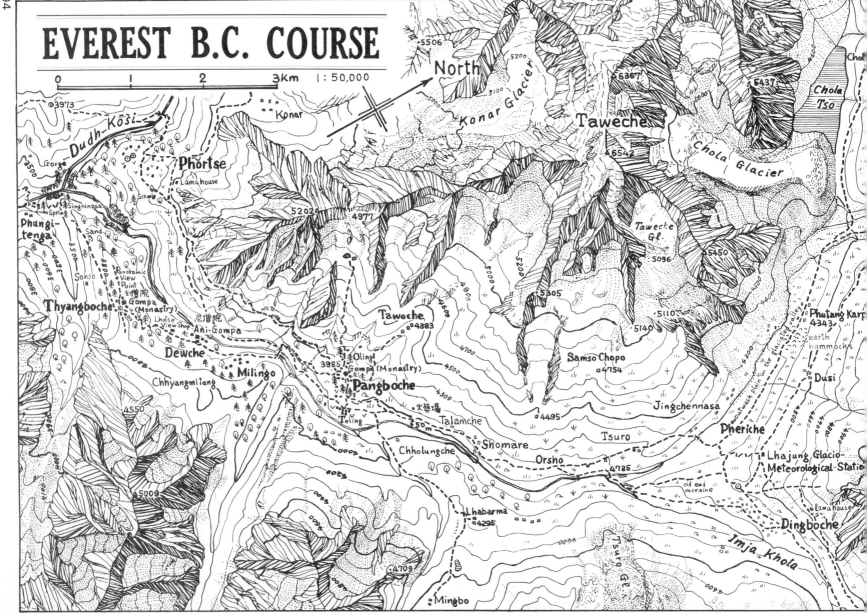

EVEREST B.C. COURSE

0   1   2   3km   1 : 50,000

Pumo Ri
7145

West Chargri Gl.
East Changri Gl.

5551
5613
5687

Kala Pattar
5630
6150

5365
5245
Lobuche Gl.

A5545
5527

Lobuche

5100
sketch point
polygon ground

lateral moraine
Gorakshep
5400

?chowins
Tsukpilarey
end moraine

Khumbu Glacier

B.C.1953
Hunt party (British)

Ice Pinnacles

4620
Hunku
(Tukla)

5456

B.C.1963
Dyhrenfurth
(U.S.A.)

5325
4668

Ice Fall

Lhola
6006

5820

5741
5799
5535 Kongma La
5806
Kongma Gl.
5880
5965
5749

6086

7205

5745
Kongma Tikpe Gl.

5638
5787

5798
5955

7030

West Ridge

Mt. Everest

Nuptse Glacier

Western
Cwm (Cirque)

5443

Nuptse
7879

A. Sozawa '75

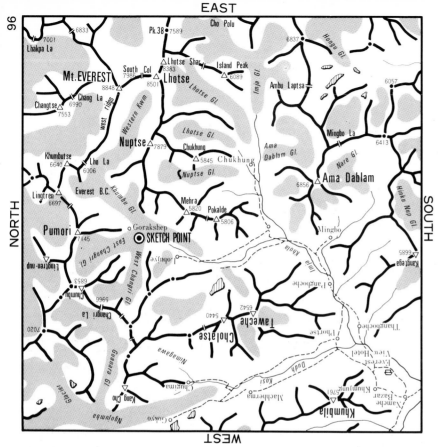

EAST

Cho Polu
Pk.38 ● 7589
● 6837
Hongu Gl.
6833
7001
Lhakpa La
Lhotse Shar
South Col △ 8383
7986 △ Lhotse
8501
Mt. EVEREST
8848 △ Island Peak
△ 6089
Imja Gl.
Ambu Laptsa —
6057
Chang La
Changtse △ 6990
7553
West ridge
Western Kwm
Lhotse Gl.
Mingbo La
6413
Nuptse △ 7879
Lhotse Gl.
Chukhung
△ 5845 Chukhung
Ama Dablam Gl.
Nare Gl.
6856
Khumbutse 6640
Lho La 6006
Nuptse Gl.
Ama Dablam
Lingtren △ 6697
Everest B.C.
Khumbu Gl.
Mehra △ 5820
Pokalde △ 5806
Hinku Nup Gl.
Mingbo
Pumori △ 7145
Gorakshep ○
◉ SKETCH POINT
East Changri Gl.
West Changri Gl.
Imja Khola
Kangtega 6899
Lingtren-nup ▽
6853
Khumbu △ 5966
Changri La
Lobujye ○
Thangboche
7020
△ 5440
Tawache △ 6542
Cholatse
Nimagawa
Phortse
Thangboche
Guanara Gl.
Kang Cho
Chuizimu ○
Dudh
Kosi
Everest Hotel
View Hotel
Glacier
Ngojumba
Tokyo ○
Machherma
5761 ○ Khumjung
Namche Bazar
Khumbila

NORTH / SOUTH / WEST

The Area of the Khumbu Glacier

The best vantage point to see the mountains surrounding the Khumbu Glacier is located between **Lobujye** and **Gorakshep** where the **West Changri Glacier** and the path across the moraine of the **East Changri Glacier** join the **Khumbu Glacier**.

Pumo Ri 7145
Kala Patter South 5545
Lingtern 6697
Khumbutse 6640
Lho La 6005
Chan

Panoramic View of the Mountains Surrounding the Khumbu Glacier

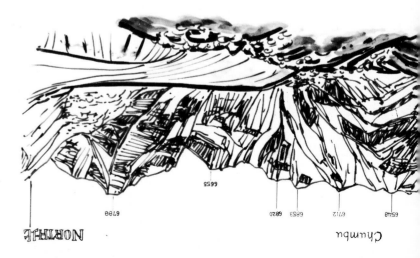

NORTHEAST

Khumbu

6788
6655
6820 6853 6712 6548

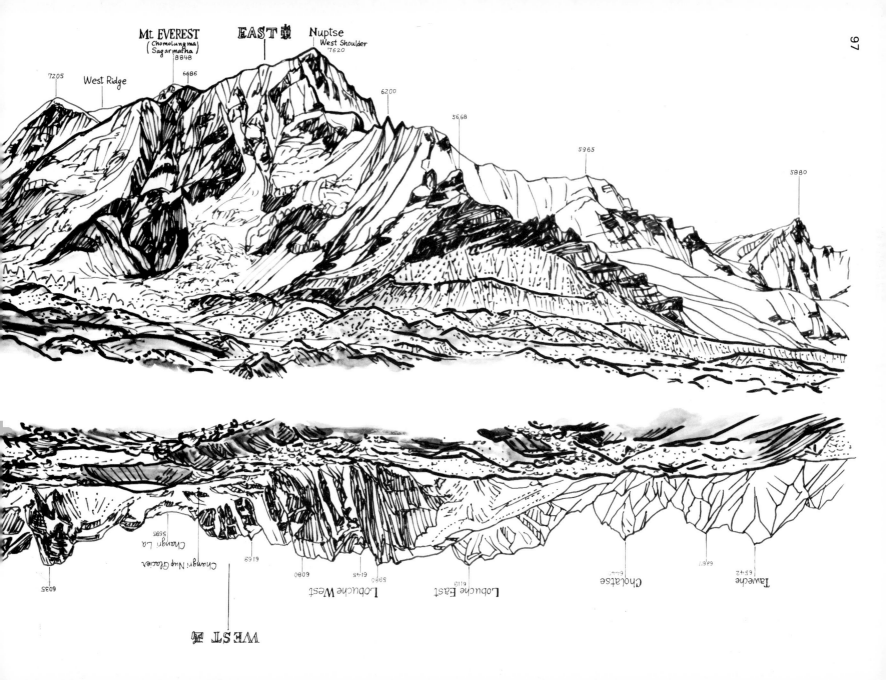

Mt. EVEREST
(Chomolungma)
(Sagarmatha)
8848

EAST 東

Nuptse
West Shoulder
7620

6686

7205 West Ridge

6200

56,68

5965

5980

WEST 西

6035

Changri La
5695

Changri Nup Glacier

6169

Lobuche West
6080

6145

5980

Lobuche East
6119

Cholatse
6440

6367

Tawache
6542

6. Imja Khola

The road from Pangboche to Pheriche, which leads ultimately to the stratified rock walls of Mt. Lhotse, traverses a vast, elevated, arid plateau, where, since here and there are the graveyards and crematoriums of the local residents, the Sherpa may be inclined to make wist-

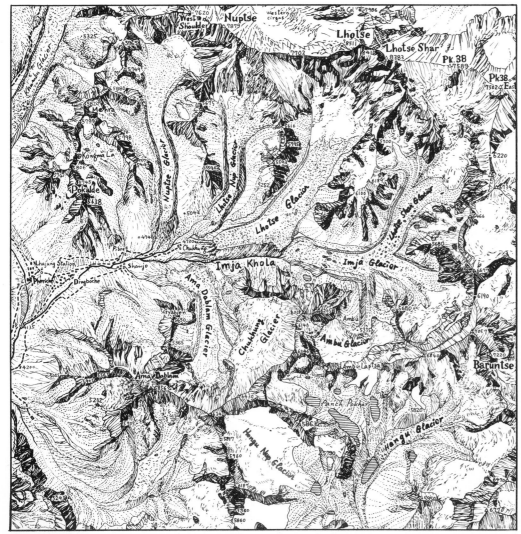

Map of Imja Khola

A Panoramic View From Lhengbo Ridge

ful comments. By following this road directly it is possible to enter the Imja Valley at the foot of Mr. Lhotse. However, since the stream from the Khumbu Glacier enters this valley on its right bank it is necessary to divert your course temporarily by scrambling down the

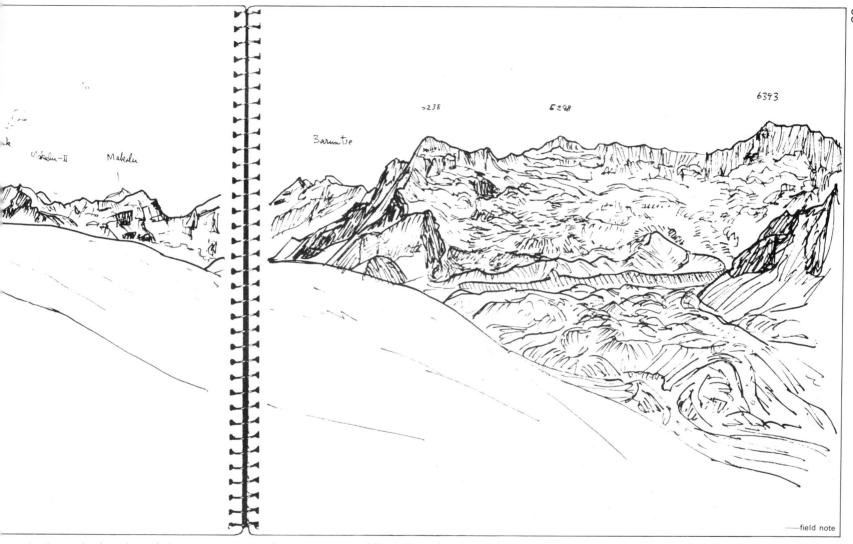

Vishala-II Makalu

Baruntje >238 6248 6393

—field note

bank to the junction of the two streams and proceeding across a bridge, where the path again ascends the cliff and reaches the village of **Dingboche**, on whose outskirts is a terminal moraine created by the Khumbu Glacier in the pleistocene Epoch. This village is located on an expanse of level ground and contains two permanent residents, an elderly couple, as well as a number of transients according to the season. The valley scene unfolds as one plods along, at first with **Ama Dablam** (6,858 meters) as a focal point, surrounded by white fields of snow and ice and, in the distance, many Himalayan Peaks, then by Mt. Makalu, Baruntse, and ultimately of course, by Nuptse and Lhotse. The life-style of the mountain people, meanwhile, seems like an ode sung by a shepherd as he tends his flock in a mountain pasture.

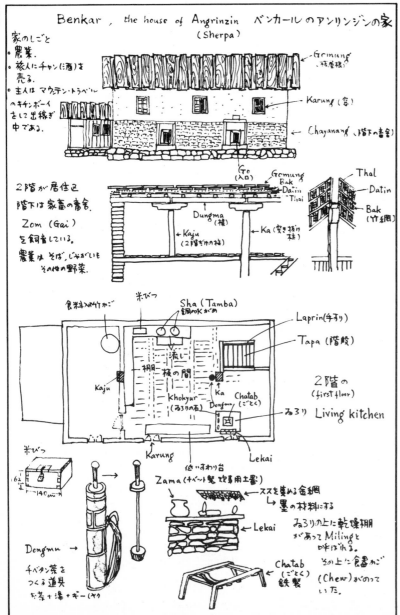

Benkar , the house of Angrinzin　ベンカールのアンリンジンの家
(Sherpa)

家のしごと
○農業
○旅人にチャン(酒)を売る
○主人は マウンテン・トラベルのキッチンボーイをして出稼ぎ中である。

Gemung (板屋根)
Karung (窓)
Chayanang (階下の畜舎)
Go (入口)
Gemung Bak
Datin
Thal
Dungma (梁)
Kaju (2階ざわけの柱)
Ka (突き抜け柱)

Thal
Datin
Bak (竹網)

2階が居住区
階下は家畜の畜舎
Zom (Gai) を飼育している。
農業は そば、じゃがいもその他の野菜。

食料入れ竹かご
米びつ
Sha (Tamba) 銅鍋やK がめ
流し
棚 板の間
Kaju
Khokyur (ゐゐりの布)
Ka
Chatab (ごとく)
Dongma
Laprin (手すり)
Tapa (階段)
ゐゐり Living kitchen

2階の (first floor)

Karung
Lekai

米びつ
162
140cm

Dongmn →
チベタン茶をつくる道具
お茶＋湯＋ギー(ヤク)

Zama (チベット製 文房用土墨)
ススを集める金網
墨の材料にする

ゐゐりの上に乾燥棚があって Miling と呼ばれる。
その上に食器が (Chew)がのっていた。

Lekai
Chatab (ごとく)鉄製

使いすわり台

7. The Sherpa Life

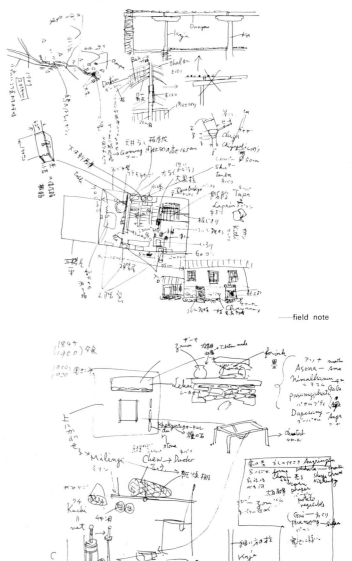

field note

Many among the tribes who dwell in the Himalayan highlands seem to reveal a superficial facial resemblance to the Japanese, and, when one considers certain likenesses in agricultural practice, even in language, there appear to be other common aspects as well. Such observations have been noted particularly by Westerners who came here initially to climb but who become interested enough in the region to record their observations.

Thanks to the hospitality of Mr. Dakau of the Sherpa tribe in the village of **Thame Og**, I was afforded an opportunity to record the details of a typical Sherpa house and its effects. (The elderly woman of the house was called **Angdami**, the adult son, **Gyelzen**, and the sister, of whom there were three all together, **Angphurba**.) December 1, 1972.

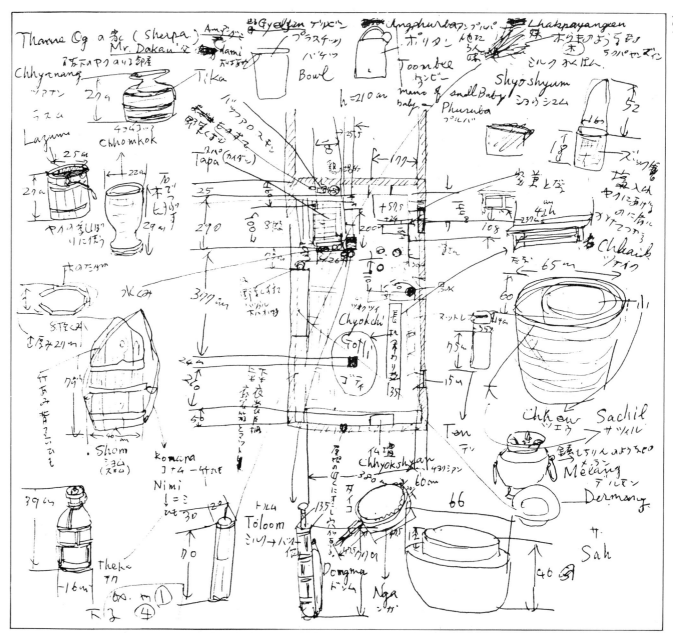

—field note

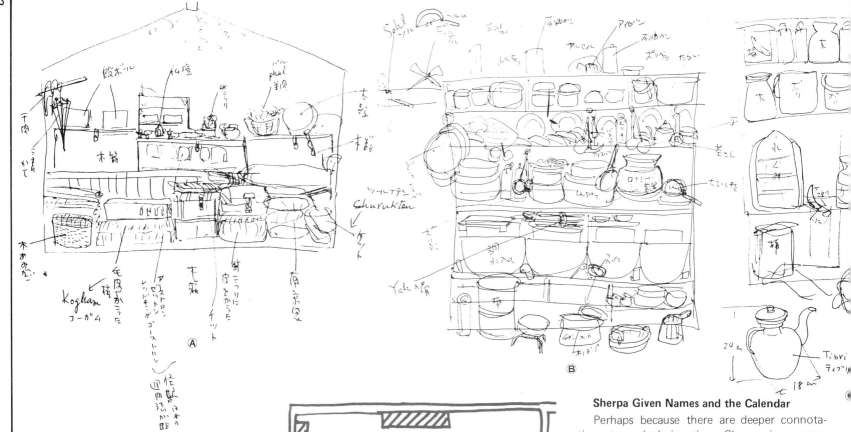

Ⓐ

Kogham
コーガム

Churukten

Yak入れ旧

Ⓑ

Tibri
ティブリ

A Sherpa House of Thame

Here, I attempted to describe in exact detail, the visible effects noted in the rooms on the second floor of the house mentioned on the preceeding page. I have also tried to capture these in both black-and-white and color film, thinking that eventually I may make a more systematic presentation in a later work.

Sherpa Given Names and the Calendar

Perhaps because there are deeper connotations, to such designations, Sherpa given names are related to the days of the week. Most of us, on the other hand, are probably ignorant of this detail of our own lives. However, since many individuals have the same name, other attributes, such as the place of residence, the style of one's house, even certain physical characteristics, are usually included in the name as well. It might be amusing to imagine what one's name would have been under these circumstances.

An Old Man of Pangboche

The village of Pangboche is probably the most remote area of permanent tribal settlement among the Sherpas. Here, an old man, **Dhawa Namgyal**, was asked about such things as local hunting, and the **Abominable Snowman**. He replied that there are four kinds of wild creatures hereabouts, the **Changu** (snow leopard), the **Jarao** (giant deer), the **Kongma** (snow grouse, or a kind of ptarmigan), and the **Danphe** (rainbow pheasant). ↘

パンボチェ・ゴンパ内院

E

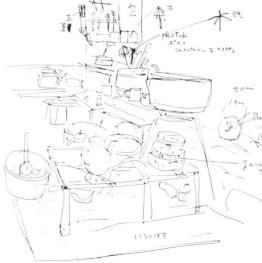

↘ As for the latter, there are two versions of **Yeti** (the Abominable Snowman). One is said to be a **manchi kantza** (cannibal), called **Miti**; the other, **Chuttee**, a **yak kantza**, or yak-eater. The two differ in that the former's body is inscribed around the waist with a girdle-like pattern which divides the torso into an upper protion, covered by blackish hair growing upward, while that below the waist grows downward. Chuttee's hair, on the other hand, envelopes the entire body, is longer, brown rather than black, and grows entirely downward. Both have cries that sound something like, 'Hew!', 'Khen!', or 'Cwaka ka ka ko!'. Having faces resembling those of bears, Yeti are sometimes seen standing clumsily upright, like bears or monkeys, but usually they crawl about on all fours.

English	Sherpa	Nepali	
Sunday	Nima	Aita Bar	आइतबार
Monday	Dhawa	Som Bar	सोमबार
Tuesday	Mingma	Mangar Bar	मंगलबार
Wednesday	Lhakpa	Budha Bar	बुधबार
Thursday	Phurbu	Brihaspati Bar	बृहस्पतिबार
Friday	Pasang	Shukra Bar	शुक्रबार
Saturday	Pemba	Shani Bar	शनिबार

—field note

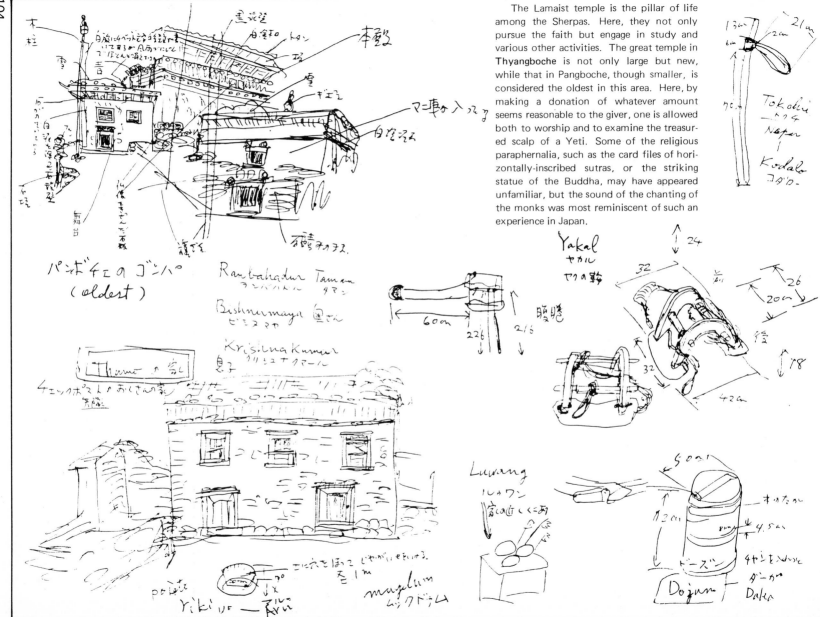

The Lamaist temple is the pillar of life among the Sherpas. Here, they not only pursue the faith but engage in study and various other activities. The great temple in **Thyangboche** is not only large but new, while that in Pangboche, though smaller, is considered the oldest in this area. Here, by making a donation of whatever amount seems reasonable to the giver, one is allowed both to worship and to examine the treasured scalp of a Yeti. Some of the religious paraphernalia, such as the card files of horizontally-inscribed sutras, or the striking statue of the Buddha, may have appeared unfamiliar, but the sound of the chanting of the monks was most reminiscent of such an experience in Japan.

(left-vertical cut) The Center of the Village of **Namche**

(right-top) Kitchen-Living-Room of a Sherpa Family.

(lower-middle) Spreading dough (**Pintaro**) with a stick roller.

(lower-right) Baking **rikru** on a stone griddle.

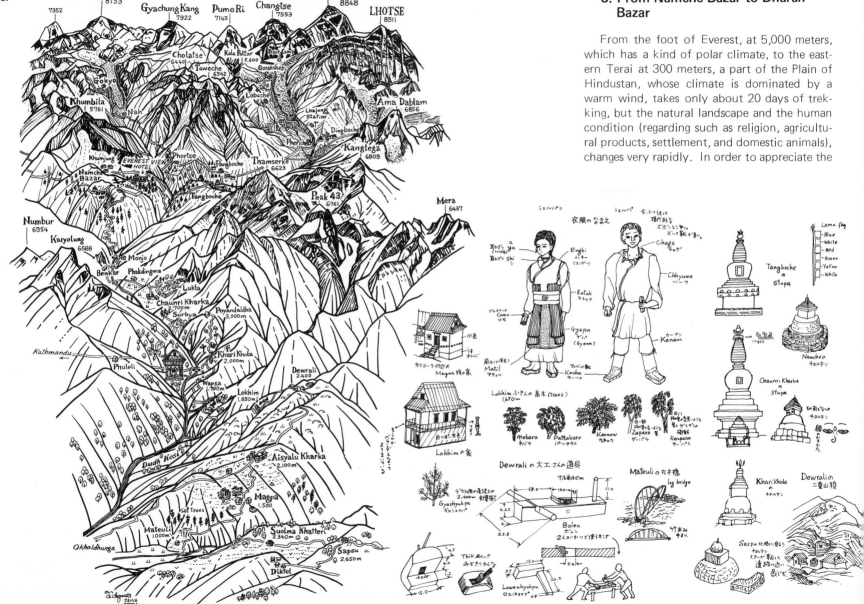

8. From Namche Bazar to Dharan Bazar

From the foot of Everest, at 5,000 meters, which has a kind of polar climate, to the eastern Terai at 300 meters, a part of the Plain of Hindustan, whose climate is dominated by a warm wind, takes only about 20 days of trekking, but the natural landscape and the human condition (regarding such as religion, agricultural products, settlement, and domestic animals), changes very rapidly. In order to appreciate the

Field Sketches, From Namche Bazar to Dharan Bazar

details of this natural and cultural transition, one should, of course, experience such a trek, laterally, along the vast mountain chain, and vertically, from one realm to the next.

In my most recent trekking experience, I was surprised to find that a new road had been constructed from **Bhojpur**, along the **Arun** River, to the **Sapt Kosi** (river). The task of hacking and hewing a ledge to fashion such a pathway must have been prodigious indeed!

But the most striking feature to this writer was the obvious vigor of those who, in their animated pace and movements, were clearly expressing their delight in this new facility. Moreover, clusters of inns, lodging places, and such, had sprung up all along the route. Here, one would constantly pass parties of ten or more persons, each with a pannier supported by a light rope attached to the head, and keeping his balance by the aid of a staff, the last of which is usually seen in a corner when the party is resting. To meet up with such a party along a narrow ledge, with a cliff on one side, always creates a difficult problem of passage.

thatched roof · galvanized · thatched roof · iron roof · thatched roof · tiled roof · galvanized iron roof · thatched roof · intersection · tiled roof · thatched roof · galvanized shingle roof · galvanized iron roof · thatched roof · tiled roof · galvanized roof · tiled roof · thatched roof

Okhaldhunga · grocery · rice shop · grocery · restaurant · grocery · dry goods · grocery · dry goods · dressmaker · camera shop · Hindu temple · hardware · grocery · dry goods · hardware · blacksmith · dry goods · grocery · tea house · cosmetics and dry goods · dressmaker (3 machines) · restaurant with attractive waitress · Dingla

← WEST

EAST →

BHOJPUR TOWNSCAPE

intersection · galvanized roof · thatched roof · galvanized roof · tiled roof · thatched roof · galvanized iron roof · tiled roof · galvanized

dry goods · groceries · pharmacy-cosmetics-grocery · family planning center · flashlights watches repair shop · watches, clocks, restaurant (crackers & doughnuts) · pictureframes electric bulbs · teahouse · restaurant (boiled potatos) · Hindu temple · pharmacy Advocate · grocery book

← NORTH

The Mahabharat Range

Although the Khumbu area may be likened to the polar or arctic regions, the Mahabharat Range is more like a temperate transition zone between the Khumbu District, on the one hand, and the Churia Hills and sub-tropical Terai Plain, on the other. If, in Japan, the area between the Kanto District and southern Tohoku, is the eastern limit of the so-called "Laurel Forest Cultural Zone", the Mahabharat Range of Nepal is the western, and since there seems to have been, from ancient times, considerable cultural exchange within these zones of roughly parallel physical conditions, I have noted as stated many common elements.

Local religious symbols

Village of **Khorsani**, with field containing chili and tobacco.

A Mahabharat village lost in the clouds.

The inhabitants of the temperate Mahabharat Range area are generally such tribes as the Sherpa, Tamang, Rais, Limbu, Chhetri, Brahman (colloquially Baun), Magar, and Gurung, who support themselves by agriculture; or the Newar, who are essentially urban and live in agglomerated settlements.

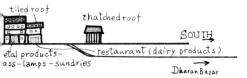

Weaving, using the roof-overhang as a support.

Ferry boat, **Arun** River.

Travelers along the **Sapt Kosi**.

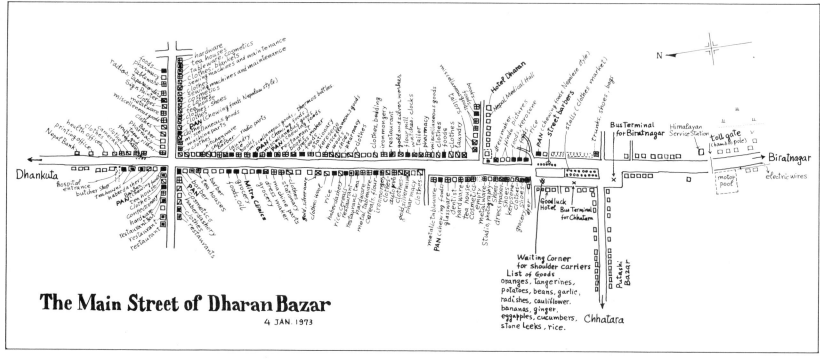

N

The Main Street of Dharan Bazar

4 JAN. 1973

Dhankuta

Biratnagar

Hotel Dharan
Nepal Medical Hall

Bus Terminal
for Biratnagar

Himalayan
Service Station

toll gate
(bamboo pole)

motor
pool

electric wires

Goodluck
Hotel

Bus Terminal
for Chhatara

Putaishi
Bazar

Waiting Corner
for shoulder carriers
List of Goods
oranges, tangerines,
potatoes, beans, garlic,
radishes, cauliflower,
bananas, ginger,
eggapples, cucumbers,
stone leeks, rice.

Chhatara

9. Dharan Bazar

Dahran Bazar is the starting point for the Himalayas of eastern Nepal, and the trip from Kathmandu to **Biratnagar** takes one-hour by airplane; two days by bus, with another hour-and-a-half to Dahran.

Our party left by bus from **Chhatara**, a local collection and distribution center for goods and products, including those of the area, located at the apex of an alluvial fan, bordered on one side by the Sapt Kosi. Upon our arrival at the bus terminal in the open area in the midst of Dahran Bazar, we were immediately struck by the great throng of people and by the wealth of goods displayed, but especially by the verve and vitality of the crowd.

Dharan Bazar filled with folk resting after carrying products from the **Mahabharat Range**.

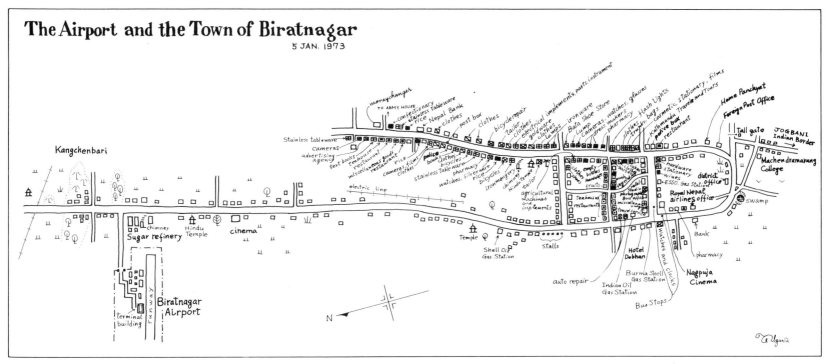

The Airport and the Town of Biratnagar
5 JAN. 1973

Kangchenbari

Stainless tableware

money changer
TO ARMY HOUSE
confectionery
stainless tableware
rice Nepal Bank
clothes
post box
clothes
bicycle repair
tailor
electrical implements, parts, instrument
goldsmith
electrical ware
clothes
Lumps
Bata Shoe Store
ironware Store
cameras, watches, glasses
dress makers
pharmacy
clothes, flash lights
trunks, bags
Kathmandu Travels and Tours
cosmetic, stationary, films
police box
restaurant
Home Panchyat
Foreign Post Office
Toll gate
JOGBANI Indian Border

Cameras
advertising agency
text books
teahouse
restaurant
miscellaneous goods
restaurant
rice
cameras, films
clothes
police
book, clothes
bicycles
pharmacy
watches, silverware
rice
bicycles
ironmongery
chimney
Hindu temple
tailor
agricultural machines and implements
fruits
Comp. books, harware
hardware
stationary
wines
ESSO Gas Station
district office
Royal Nepal airlines office
Teahouse
restaurants
miscellaneous
Travel Service
Machendramarang College
swamp
Bank
pharmacy

electric line

chimney
Sugar refinery
Hindu Temple
cinema
Temple
Shell Oil Gas Station
stalls
Hotel Dobhan
auto repair
Indian Oil Gas Station
Burma Shell Gas Station
watches and clocks
Bus Stops
Nagpuja Cinema

N

terminal building
runway
Biratnagar Airport

On reaching **Biratnagar**, both in the animals and the inhabitants, one again detects the flavor of India.

10. Biratnagar

The town of Biratnagar, stretched out in the midst of paddy fields and vegetable plots, boasts an airport, a sugar refinery, and a business district composed of two, rather than the usual one main shopping street. However, despite these facilites and the activity generated, the atmosphere of vitality noted for Dahran Bazar, was simply not in evidence.

Biratnagar, on the other hand, does have many inns and hotels, including the Biratnagar Himalayan Hotel, the Hotel Milan, Hotel Dobhan, and the Hotel Birat.

One more impression upon quitting the mountains for the plains that may be worthy of note, is that here there appear to be more swarthy people, and the sight of humped-back bullocks pulling their traditional wagons takes us into a new and different world.

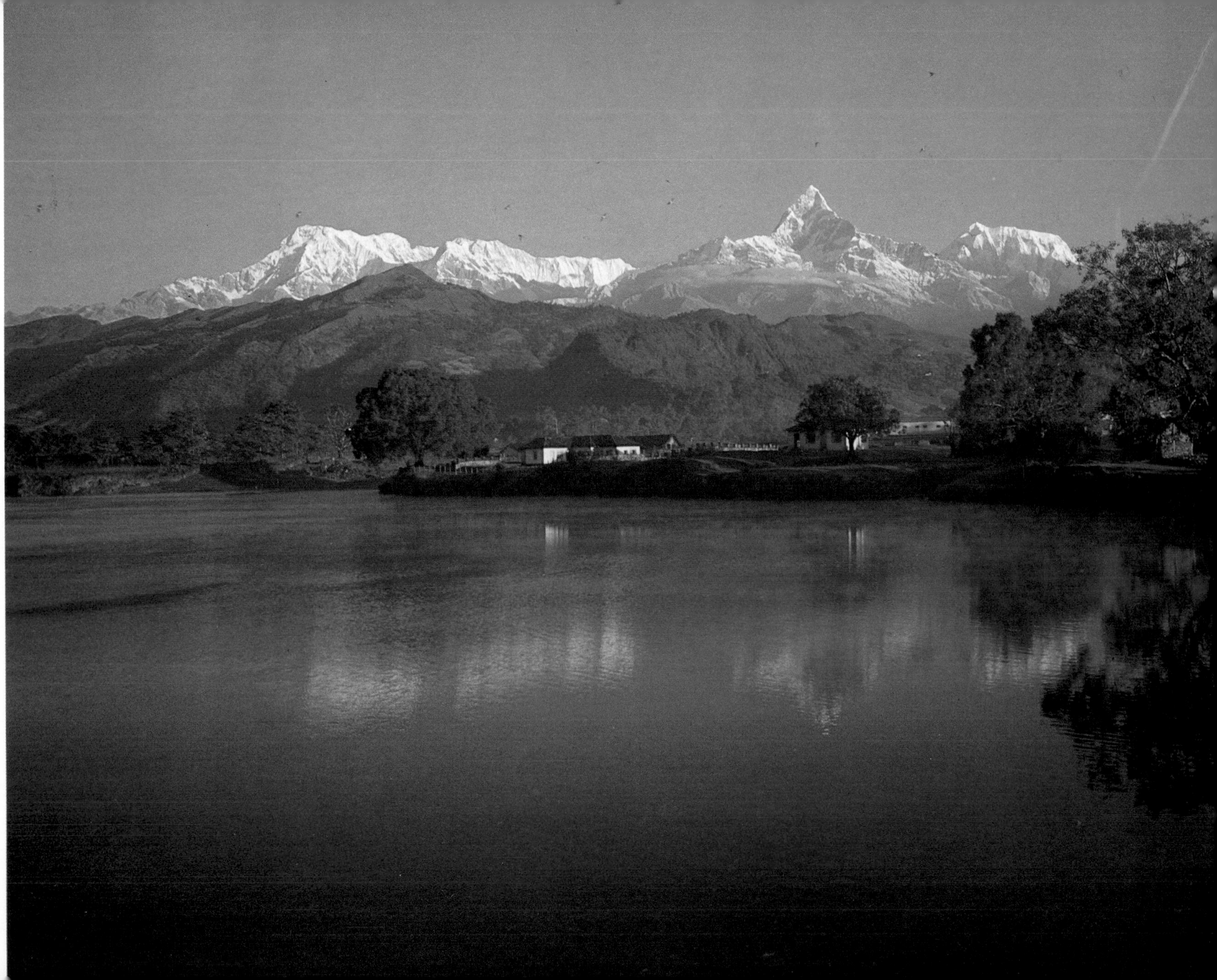

Pokhara is a beautiful lake-side town, whose formerly cobblestone street has been replaced by an asphalted highway which runs from **Bhairhwa** at the Indian border, and extends beyond Pokhara to Kathmandu. Naturally, this development has quickened the movement of people and goods and has promoted the spread of settlement in the outskirts of the town, where many new houses are seen. However, basically this remains a Nepalese country town with all the traditional inconveniences that such would imply. On the other hand, the magnificent views of **Machhapuchhare** and **Annapurna** that are visible over the roof tiles roundabout are only slowly being obstructed by electric wires that have been strung about at random. Notwithstanding, when one ventures out of town as far as the lake, it is reassuring to find its waters and the mountain panorama, as awe-inspiring as ever.

1. Planning and Preparation

Of the main trekking courses leading from Pokhara, the ten to fifteen listed in the table on pages 80-81 are the most popular. (It should be noted that in Number 14, in 1977, one was allowed to go as far as **Muktinath**.)

In eastern Nepal, the highest points of the Himalayan chain are represented by border posts with the Peoples Republic of China, but in the center, as the mountain arc swings southward, the higher peaks lie well within Nepal itself. Therefore, in the east, one can note the highest mountains in the background, beyond

Morning on **Phewa Tal (Lake)**, south of Pokhara. More recently, however, a break in the dam has caused the water to recede.

lower summits that are obviously closer, but in the center, ice and snow-covered peaks are much more a part of the immediate scene. Pokhara lies at about 800 meters (much lower than Kathmandu) and even in winter temperatures are mild enough that tangerines are a local specialty crop.

Here, since even the aged and infirm come to enjoy the magnificent panorama of distant peaks, which often reach 8,000 meters, there are a number of one to three-day trekking courses specifically designed for such clientele, for which the goal is simply to enjoy the views of lakes and other scenery. Also, through the wise use of public buses and taxis which run to such destinations as Kathmandu, **Butwal**, and **Tansen**, it may be interesting to plan individual treks to unusual places en route. Some may wish to ascend the **Kali Gandaki** Valley, although Jomosom is the usual point for which permission is granted by the Government. On the other hand, subsidiary treks can be entered into the itinerary as circumstances may dictate. Permission is also occasionally granted for **Tilitso**. Those whose ambitions lie downstream should be sure to visit **Beni, Baglung, Kusma, Tansen, Butwal,** and **Bhairhwa** and for those

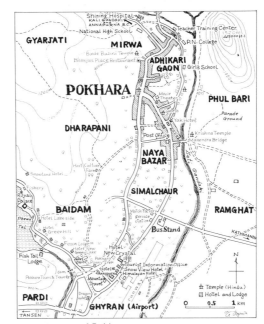

A simple map of Pokhara.

who wish to see the birthplace of the Buddha, there is an extra fee (150 − 200 Rps.), to cover the rental of a jeep, since **Lumbini** must be included in the itinerary.

For the foot-hills of Mt. **Machhapuchhare, Ghachok, Ghandrung,** and **Annapurna Base Camp (B.C.)** should be inserted in order to provide the widest possible trekking opportunities. But for **Namun Bhanjyang, Thonje,** on the opposite side of the mountain might also be entered, along with **Siklis,** although if such permission cannot be obtained, you should be prepared to return by the same route.

A guide for such trekking could either be hired at Kathmandu or chosen from among the Sherpas who may be soliciting such employment at the (Pokhara) airport. In order to be more sure of such personnel, one could gain an introduction to a specific party through predecessors or acquaintances, or be provided with an introductory note or letter from a trusted person in Kathmandu. As for provisions, most needed items are purchasable in Pokhara, but there is a greater variety of stores and a richer assortment of goods available in **Tatopani**. If the trek is downstream along the Kali Gandaki, there are many facilities for food and lodging along the way, especially if one chooses those run by members of the **Thakali** tribe, who maintain a good reputation for hospitality and honesty to travellers.

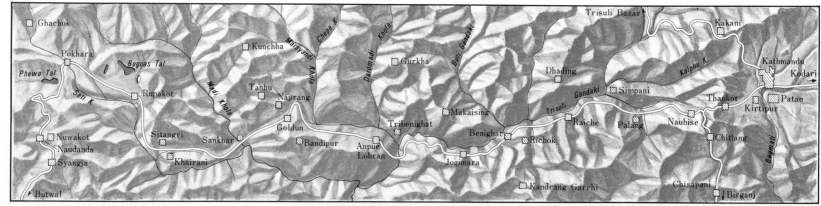

From **Kathmandu** to **Pokhara**.

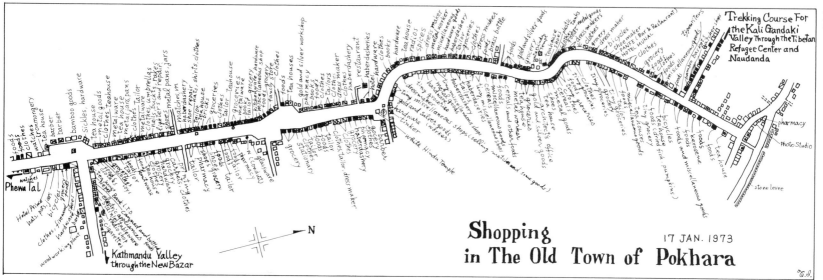

Shopping in The Old Town of Pokhara

17 JAN. 1973

2. Pokhara Bazar

The place known as Pokhara Bazar once referred only to the area shown in the accompanying sketch. However, since highway communications have been put through to Kathmandu, modern shops and traditional streetside stalls have sprung up all along the road east of the town. In addition, many hotels and lodging places have been built around the shores of (Lake) **Phewa Tal**, in the vicinity of the airport, and between the new market area and the old bazar. The atmosphere of Pokhara has thus now grown considerably more complex. Another aspect of this is seen in the expansion of housing enclaves in the southern reaches of the town, and it is evident that this kind of growth will continue for the time being.

My personal wish, however, is that this rapid transition will not efface the beauties of the setting, such as may be occurring as power lines are strung across once-uncluttered views of mountain landscapes.

As was my policy in Kathmandu, I have recorded the details of the old bazar of Pokhara on eleven rolls (400 pictures) of film, considering this a relatively simple method of preserving the scene, including details of all houses and stores, as well as of goods, store-keepers, customers, folk in native costumes, domestic animals — all combined into interesting and impromptu capsulations of moments in time.

The plain which houses the town of Pokhara and its airport is dissected by a gorge, 10 meters in width by 80 meters in depth, which runs roughly from north to south and passes along the eastern border of the airport. By descending to the river bed north of the bazar, behind the hospital, and looking downstream, the entrance to this gorge appears like the door to the nether regions. And if one follows the road leading southeast of the airport, there is a view of the gorge opening and the valley head.

Hotels and Lodges in Pokhara (as of January 1977)
[Rates in Nepal Rupees, Including Service charge of 5% and Tax of 10%]

A. Ordinary Hotels

Name	District	No. of Rooms	Beds	Rates Twin	Single
1 Fish Tail Lodge	Phewa Tal	16	32	164 34	119 52
2 New Hotel Crystal	Airport	46	90	217.35	147 00
3 Hotel Mt. Annapurna (Ph 31)	Airport	28	56	162.00 (US $13)* 224.00**	112.00 (US $9)* 149.00**
4 Hotel New Snow View	Airport	14	28	110.00	80.00
5 Hotel Mandara	Mahendra Pool				
6 Hotel Dragon	Pardi	20	40		

(*=bed & breakfast **=with tax and full board)

B. Economy Class and Lodges

Name	District	No. of Rooms	Beds	Twin	Single
7 The Himalayan Hotel	Airport	11	28	15.00	5 00
8 The Raju Hotel	Airport	6	17	12.00	6 00
9 The New Baba Lodge	Baidam	9	24	20.00	—
10 Phewa Lodge	Baidam	9	10	20.00	15 00
11 Hotel Mountain View	Pardi	7	14	10.00	7 00
12 Hotel Pokhara View	Pardi	8	15	6.00	4 00
13 Hotel Quality	Mahendra Pool	5	11	12.00	8 00
14 Hotel Dhaulagiri	Mahendra Pool	3	7	—	4 00
15 Hotel Snow Land	Baidam	12	26	10.00	
16 Hotel Madan	Pardi	5	10	6.00	4 00
17 Hotel Gorkha Cravern	Pardi	7	14	6.00	4 00
18 Hotel Raji	Baidam	3	5	5.00	4 00
19 Hotel New Green Lake	Baidam	8	16	10.00	6 00
20 Hotel Lakeside	Baidam	10	20	20.00	10 00
21 Trekkers Retreat Lodge	Baidam	7	14	15.00	10 00
22 Hotel Green Hill	Baidam	5	10	10.00	7 00
23 Hotel Phewa Lakeside	Baidam	11	22	30.00 7 00* 16 20	20 00 1 00* 10 00
24 Hotel Muktinath (Ph 182)	Mahendra Pool	11	27	25.00***	

(*twin room, **single room, ***triple room.
Note also, Hotel Muktinath has dormitory accommodations with single beds for 1 Rupee (6 beds in all))

ANNAPURNA and DHAULAGIRI

T. IOZAWA

Mustang

Muktin

Dhaulagiri-IV
7661

D-V
7618

D-III
7715

D-II
7751

Dhaulagiri-I
8167

Sita Chuchura
6611

Tukche Pk.
6920

Annapurn
8091

Gurja Himal
7193

6395

Nilgiri-North
7061

Tiliteo-Pk.
7132

N-South
6839

6940

Annapurna S
7219

6620

Jirbang
6062

Tukuche

5130

Gandaki

Larjung

Myagdi

Khola

Lete

Miristi Khola

Chhmro

Hinko

Lipsiba

Asnam Dhuli
3507

Dwari

Ghasa

Sidi

Sonakosh

Chaurakhan

Thulo Khola

Kali

Dana

Sikha

Ghorapani

Ghandrung

Landrung

Jamruk

Beni

Talopani

Ullerin

Lumle

Khare

Naudanda

Bium

Okhrent

Birethanti

Sallyan

Kaski

Baglung

2511

Modi Khola

Tilbar

Panchase
2509

Kusma

Gijan

Karkineta

Bhaira

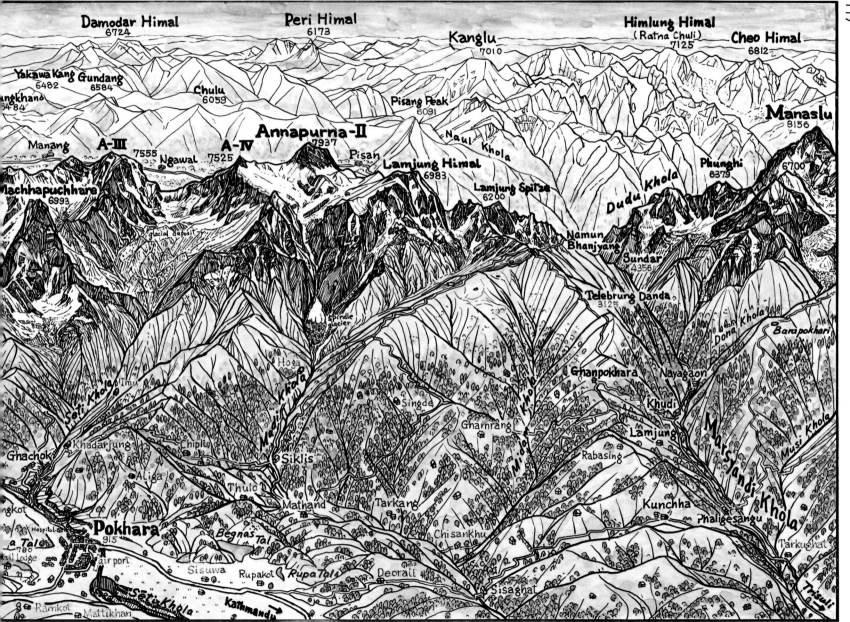

Damodar Himal
6724

Peri Himal
6173

Himlung Himal
(Ratna Chuli)
7125

Kanglu
7010

Cheo Himal
6812

Yakawa Kang
6482

Gundang
6584

angkhang
484

Chulu
6059

Pisang Peak
6091

Manaslu
8156

Manang

A-III
7555

A-IV
7525

Ngawal

Annapurna-II
7937

Naul Khola

Pisan

Lamjung Himal
6983

Phunghi
6379

6700

Machhapuchhare
6993

Lamjung Spitze
6200

glacial deposit

Dudu Khola

Namun
Bhanjyang

Sundar
4356

Telebrung Danda
3125

Spindle
glacier

Hoga

Barapokhari

Dona Khola

Seti Khola

Imu

Madi Khola

Singde

Ghanpokhara

Nayagaon

Khudi

Ghamrang

Midi Khola

Marsyandi Khola

Ghachok

Khadarjung

Chiplu

Siklis

Lamjung

Rabasing

Musi Khola

Aliga

Thulo

Mathand

Tarkang

Kunchha

Phaligesangu

ngkot

Hospital

Pokhara
915

Begnas
Tal

Chisankhu

a Tal
780

il lodge

Sisuwa

airport

Rupakot

Rupa Tal

Deorali

Sisaghat

Tarkughat

Ramkot

Mattikhan

Seti Khola

Kathmandu

Trisuli

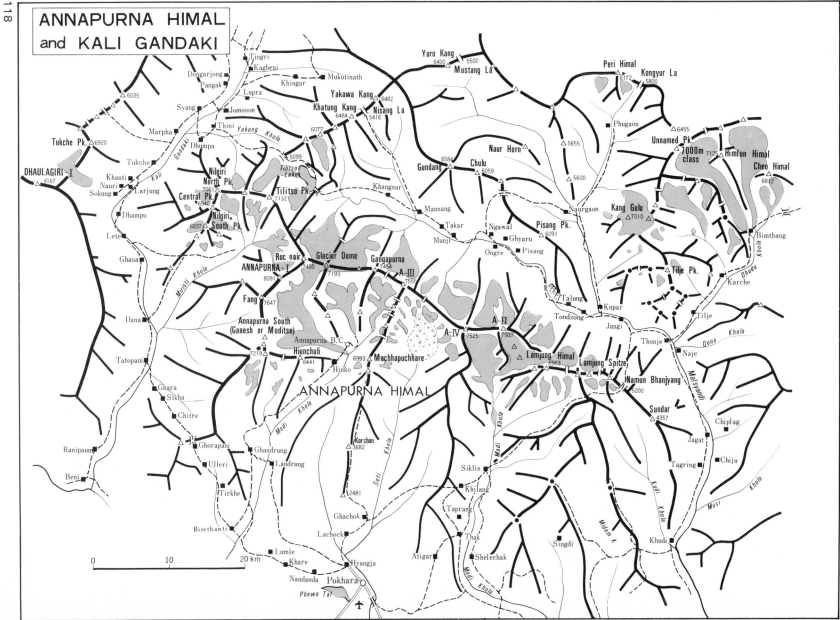

ANNAPURNA HIMAL
and KALI GANDAKI

Tingri
Kagbeni
Dongarjong
Pangak
Khingar
Mukutinath
△6035
Lupra
Syang
Jomoson
Yakawa Kang
△6482
Thini
Khatung Kang
Nisang La
△6484
△5416
Marpha
Dhumpa
6077
Tukche Pk.
△6920
Tukche
5099
Nilgiri
North Pk.
Tilitso Lake
7061
Khanti
Nauri
Larjung
Central Pk.
Tilitso Pk.
6940
7132
Sokung
Nilgiri
Dhampu
South Pk.
6837
Lete
Khangsar
Ghasa
Roc noir
Glacier Dome
7485
ANNAPURNA-I
7193
Gangapurna
8091
7454
A-III
Fang
7555
7647
Annapurna South
(Ganesh or Moditse)
Annapurna B.C.
7219
Hiunchuli
A-IV
6441
6993
7525
Hinko
Machhapuchhare

Yuro Kang
5500
6400
Mustang La
Peri Himal
Kongyur La
6172
5800
Phugaon
△6455
Naur Horn
Unnamed Pk.
△5655
7125
Himlun Himal
7000m class
Cheo Himal
6584
Gundang
Chulu
6059
△5600
6812
Mannang
Kang Gulu
△7010
Takar
Bimthang
Ngawal
Pisang Pk.
Munji
Ghyaru
6091
Naurgaon
Ongre
Pisang
Tilje Pk.
Karche
Dhudu
Talung
Kupar
Tondzong
Tilje
A-II
Jangi
7937
Thonje
Lamjung Himal
Naje
A-II
6983
7525
Lamjung Spitze
Namun Bhanjyang
5200

ANNAPURNA HIMAL

Dana
Tatopani
Ghara
Slkha
Chitre
Ranipaum
Ghorapani
Beni
Ulleri
Landrung
Tirkhe
Birethanti
Lumle
Khare
Naudanda
Pokhara
Phewa Tal

Korchon
3682
2481
Ghachok
Lachock
Atigart
Thak
Shelechak
Siklis
Khilang
Taprang
Singdi
Midam K.
Kudi Khola
Sundar
4357
Chiplag
Tagring
Jagat
Chiju
Khudi
Musi Khola

0   10   20 km

3. At the Foot of Mount Machhapuchhare

If the representative peak in the Alps is the **Matterhorn**, then **Machhapuchhare** is its counterpart in the Himalayas.

The name appears to have originally referred to its resemblance to the tail of a fish, and, in fact, when seen from a western sector, the curved ridge line connecting its two pinnacles, does suggest such an association. From the town of Pokhara, this beautiful mountain (the closest peak of fame in this region) gives the appearance of a narrow, elongate pyramid. And, although the various trekking courses at the base of the mountain, in and around the grass-covered, glaciated features found there, afford the visitor many interesting opportunities, the area is surprisingly little-known. It is the writer's ambition to trek here one day and, beginning with visits to the villages in the foot-hills, to reveal the secrets of this region, one by one.

For the beginner, typical one-day trekking courses might be to places like **Naudanda**, west of Pokhara; **Ghachok**, to the northwest, and **Arghoun** in the hills to the east.

120

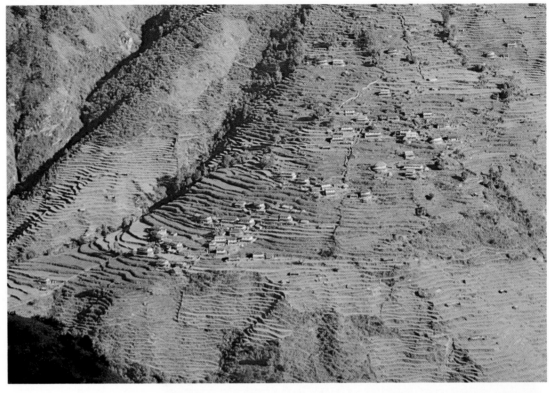

(top-left)
Banana tree in the Village of **Ghachok**, backed by a view of **Mt. Machhapuchhare** (6,993 meters).

(lower-left)
Mt. Machhapuchhare as seen from the old Pokhara Bazar gives perhaps a hint of Switzerland.

(top-right)
Terrace cultivation around the village of **Ghandrung**.

(lower-right)
Annapurna South (7,219 meters) as viewed from Ghandrung.

Nilgiri South Peak (6,839 meters) seen from Tatopani.

Ms Pool Kumari, of Tatopani.

A view of Dhaulagiri I (8,167 meters) from the western summit of Ghorapani Pass.

A woman and child of Ghasa.

Houses and willow trees along a river bank in the Village of **Larjung**.

Temple, Larjung.

Road, tunneling under a house in the Village of **Khati** (Khanti) upstream of Larjung.

Tukche, the largest settlement of the area is virtually deserted in winter when most of the inhabitants work elsewhere.

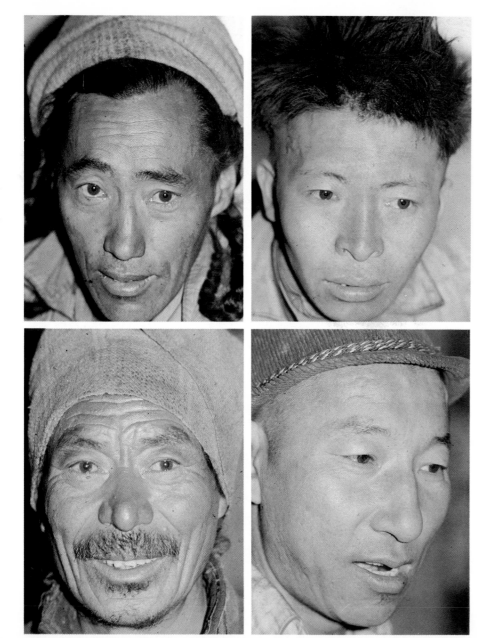

↑ page 124 The flat-roofed houses and backyards of Jomosom demonstrate the court-yard style of animal husbandry.

A child encountered in the river-bed of the Kali Gandaki.

←
This group of Tibetans, met in the Matsang Restaurant at the southern entrance to Jomosom agreed to pose for portraits. The girls, unfortunately, all fled.

A flowering vine along a stone fence.

Along the road from Ghandrung.

SCENES IN TANSEN

(upper-left) Street flanked by brick houses.
(lower-left) Metalworker in a corner of the town.
(lower-right) Workers bagging grain.

Out-door shop, Tansen.

4. Ghandrung to Tatopani

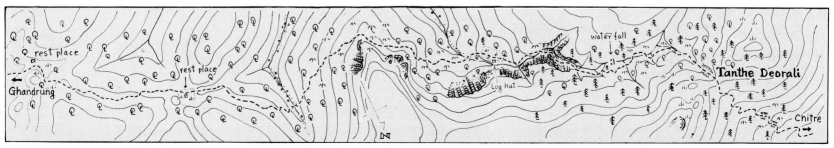

If one wishes to have only one trekking experience in the Himalayas, I would like to recommend a course centering on the valley of **Kali Gandaki**, and across the mountain range. This would reveal the influence of the great range in producing two kinds of atmospheric conditions, arid and humid; it would allow one to experience the rapid vertical transition in scenery, from extremely cool to subtropical; to note the changes in house-types and agricultural practises, and in addition to all this, such a trip is inordinately romantic. This region may not contain the world's highest peak, but it does have at least three which lie above 8,000 meters and, best of all,

the dangers of high altitude sickness are minimal. On the other hand, if one is particularly acclimatized to high-altitude conditions, side treks to such places as Lake **Tilitso** and **Annapurna Base Camp** (B.C.), can be added to the itinerary.

The most likely course from Pokhara to Kali Gandaki is a trek of three night and four days, via **Hyangja** and **Naudanda** (first day); **Khare, Lumle, Birethanti,** and **Trikhe** (second day); **Ulleri** and the **Ghorapani Pass** (third day), and finally to **Sikha, Ghara,** and **Tatopani**. The path along the ridge from Naudanda to Khare, which affords marvellous views of the Annapurna Himal, centered on Machhupachhare, or the moment when one stands on a grassy slope at about 3,000 meters, west of the Ghorapani Pass facing **Mount Dhaulagiri** in the distance, are the highlights of the entire trek.

Recently, it has become rather popular to branch off this course at Birethanti and ascend the **Modi Khola**, via **Ghandrung**, regional center of the **Gurung** people, to Annapurna Base Camp. However, since access from Ghandrung to the Kali Gandaki is difficult because the pass does not, as is usually the case, conform to the surface configuration and the passage is more complicated than might be expected, it would be well to have the guidance of an experienced Sherpa. The attached sketch-maps, compiled during such a trek, contain the main points of reference.

5. Tatopani to Jomosom

The deep gorge containing the Kali Gandaki, whose bed lies at only 2,600 meters, roughly bisects the some 40 kilometers that separate **Dhaulagiri I**, at 8,167 meters, in the west, and Annapurna I, at 8,091 meters, in the east, and is an earth feature of spectacular proportions, even by global standards. This valley, whose walls rise to a height of 5,000 meters, is an opening through which blow the dry, cold winds off the Tibetan Plateau, which rush through to mingle with the warm moist air of the Indian realm. Thus, since the northerly winds concentrate in this valley, the portion of the course between **Lete** and **Jomosom** is constantly subjected to swirling, blustery dust storms whose intensity is enhanced by the peculiar surface conditons.

However, these winds become gentle in the lower part of the gorge, at about **Kabre**, and in Tatopani the mildness of the climate is well-known, if one is to judge by the clusters of young westerners of both sexes, who obviously have been attracted by the pleasant living conditions.

Tatopani, whose name indicates the presence of a hot-spring, is a small village stretched out along the road and features a number of shops, restaurants and inns which, probably in response to the demands of tourists and despite their rather limited number, offer a surprisingly large array of goods and services. In the narrow store-fronts, for example, one sees such items being displayed as de-hydrated vegetables and instant foods — goods which are often unobtainable, even in Kathmandu.

Since the hot-spring is rumored to have four sources, all told, it would be well to visit at least one, which can be reached by walking eastward from the village center and descending the natural terrace to the river bank. Here, in all directions, are chips of **gneiss**, recognizable

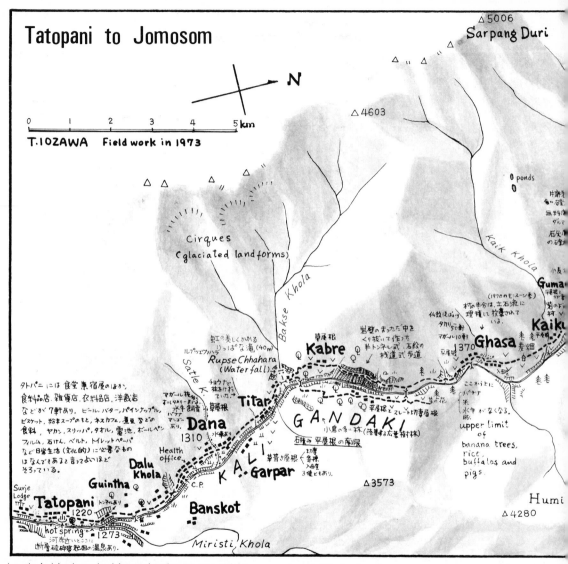

by their black and white striped patterns, which appear to glisten in the bright sunshine. Between these stones, one can notice numerous pools of reddish-brown water, and by observing closely where air-bubbles are rising and steam is emitted, the hot water can be identified. Since these are natural bathing pools, moreover, one can enter the water directly at this point, even though partly dressed, and discover that this is truly an excellent hot-spring. The scene,

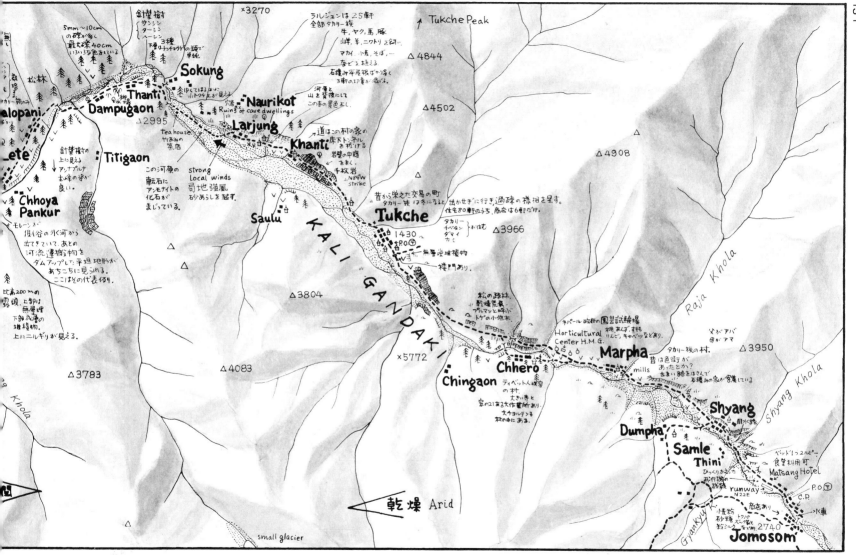

which is likely to include local women doing laundry or the aforementioned western visitors, playing flutes or reading, is impressive, especially when backed by the deep green hue of the opposite river bank and experienced to the ac-

companyment of the bubbling of the stream as it flows rapidly along its course.

The Kali Gandaki valley was used by Ekai Kawaguchi, who entered Nepal in 1899 as the first Japanese visitor to that country, and ulti-

mately it became his avenue into Tibet. But for one year, before entering Tibet in July 1900, he resided in the village of **Charang** in the **Mustang** district in the upper course of the river. An examination of his travel log makes an interest-

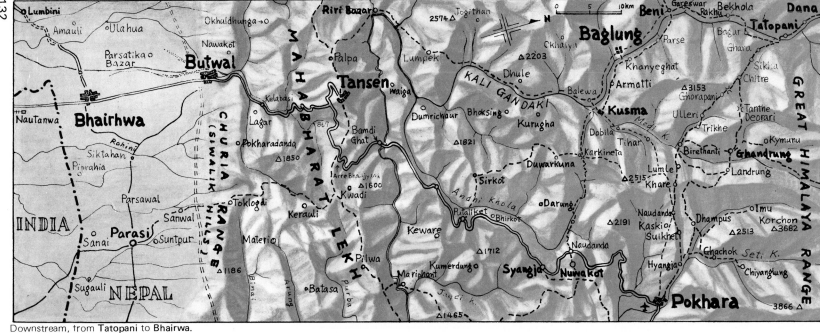

Downstream, from **Tatopani** to **Bhairwa**.

ing comparison with current conditions.

The trek from Tatopani to **Tukche** can be covered in two days, and to **Jomosom** in one day more. Since the first half of this is in an area of humid climate where house-roofs are decidedly hipped, and the latter is in a region of steppe-like climate, where roofs are flat, it can be observed that house-types change according to changes in atmospheric conditions and the availability of local building materials. In the accompanying sketch-map, which contains the details of this course, at the point where the river reaches its 'upper' bend — at about **Thanti** — as seen through openings in the coniferous forest, the valley widens out suddenly, and there, standing in miniature in the distance, surrounded by an arid, dusty landscape that differs markedly from that just traversed, is the town of Tukche. The exotic quality of this

scene is heightened by the cover of azure sky, which one knows extends into the very heart of the Asian landmass. All together, this is a sight to stir the emotions of even the most sophisticated! One should wear some form of goggles, however when trekking along this river, to protect the eyes from swirling sand and dust. And, in the two kilometers between Tukche and **Larjung**, one should note the presence of blackish stones, which are **ammonite (cephalopod fossil)** fragments.

The upper Kali Gandaki area is known as **Thak Khola**, the home country of the Thakali people. As mentioned, the Kali Gandaki gorge seems to have been fashioned by nature as a major economic and cultural access trail between the continental Plateau of Tibet and the sub-continental Indian lowland. Moreover, this route is revered by pilgrims as a path to the seat of the Hindu holy land, known as **Muktinath**,

at the heart of which is a cave lighted by a flame of natural gas. Followers of Hinduism and Lamaism customarily designate as holy places, sites where there are unusual physical conditions. Hence, **Amarnath** of Kashmir, and Manikaran of Himachal, which are famous for such formerly mysterious qualities as hot-spring's, or for caverns with stalactites and stalagmites, are known as holy places where pilgrims visit. Even in Japan, certain sects of Buddhism (i.e. **Mikkyo,** or esoteric Buddhism) follow such practise, as is seen in the attitude toward the stupa-like hot-spring of Yudonosan, in Yamagata Prefecture.

6. From Tatopani Downstream to Bhairhwa

Recently, since the completion of the Shidarda motor highway from Pokhara to

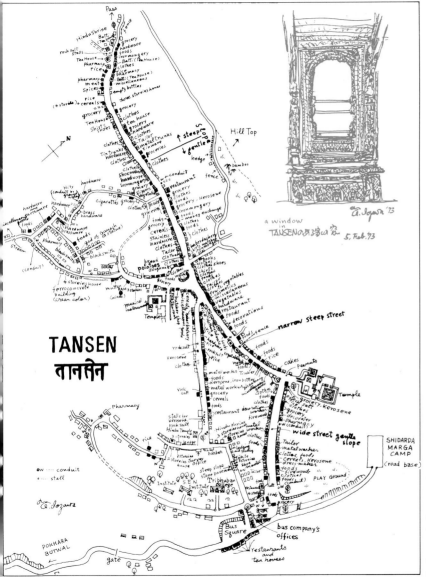

TANSEN तानसेन

a window in TANSENの部分山窓 5. Feb. '73

BUTWAL बुटवल

was formerly a series of terraced rice plots and is now a major thoroughfare, in its generally widened and trampled appearance, bears the imprint of the feet of countless travellers. Other evidence is seen in the numerous bamboo tea houses that have crowded along the road,

Tansen, at 1,500 meters, is a hill city in the Mahabharat Range. Its large, solidly-built temples, its specialized (though rather small) stores, lend a distinctly urban atmosphere that sets it apart from, say, the more newly-built hill stations of middle-western India. One must take care in bus travel, however, as some by-pass the town on their way to Butwal.

Butwal, in contrast, sits at the foot of the mountains, where the Himalayas join the Plain of Hindustan, and since the town commands the valley mouth of the **Tinau** River, it functions as the place of contact between, the plains and the highlands. Here, along the motor road, one sees numerous plants and facilities for highways, construction in general, and for the maintenance of highways and vehicles, together with a university and attendant housing. Along the old main street are shops, schools and miscellaneous facilities. Most of the buses from Pokhara end their runs here, and if one wishes to proceed to Bhairwha, it is necessary at this point, to transfer.

Bhairwha, close to the international boundary, is a town on the plain to which, from Kathmandu, there are four scheduled flights

have been altered and a fairly level path oriented to stops along the bus road has become preferred. For example, from **Kusma**, this course crosses the **Modi Khola**, climbs the eastern bank to the village of **Karkineta**, continues downstream to **Lankuri**, from whence it again rises gently to the town of **Naudanda** (not the aforementioned place, but a village of the same name), where there is a bus stop. Here, land that

Bhairhwa, which permits regular bus service between the two points, the old trekking courses

each week. Most of the buses pass by the eastern reaches of the town, however, on their way to India, so again the traveller must be aware that this is not a regular bus terminus. From Bhairhwa, by jeep, it is possible in one day, with two river-crossings, to reach **Lumbini**, birthplace of the Buddha.

Local people, even without a visa, can travel by bus from India (to Lumbini), but this means is not available to foreigners.

Dhaulagiri I

Annapurna-I

**POKHARA
TANSEN
BUTWAL**

N

BHAIRHWA
ग्रेरह्वा

**SONAULI
INDIA**

TREKKING IN THE LANGTANG VALLEY

1. Planning and Preparation

Trisuli Bazar, Dhunche, and **Langtang** should all be included in the officially-sanctioned itinerary, but if one wishes side treks to such places as **Helambu**, via the **Kangja La (pass)**, or, in mid-course, to **Gosainkund**, these names should also be inserted.

In this area, except for the yak milk, butter, and cheese that may be available in the meadows around **Kyanjung**, and since shops are few and most food items scarce, such supplies should be purchased beforehand in Kathmandu.

The transport of luggage is not difficult, however, since buses regularly serve Trisuli Bazar, and it is possible to proceed as far as **Betorawati** by taxi. Porters, on the other hand, are more easily procured in Kathmandu.

Along the course, food is obtainable at Trisuli, **Betorawati, Ramche, Dhunche, Syabru Bensi,** and **Gola Tabera.** Otherwise, one must implore the local residents to share what they may have, and although it is possible to lodge in the houses of the neighborhood, if the course is in the upper stream valley, it is best to be equipped with a tent.

2. Trisuli Bazar

If one proceeds west

from the dairy in Kathmandu, crosses an intersection and continues to where a street enters from the left, the next turn right is a road

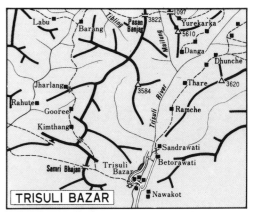

TRISULI BAZAR

leading out of the city down into an open area. This is at the northern edge of the Kathmandu Plateau (**Tar**), and the medieval brick walls that surround the city will be seen to have followed the fork in the road. This section is called **Paknajol**, and from here the highway, flanked on both sides by houses, heads northward down the slope toward **Trisuli Bazar**. Buses run form **Sorakhutte Pati**, where seat reservations can be made, preferrably one day ahead.

The bus road proceeds through **Balaju** and then winds its way northward along the western edge of the basin, passing over the stream divide, then westward, snaking down along the southern slope of the west-trending ridges, which originate at the northern edge of the basin. On the ridge line at **Kakani**, as noted, is an observation platform and rest-house, connected by a jeep road, but further along the bus road at the check point, the scenery is not notable. However, at **Ranipoa,** where the bus takes a lengthy break, one has at least 20-minutes for rest and refreshment. Here, there are about ten combination inns and eating establishments where such fare as Nepalese-style rice, **dal** (chick-pea) soup, and a kind of curried stew, is offered. The view here is similar to that of Kakani. That is, one can see **Annapurna II, Himal Chuli, Manaslu, Ganesh Himal,** and **Langtang Lirung.** Of these, **Himal Chuli,** rising like an ebony tower from a sea of snowy white, is the most conspicuous. The Trisuli area, at about 600 meters elevation, is a fluvial terrace surrounded by a mantel of reddish, lateritic soil, and is located at the eastern edge of the Gandaki River system where the **Tadi Khola,** which flows from the south slope of **Gosainkund,** joins the **Trisuli Gandaki,** which comes from the direction of Tibet and crosses the main range. Into the narrow confluence area, extending like a kind of headland of red soil, is an arm of the plateau containing part of the town of Trisuli — which continues to the other bank of the river — and at the end of the bridge linking the two sides of the town, is the bus terminus. However, if the destination is the town of **Betorawati,** though the road may be more appropriate for wagons and carts, it may be best to continue northward up the slope, rather than to cross the river and descend into **Trisuli Bazar.**

To enter the bazar on foot from the bus terminus, it is necessary to leave the motor road and turn right into an alley. The road, meanwhile, turns left, and then at the power station, right again, and follows the circuitous upstream course of the canal. The trekker, on the other hand, must walk down the sloping street of the bazar, pass through the town, cross the paddy fields which stretch toward the canal and through a hot, sun-baked but heavily-trafficked area along the canal, and finally cross the bridge over the dam to the opposite bank.

3. The Trail to Langtang

Since the automobile road ends at **Betorawati,** this is the starting point of the trekking course. Here, at various distances from the river, rise a series of terraces. For example, Betorawati itself lies at about 5 meters above the flood-plain, while the next step is a rather extensively-developed terrace at about 15 meters, above which are three more broad terraces lying at about 50, 100, and 200 meters in elevation. The terrace at 200 meters is composed of sedimentary materials, including giant conglomerates, and across the river from Betorawati, at the top of the opposite bank, is an outcropping which suggests Pleistocene ice activity. Also on the further bank, located on a point-like ridge, is the village of **Sandrawati,** from whence an excellent, recently-completed road of 3 meters width, twists along the river course to a point near **Dhunche.** As one proceeds upward along this course, the view broadens to include waterfalls where streams plunge into the riverine terraces of the downstream portion, or into the precipices of the upstream valley. The Nepal Himalayas lie generally from here northward to the junction of the **Langtang Valley** at **Syabru Bensi** — an area that seems to reveal the recency of the tectonic upheaval, in that the valley walls appear unusually rigid, free of any hint of slackness. When passing through the towns of **Boutalou, Manigaon,** and **Ramche,** it will be noticed that the roofs, which have been hipped and made of thatch, are gradually superseded by roofs of

shingle, held in place by stones. From here, through **Thare** and as far as **Dhunche,** the trail crosses a laterally sloping surface. Dhunche, at a junction of routes, is a settled colony with a number of houses. The road to Gosainkund forks off to the right here, while that headed for Langtang descends to the Trisuli Khola, into which, near a **chorten** (stupa) at the edge of the village, a secondary stream pours into the river. One can now either cross the bridge and climb along the winding course of the left bank or take the path to Gosainkund, ascend to a summit area and cross over to the Langtang

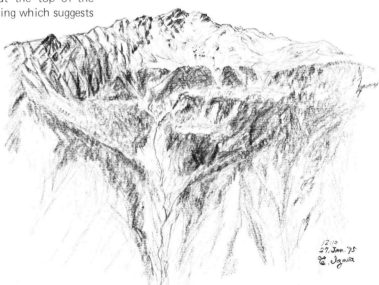

Cirque and morainal deposit on the southwestern edge of Gosainkund, Langtang Valley.

trail. If one takes the former and circles around to the rear of Dhunche, the trail again proceeds along the sloping wall of the valley, passes through two villages, **Bhargu** and **Sanobhargu,** and descends once more to the river bank. A newly-built road to **Syabru** rises along the slope from here, but where the crystalline rocks,

Source Maps of Collation Table

A: Attached map of Gakujin (The Alpinists) 1:250,000
B: Trekking map (1:126,720) "Gosainkund, Helambu, Langtang" (Mandara Maps)
   Supplied by 1:63,500 (1 inch — 1 mile) map No. 71 $\frac{H}{12}$ (SURVEY OF INDIA, 1959) and Route map in Pamphlet issued by Nepal government.
C: Sketch map, made by Peter Aufschnaider (Die Alpen, 35:4Q, 1959, S.197)
D: Sketch map, made by an Italian party (1963)
E. Sketch map, made by T. Kondo (Japan), 1964.
F: Illustrations, drawn by Eizo Suwata (Japan), 1968.
G: List of mountains in "The Himalayas" by David Mordecal, 1966, Calcutta.
H: Elevations, in data showed by Yoshimi Yakushi (Japan) 1971.

COLLATION TABLE OF GEOGRAPHICAL NAME AMONG SEVERAL MAPS OF LANGTANG HIMAL AND JUGAL HIMAL

A	B	C	D	E	F	G	H
PHURBI CHACHU(6440m)	PHURBI CHYACHU(6722m) (21844ft)					PHURBI CHYACHU(21844ft)	6658m
LADIES PEAK(6000m)	—						
GYALZEN PEAK(6705m)						GYALTZEN(22000ft)	
MADIYA PEAK(6800m)						MADIZA(22310ft)	
BIG WHITE PEAK(7083m)	LEONPO GANG(7083m) BIG WHITE PEAK(23238ft)	LONPO GANG(7083m)	LOMPO GANG(7083m)	BIG WHITE PEAK(7083m)	LONPO GANG(7083m)	BIG WHITE PEAK(23240ft)	
DORJE LAKPA(6989m)	DORJE LAKPA(6990m) (22929ft)	DORJE LHAGPA(6988m)	DORJE LAKPA(6988m)	DORJE LHAKPA(6988m)	DORJE LHAGPS(6988m)	DORJE LAKPA I (22929ft)	
KANSHURM (——)	LINGSHING(6078m) (19942ft)						
URKINMANG(6397m)	HIMAL(6151m) (20180ft)				URKINMANG		
GANCHEMPO(Kanjin)	(6387m) (20986ft) (20954ft)	GANG CHHENPO(6397m)	GANG·CHHENPO(6397m)	KYANGJIN(——)	GANG CHHENPO(6397m)	FLUTED PEAK(21800ft)	6387m
PONGGEN DOPKU(5889m)	(5930m) (19454ft)			PONGEN DOPK(5889m)			
GANJA LA(5200m)	KANGJA LA(5132m) (16805ft)	GANGJA LA(——)	GANGIA LA(5623m)	GANGJA LA(5625m)			5122m
NAYA KANGA (——)	(5846m) (19180ft)			NAYAKANGA(——)			
LANGTANG LIRUNG(7245m)	LANG TANG LIRUNG(7246m) (23771ft)	GANGCHHEN LEDRUB (7245m)	LANGTANG LIRUNG(7245m)	LANGTANG LIRUNG(7245m)	GANGCHHEN LEDRUB (7245m)	LANGTANG LIRUNG (23770ft)	
KIMSHUN(6745m)	(22130ft)	TSANGBU RI(5745m)	TSANGBU RI(5745m)	KIMUSHYUM(6745m)			
YANSA TSENJI(6543m)	(21467ft)	DRAGPOCHHE RI (6543m)	DRAGPOCHHE(6543m)	YANSA TSHENJI(6543m)	DRAGPOCHHE RI(6543m)		
KYANJIN GOMPA	KYANGJ IN GOMPA	KYANJIN GYANG GYALLSHAN GOMPA		KYANJIN GYANG		(現地チーズ小屋には Kyangchin Cheese Plant と書いてあった)	
SHALBACHUM(6918m)		PHRUL RANGJEN RI(6918m)	PHRUL·RANDEN·RI(6918m)	SHALBACHUM(6700m)	PHRUL RANGJEN RI(6918m)	SHALBACHUM(22000ft)	
SHALBACHUM GLACIER		PHRUL RANGJEN GLACIER	PHRUL·RANGJEN GLACIER	SHALBACHUM GLACIER			
TRUPAIKU GLACIER	LANGSISA JHANG	TRUPAIKU GLACIER	TRUPAIKU GLACIER	TRUPAIKU GLACIER			
LANGSHISA RI(6294m)	(6145m) (20161ft)	LANGSHISA RI(6294m)	LANGSISA·RI(6387m)	LANGSHISA PEAK(6294m)	LANGSHISA RI(6294m)		6400m
	(6874m)	GUR KARPO RI	GUR·KARPO·RI		GUR KARPO RI		
KANKARMO (6830m)		DOME BLANC(6830m)	DOME BLANC(6830m)	KAN KARMO(DOME BLANC) (6830m)	PEMTHANG KARPO RI (DOME BLANC) (6830m)	PEMTHANG KARPO (22447ft)	
PENTHANG KARPO *		PEMTHANG RI(6842m)	PEMTHANG·RI(6842m)	PEMTHANG KARPO(6842m)	PEMTHANG RI(6842m)		
KYUNGKA RI(6979m)		KYUNGKA RI(6979m)	KYUNGKA·RI(6979m)	KYUNGKA RI(6979m)	KYUNGKA PEAK(6979m)	KYUNGKA(22897ft)	
GOLDUM(6947m)		GOLDOM(6447m)	GOLDUM(6447m)	GOLDUM(6447m)	GOLDUM(6447m)		
CHUSMUDO(6248m)		CHUSUMDO RI:6500 無名峰 (6248m)	CHHUSUMDO RI(6508m)	MORIMOTO PEAK(6750m)			
LANGTANG RI(7239m)		LANGTANG RI(7239m)	LANTANG·RI(7239m)	TSUNGA PEAK(7284m)	LANGTANG RI(7239m)	TSUNGA RI(23900ft)	
LANGTANG GLACIER	LANG TANG JHANG	LANGTANG GLACIER	LANGTANG GLACIER	LANGTANG GLACIER	LANGTANG GLACIER		
PONRONG RI(7284m)		PORONG RI(7284m)	PORONG·RI(7284m)		PORONG RI(7284m)		
RISUM		RISUM	RISUM		RISUM		
GOSAINTHAN (SHISHA-PANGMA) (8013m)		SHISHA PANGMA(8013m)	GOSAINTHAN (SHISHA-PANGMA) (8013m)	GOSAINTHAN (SHISHA-PANGMA) (8013m)	SHISHA PANGMA(8013m)	GOSAINTHAN (SHISHA PANGMA) (2629ft)	
PHOLA GANGCHEN(7661m)		PHOLA GANGCHEEN(7445m)					
NYANANG RI(7071m)		NYANANG RI(7071m)	NYANANG·RI (7071m)		NYANANG RI(7071m)	NYONNO RI(22142ft)	

* Position is showed at Triangle Peak

which have been glittering like gold, take on tinges of white, one is already close upon **Syabru Bensi**. The re-appearance of terrace formations along the stream indicate the junction of the Langtang Valley which, becoming a narrow and precipitous gorge at this point, extends eastward. The trail to Langtang from Syabru Bensi follows the left bank of the Langtang Khola, and from **Wangai**, turns left into the mountains. Thus, after passing upward through a pine forest and emerging into a cropped area marked by fields of wheat, buckwheat, and maize, the trail enters the **Khangema** district, whose farmhouses are surrounded by stone walls, like the fortresses of a western movie. From here, if one continues up the slope for an hour or so, the climb finally ends and the path, narrower still, simply winds along the cliff face for one more day. When the surroundings become unusually steep and covered with grass and there are long-needled pines here and there, and after passing through the villages of **Suruka** and **Syarpa**, the trail enters open country with only occasional houses and no agglomerated settlements until it reaches the mainly Tibetan village of **Gola Tabera**, where it again drops to the floodplain and joins the road from Syabru. It then passes through a moist pine forest, followed by grassy country along

the river, and when it climbs to an elevation of about 2,800 meters, one should recognize the moraine marking the end of the U-shaped Langtang Valley. Here, if one ascends into the valley and continues along the trail, it will be found that the going is comfortable for the remainder of the trek. **Langtang** should be reached from here in about half a day and **Kyangchin (Kyanjung)** in one day.

Mountains of the Langtang Valley.

85°30'E. 7246
Langtang Lirung
(Gangchhen Ledrub)

Ghenge Liru
657

85°35'E.

5951

85°40'E.

6054

Shalbachum Glacier

Langtang Glacier

Lirung Glacier

Chhalr Pochln

5002

5311

base line for photographing works
4773

Pasari Golddum
Kijung Phu

Pemdang Karpu
4155

3514 Mund Singdum

Langtang
3496
3682

Papal

Chnaha

Kyanjung Gompa

Tharche Pisa
4884 Yala

5033

Tsergo Ri

5125

Langsisa Kharuka

Lanshisa Ri
6145

3906 Chamki
Thangsep

4497

Chhongdu
STOL field
Marku
Kingur Chin

Thikyapsa

Nubama Dhang

3960

Langtang Khola

Ghora Tabela

Parigante Long
3738

4687

3877

Langsisa Glacier

3997
t moraine of Langtang Khola

4757

4762

5252

4404

4963

5270

28°20'N.

Naya Kanga
5846

5103

Ganchempo
6387

Urkinmang
6151

5822

Pou88en Dopku
5930

Chimisedang Lekh

Kangja La 5132
(Ganja La)

Kangja La Himal

5543

5845

Himal

Ling

5825

5862

5576

5551

5846

Naya Kanga 5846m
19180

4957m
16263

Kangja La Himal

5267m
17280

Chimisedang Lekh

4762
15624

5845m
19176

5700m
18700

4968m
16300

5643m
18515

5334m
17500

5212m
17100

5270m
17289

5822m
19100

5304m
17400

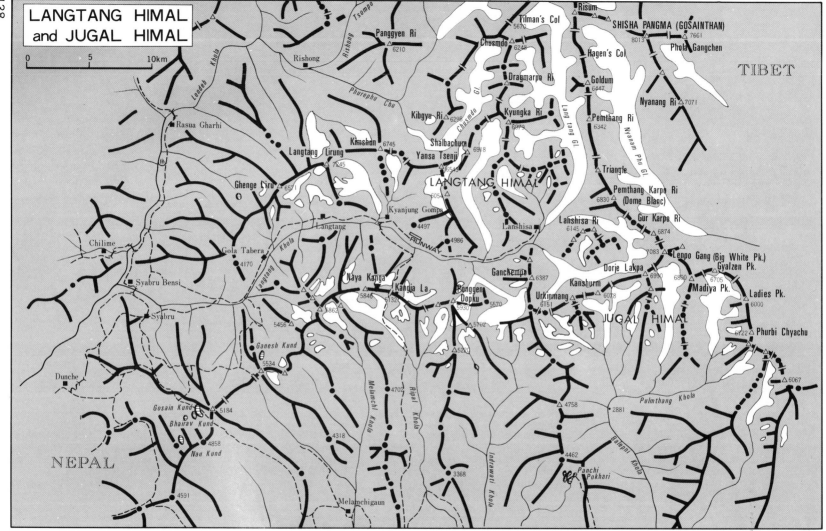

LANGTANG HIMAL and JUGAL HIMAL

0   5   10km

TIBET

NEPAL

Risum

Tilman's Col 5670

SHISHA PANGMA (GOSAINTHAN) 8013 △7661

Panggyen Ri 6210

Chusmdo 6245

Hagen's Col

Phola Gangchen

Rishong

Dragmarpo Ri

Goldum 6447

Nyanang Ri △7071

Rasua Gharhi

Kibgyu Ri △6298

Kyungka Ri 6979

Pemthang Ri 6342

Kimshun 6745

Langtang Lirung △7245

Shalbachum

Yansa Tsenji △6543 6918

LANGTANG HIMAL

Triangle

Ghenge Liru △6571

Pemthang Karpo Ri (Dome Blanc) 6830

Kyanjung Gompa

6054

Lanshisa Ri 6145

Gur Karpo Ri △6874

Langtang

4497

Lanshisa

Chilime

Gola Tabera 4170

4986

RUNWAY

7083 △Lenpo Gang (Big White Pk.) Gyalzen Pk.

Syabru Bensi

Ganchempa △6387

Dorje Lakpa 6990 6860 △6705

Madiya Pk.

Syabru

Naya Kanga 5846

Kangja La 5320

Bonggen Dopku 5930

Urkinmang 6151

Kanshurm 6078

Ladies Pk. 6000

5456 △5862

5570

JUGAL HIMAL

6722 △Phurbi Chyachu

Ganesh Kund 5534

5702

5220

4702

Pulmthang Khola

6067

Dunche

Gosain Kund △5184

Bhairav Kund

4318

Ripal Khola

Melamchi Khola

4758

2881

Nau Kund 4858

3368

4462

Panchi Pokhari

Indrawati Khola

Balepni Khola

4591

Melamchigaun

Lendeb Khola

Phurephu Chu

Tsompo

Rishong

Chusmdo Gl.

Lang tang Gl.

Nyanam Phu Gl.

Langtang Khola

4. Langtang and the Jugal Himal

Each of these mountain clusters is distinctive for its individual drainage system but since these lie virtually back-to-back, they form a common stream divide.

As the Langtang Valley belongs to the Gandaki drainage system, and the Jugal Valley to the Kosi, the access routes to each contain tribes of differing cultures and languages. Moreover, when these respective areas have been visited by mountain-climbers from such foreign lands as Germany, Italy, Japan, Britain, and the United States, and there has been relatively little contact between the groups there have arisen certain differences of opinion concerning even the identification of some of the mountains. For example, until very recently there have been many questions about the layout of ridges and valleys, especially about their mutual accessibility. **Mandala** (trekking) **Maps**, obtainable in Kathmandu, to carry this further, simply do not show the details of the relationships between the Langtang Valley and the international boundary (with the Chinese Peoples Republic), obviously because the maps are based on old data, and since the boundaries were drawn from past knowledge of the ridge lines, even if the proper surface contours are now known, the exact locations are difficult to demonstrate.

In view of these circumstances, a simple table is shown here, which tries to incorporate references from various languages in showing the pattern of the valleys and the association of the ridges. This table was originally published in the journal GAKUJIN (**The Alpinists**) in 1972, but has been updated and revised for inclusion in this volume.

5. Helambu

Also known as Helmu, Helambu is really an assortment of Tamang-Sherpa villages, distributed over a wide area, roughly associated by a series of mountains lying at about 5,000 to 6,000 meters, between the **Jugal Himal** group in the east, and **Gosainkund**, to its southwest. The region is further divided by a number of north-south trending valleys which are generally tributary to the **Indrawati** River system, the upstream portion of the **Sun Kosi**. Of these, the westernmost is known as the **Melamchi Khola**, followed by two branches of the Indrawati, the **Yangri Khola**, and the **Larke Khola**, while the **Tadi Khola**, in the extreme western sector, is a part of the Trisuli drainage system, as previously mentioned. The entire area containing these valleys and the ridges which separate them,

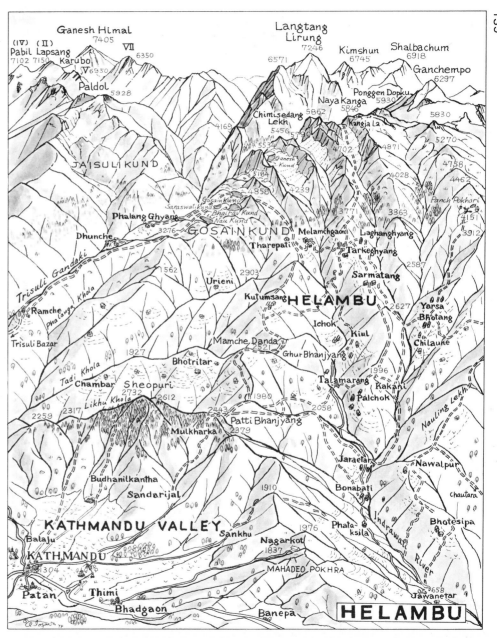

with a local relief of between 1,200 and 3,600 meters, is known as Helambu.

Among the notable settlements of this region are **Tarke Ghyang, Melamchigaon** (also **Melemchigaon**), **Sermathang, Kakani** (a different settlement from the aforementioned), and **Icchok**. And since there are no such peaks of the 8,000 meter class as Annapurna or Khumbu, the general landscape may arouse feelings of mild disappointment. There is also little of the distinctive flavor to the villages that was noted for those in more arid locations, such as in the Kali Gandaki Valley, or in its upstream portion, the Thak Khola.

Proximity to Kathmandu is an advantage here, especially for those whose time for trekking is limited, or during the rainy season, as one can rely almost entirely on his own powers of locomotion.

The first day, if one travels form Kathamandu by jeep, via **Bodhnath**, to **Sundarijal**, it is possible on the second day, to trek on foot as far as **Pati Bhanjyang**. Caution should be exercised at Sundarijal, however, when passing under the pipes of the hydro-electric station and across the elevated dam of the reservoir, in attempting to reach **Mulkharka**, as the route may be somewhat confusing.

The best views are to be had along this course in good weather, by proceeding northward from Pati Bhangyang, via **Chipling** and **Ghur Bhanjyang**, and by spending the night at **Bhanjyang**, and by spending the night at **Kutumsang**, rising early the next morning and continuing on foot all the way to Melamchigaon. If the weather is foul, however, the valley route is best by proceeding from Pati Bhanjyang, descending eastward to the **Talamarang Khola**, then by proceeding via **Mahankal, Keul, Timbu Kakani,** and **Tarke Ghyang**, to Melamchigaon.

Melamchigaon will probably offer the traveller more comfortable and cordial lodgings than Tarke Ghyang, but it is from the latter that the trail out of the region northward along the ridge and via the **Kangja La** (or **Ganja La [pass]**), at 5,132 meters, to the Langtang Valley, should be taken. Another trail crosses the Indrawati Khola toward the east and climbs over the next ridge to **Panchi Pokhari**, an area of glacial lakes at about 5,000 meters — the name means 'Five Lakes' — which is a well-known holy site. From here there are excellent views of **Dorje Lakpa** (6,990 meters), and **Phurbi Chyachu** (6,722 meters).

While trekking eastward from the lakes to the **Kodari Highway** may be a project for the future (though it has often been tried), it is possible to proceed directly across the ridges and descend to the large settlement of **Chautara**. And from the village of **Talamarang** on the Melamchi Khola, in a light vehicle, one can also descend downstream along a narrow road and reach the Kodari Highway at **Panchkal**. Furthermore, even though this road is often strewn with fallen rocks or collapsed side walls which may obstruct automobile traffic, passage may still be possible by motor bicycle.

OTHER TREKKING COURSES IN NEPAL

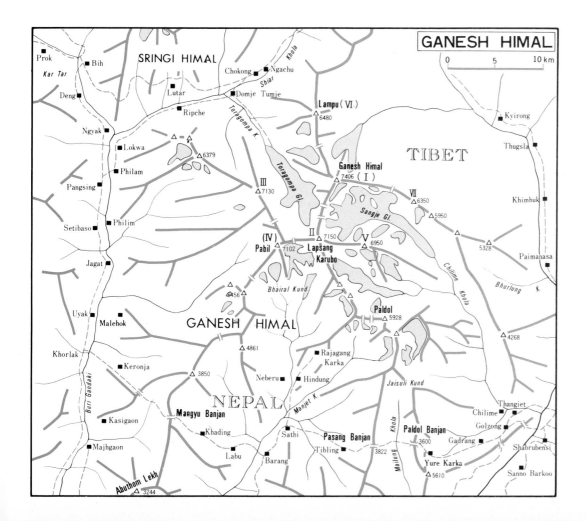

GANESH HIMAL

SRINGI HIMAL

TIBET

GANESH HIMAL

NEPAL

Prok
Bih
Kar Tar
Deng
Ngyak
Lokwa
Philam
Pangsing
Setibaso
Philim
Jagat
Uyak
Malehok
Khorlak
Keronja
Kasigaon
Majhgaon
Ripche
Lutar
Chokong
Ngachu
Domje Tumje
Lampu (VI.)
△6480
△6379
III △7130
Ganesh Himal
7406 (I)
VII △6350
△5950
Sangie Gl.
II △7150
(IV) △
Pabil 7102
Lapsang Karubo
V △6950
△5328
△456
Bhairal Kund
Paldol
△5928
△4268
△4861
△3850
Neberu
Hindung
Rajagang Karka
Jaisuli Kund
Mangyu Banjan
Khading
Sathi
Pasang Banjan
Labu
Barang
Tibling
3822
Manjur K.
Paldol Banjan
3600
Mailung Khola
Yure Karka
△5610
Thangiet
Chilime
Golzong
Gadrang
Shabrubensi
Sanno Barkoo
Kyirong
Thugsla
Khimhuk
Paimanasa
Bhurlung K.
Chilime Khola
Toragompa K.
Shiar Khola
Buri Gandaki
Abuthom Lekh
△3244

0   5   10 km

1. The Ganesh Himal

This is an area where recently the Japanese have been conducting reconnaissance trekking missions designed to provide information for subsequent climbing efforts.

As far as **Syabru Bensi**, this course is the same as that to Langtang, but from here one should enter westward into the **Chilime Khola** Valley, or veer to the southwest and circle around the foot-hills of **Jaisuli Kund,** which lies south of **Paldol** (5,928 meters), and observe the southern faces of **Lapsang Karubo**, or Peak II (7,150 meters), and **Pabil**, or Peak IV (7,102 meters), respectively. West from here, by crossing **Mangyu Bhanjyang** (pass), the course descends to the **Buri Gandaki**.

The trek across these passes and **cols** is rather strenuous and there may be difficulty in securing appropriate lodgings. Nonetheless, since this area has been little explored and consequently is not well-known, this course may appeal to those with a keen sense of adventure. The attached map, based on personal aerial observation and drawn by the writer, is about as close to reality as is possible under the circumstances.

2. Kanjiroba and the Western Nepal Himalayas

Until the present, the ancient city of **Jumla** has been considered a place of some mystery, but recently it has become the terminus of regularly-scheduled flights by the RNAC from Kathmandu. However, since return flight schedules are uncertain, it is best to plan a return trek on foot, for which courses the reader should refer to the aforementioned table. In any case, in planning such a trek, one should allow enough time to leisurely observe the scenery from atop small hills en route.

The **Kanjiroba Group**, Hiunchuli Patan

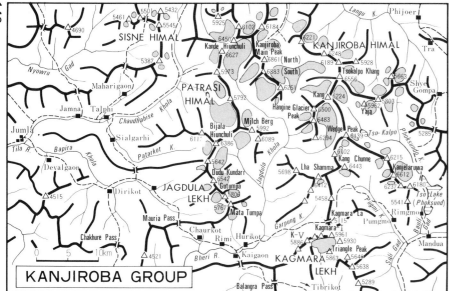

KANJIROBA GROUP

of the major **thrust fault** that characterizes the southern slopes of the **Greater Himalayas,** and in the upper portion of the cliff face, one can see white-ish limestone, typical of Tibet to the north, but of which this is the terminal occurrence. The lower cliff face, on the other hand, includes layers of **gneiss,** and, because of the depth of the fault, the rock found in the vicinity of the **Myagdi Khola** is revealed. From **Beni,** in the mid-course of the **Kali Gandaki,** one can ascend the **Myagdi Khola** and reach **French Col,** on the glacier to the west of the main peak. It is also possible to climb from the village of **Muri,** westward along the **Dara Khola** and, via the **Jaljala Bhanjyang** (pass), to cross to **Dhorpatan;** and finally there is a course from **Gurjakani,** which crosses the glaciated terrain spreading southwest from **Putha Hiunchuli** (7,246 meters), and around to the western side of **Dhaulagiri.** Each of these treks —

(5,916 meters), and **Chalike Panar** (5,145 meters), are not particularly high, but within these are places which exhibit remarkably few human traces. Generally, as a matter of course, one's trekking experiences can be enhanced if all that is heard and seen is recorded in notes and text, so that ultimately these can be collated and reviewed. In this vein, since the drainage system of the **Karnali River** is relatively little-known, this area might be an appropriate one to test this premise, as by such means, one might reveal impressions of mountains like **Api** (7,132 meters), **Saipal** (7,025 meters), and **Gurla Mandhata** (7,728 meters).

3. The Southern Sector of Dhaulagiri

Along the southern slopes of **Myagdi Matha** (6,273 meters) and the **Gurja Himal** (7,193 meters) — two of the most prominent peaks of this area — are a series of magnificent cliffs, so sheer as to give the impression of having been hacked apart with an axe. These are evidence

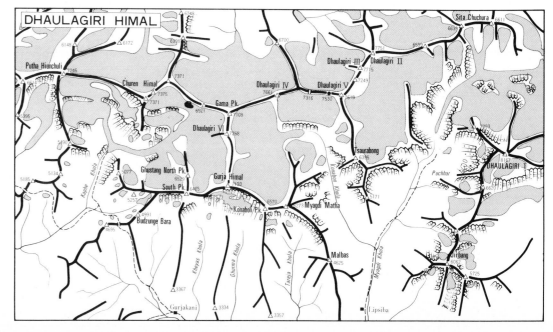

DHAULAGIRI HIMAL

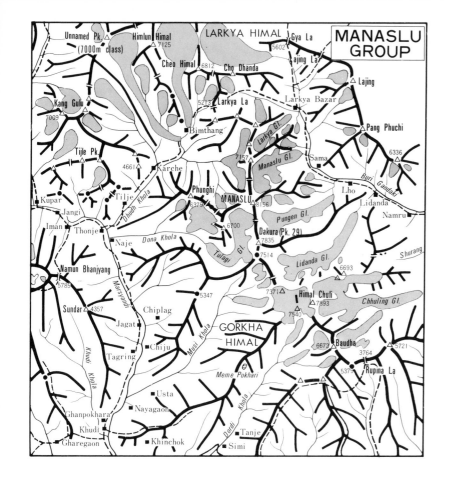

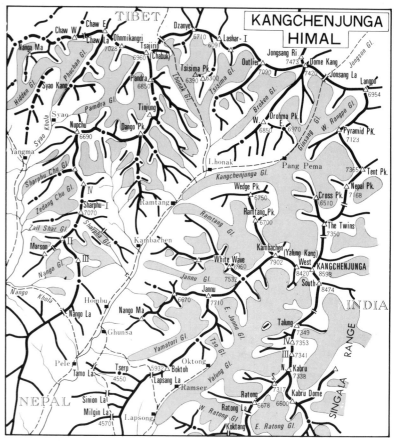

— passes and valleys included — traverses open, uncluttered landscapes which afford excellent views of the Dhaulagiri Himal's southern sector.

4. The Manaslu Group

The three mountains of the Manaslu Group, **Manaslu** (8,156 meters), **P-29** or **Dakra** (7,835 meters), and **Himal Chuli** (7,893 meters), were first climbed by Japanese mountaineers associated with the late Fukada Hisaya, whose ardent

wish was to produce a reliable and detailed map of the region, a desire which, although the writer was among his followers, has yet to be accomplished. This regrettable situation may be attributable, in Japan and elsewhere, to the frequent impression that the art of cartography is of rather little moment.

The Manaslu area, however, both the eastern and western portions, has been well-described by the Japanese, whose field notes provide a

rich fund of knowledge about this particular cluster. Perhaps for this reason, the area is regarded as somewhat too familiar to be a favorite trekking site.

The region is best reached by a flight to **Gurkha**, and from there by either of two routes. The easternmost leads to the **Buri Gandaki** via **Ali Bhanjyang, Khanchok,** the **Mukhti Khola,** and **Arughat.** The westernmost aims at the **Marsyangdi** (or **Matsyandi**) Valley,

The highest peak of the group in the foreground, see on the right, is **Bijala Hiunchuli** (6,386 meters). The summit in the background is **Kanjiroba Main Peak** (6,883 meters).

meters), an elevation to its south, were also made accessible. It can be seen, therefore, that after 1970, the available trekking areas in this sector must have been considerably enlarged.

For access to this mountain region, the reader is advised to consult the previous section entitled, **Trekking In The Foot-Hills of the Himalayas**, Part 9, **Dahran Bazar**, and Part 10, **Biratnagar**. If the air ticket is made out to Biratnagar and the flight ends in Calcutta, the traveller should both insist on being delivered to his ultimate destination, and should remind the officials that since his flight should have begun and ended in Nepal, cutoms inspection by the government of India is unnecessary.

By bus from Kathmandu, one should head south for **Birganj**, then transfer to a bus running east to **Biratnagar**. This trip should take about two days from Kathmandu, all told. Lodgings at Nepalese-style hotels in places like Birganj or Janakpur should be reasonably comfortable. In fact, it may be something of a treat to sleep in a bed, under a mosquito netting.

Both the **Tamur** and **Arun** Rivers contain numerous fragments of such materials as tourmaline and garnet, whose sands tinge the floodplain dark red, the color of **beefsteak plant** (perilla frutescens crispa). Views from the ridges around **Dhankuta**, or **Taplejung** to its northwest, are excellent, but some may have only enough available time to see these and return. Those with more leisure, however, may feel adventurous enough to enter the little-visited **Lumbasamba** mountain group to the north.

which is reached by one of two courses of roughly equal length, by taking either the **Ampipal** (pass), or the **Luitel Bhanjyang** (pass) to **Tadi Pokhari**, and finally to **Tarkughat**. Otherwise, if conditions are tranquil among the people of Tibetan culture to the north, and in such places as the **Larkya La** (pass), trekking in this area can be quite attractive.

5. The Kanchenjunga Himal

When climbing authorization was liberalized in 1970, **Yalung Kang** (8,420 meters, although survey work of a recent Japanese expedition shows the elevation as 8,050), the westernmost peak in this group, was included. At the same time, parts of the western edge at **Kambachen** (7,902 meters), and at **Jannu** (7,710

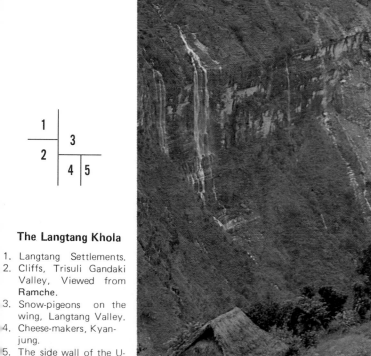

The Langtang Khola

1. Langtang Settlements.
2. Cliffs, Trisuli Gandaki Valley, Viewed from **Ramche**.
3. Snow-pigeons on the wing, Langtang Valley.
4. Cheese-makers, Kyanjung.
5. The side wall of the U-shaped Langtang Valley reveals former glacial activity.

1 | 2 | 3

1. **Kimshun Peak** (6,745 meters) at night, with the North Star visible in the right of the sky.
2. Ice fall, **Kimshun Glacier**.
3. **Shisha Pangma or Gosainthan** (8,013 meters).

↑ Hiunchuli Patan (5,916 meters).

↑ Dhaulagiri Main Peak (8,167 meters).

Dhaulagiri the and ,foreground left the in) meters 7,193) Himal Gurja ↑

Range Dhaulagiri the and

❶

❺

❷

1. Putha Hiunchuli (left) Churen Himal (right).
2. Manaslu (left) Dakura (Peak 29) (right).
3. Himal Chuli (center): Baudha Peak (right).
4. The Manaslu Group seen from the south; Himal Chuli (left) Manaslu (center).
5. The Ganesh Himal: Main Peak (left), 7th peak (center), 6th Peak (right).
6. Gauri Shankar (left); Menlungtse (right).
7. The Kanchenjunga Himal seen from the south. The white massif on the left is Jongsang Peak; the tower-like figure slightly left of center is Jannu; the rocky peak to the right of center is Kanchenjunga.

❸
❼
❹

TIGER TOPS JUNGLE LODGE

For those who wish to enjoy the wildlife of the Royal Chitwan National Park, there are three such resort hotels as Tiger Tops, the Guida Wildlife Camp, and the Hotel Elephant Camp.

DHAULAGIR
816

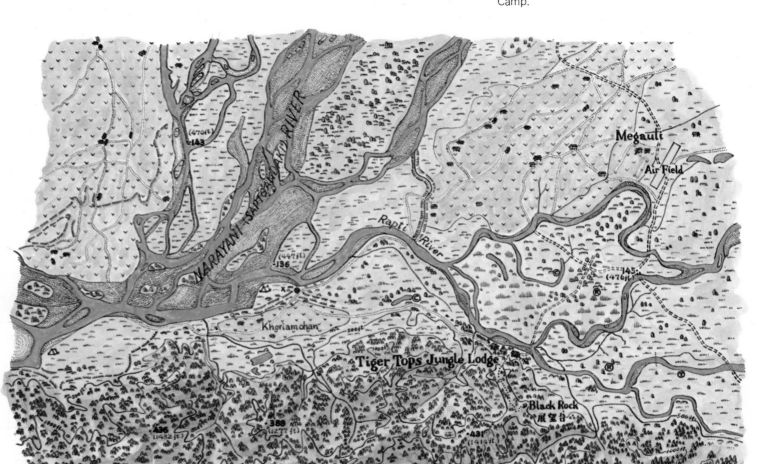

NARAYANI SAPTGANAKI RIVER

(470ft)
-143

(447ft)
-136

Rapti River

Megauli

Air Field

145-
(476ft)

Khoriamchan

500ft

Tiger Tops Jungle Lodge

Black Rock
展望台

496-
(432ft)

389-
(277ft)

431-
(414ft)

543-
(982ft)

412-
(351ft)

△ camp Ⓣ tigers Ⓡ rhinoceroses
Ⓒ crocodiles

0   1   2   3   4   5   6 Kilometers

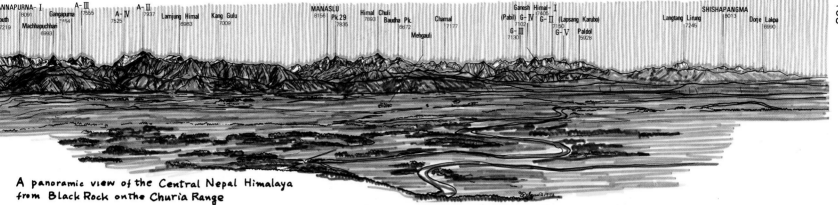

ANNAPURNA-I 8091 · A-South 7219 · Machhapuchhan 6993 · Gangapurna 7454 · A-III 7555 · A-IV 7525 · A-II 7937 · Lamjung Himal 6983 · Kang Gulu 7009 · MANASLU 8156 · Pk 29 7835 · Himal Chuli 7893 · Baudha Pk. 6872 · Chamal 7177 · Mehgauli · Ganesh Himal-I (Pabil) G-IV 7405 · G-II (Lapsang Karubo) 7150 · G-III 7130 · G-V 7102 · Paldol 5928 · Langtang Lirung 7245 · SHISHAPANGMA 8013 · Dorje Lakpa 6990

A panoramic view of the Central Nepal Himalaya from Black Rock on the Churia Range

Visas to Nepal generally include permission to visit Kathmandu, Pokhara, and **Chitwon**, but to trek anywhere else, one must apply for further authorization.

One is likely to wonder at this point why **Chitwon**, which is so hard to find even on rather large-scale maps of the region, is included among the allowed places. The village lies south of Pokhara, precisely where the Gandaki River system enters a low area, in which it meanders around here and there, and finally flows out of the Churia Hills section of the Mahabharat Range, and into the inner Terai Plain to the south. Meanwhile, the **Rapti** River enters the basinlike area around Chitwon, from the east, and in its twisting lower course, forms a vast area of marsh. This region of sub-tropical jungles and swamps, since it has been difficult to develop for other uses, has become a natural preserve for the flora and fauna of the Himalayan foothills, as well as a favorite hunting ground of the royal family, and it is not surprising that it has been designated a national park.

Since Tiger Tops Jungle Lodge, managed by an American, is located here, the traveller is able to enjoy the experience of viewing tigers, rhinoceroses, and other elements of the jungle,

at first hand, from elephant back, in true local tradition. Furthermore, one is welcomed by a gracious host, Mr. James Edwards and his splendid staff, who provide delicious meals and other services.

Life at Tiger Tops begins with your landing on the grassy air-strip at **Megauli**. Here, you will be greeted by members of the staff and guided to your elephant transport, on whose back is a kind of wooden platform-like structure into which you must climb. As at each of the four corners of this device there is a supporting column, the rider is asked to sit astride one of these, and in order to enjoy the experience, to learn to accommodate to the animal's gate. The elephants also, with clever use of the trunk, will guard the riders from being struck by brush through which it may be passing, and I have even seen an elephant, with extraordinarily sensitive use of its trunk, retrieve a dropped lens cap from a stream. The traveller must also anticipate that these marvellous creatures, which provide such convenient transport by gliding smoothly over a difficult landscape or climbing angular features, can also punctuate their efforts and enliven your experience by committing such natural acts as defecation and farting.

By the time you have reached the lodge you will have probably seen at least some deer and crocodiles. It is essential, when meeting animals in the wild, not to behave so as to surprise or disturb them. Therefore, one should be careful to curb loud talk and sudden laughter, and it is best to wear clothing of an earthen or grassy shade.

Prices for hotel accommodations and even drinks, are high here, but since the use of the elephants and the attentions of the staff are included, there should be little cause for complaint. The meals also, are reputed to be among the finest restaurant fare in the country.

Following an explanation by Mr. Edwards of the current conditions of the wild life preserve and an announcement of plans for the next day, one has free time to relax in the lounge. Drinks can be ordered from the bar, and there is ample time for easy conversation with the other guests, who come from all over the world. It is also diverting to

field note

A Nepalese Tiger Crossing A Stream In Daylight.

examine the remarks by former visitors contributed in the guest book, or to look through the albums of photographs of the local fauna. At 8 o'clock there is the tinkle of a bell, reminiscent of a country school in Japan, announcing the beginning of the dinner hour.

The following morning, perhaps through a thick fog, the animals, each with their quota of riders, move out into the jungle, and soon take up prearranged positions around a clearing,

—— field note

deployed so that if tigers are about, they will be corralled and made visible to the guests. But since no-one knows the whereabouts of the beasts, there is considerable tension during this interval.

Meanwhile, the bullet-shaped birds, with round heads and long tails, which dart across the sky, are either parakeets or other parrots. And the flashes of red and yellow that appear and disappear among the jungle branches, are really the movements of countless **scarlet minivets**, though only the males are red, the females being yellow.

Even the sounds of the forest enhance the atmosphere of the semitropical jungle. For example, there is a cry sounding like, 'ki...ki-ki-ki', or 'chikki-chikki-kyah'. And when the song, 'Jyui'ji-chippy-chippy', is heard, if one looks closely, the **Simla Black Tit**, or **Indian Grey Tit**, is bound to be seen. Pigeons are also profuse,

along with the brown figures of ducks floating on a stream. And on the branches of large trees, standing isolated in the plain, peacocks are perched, with their long tails dangling below. The sound of the peacock varies, from the comic bellow of a bassoon, to the mewling or piercing cry of a baby.

Water birds stand calmly by where crocodiles are present, and one must be quick to realize when he is being stared at through tall grass by a one-horned rhinoceros, together with its off-spring, who may suddenly wheel about and make off, with their armored rumps rustling and clanking an accompaniment to their retreat.

In our trip, we finally concluded that there were no tigers in our clearing. All we saw was the shadow of one as it leapt across a stream. Still, even this provided the satisfaction of knowing that this majestic animal was within our realm, and we were nonetheless gratified.

3

THE WESTERN HIMALAYAS

A girl of Manali.

In 1964, for the Indian Government's national atlas, the Natural Geographical Division decided that since Nepal represented the **Central Himalayas**, the chains to the west of this should be known as the **Western Himalayas**. This vast region is further divided into four sections, the **Northern Kashmir, Southern Kashmir, Punjab,** and the **Kumaun Himalayas,** respectively. Of these, the first, since it contains portions of the **Karakorum** and **Zaskar** Ranges, is somewhat a-typical and will therefore, insofar as most of the details are concerned, be omitted from this discussion. That which follows will concern mountain-climbing, trekking bases, and the main trekking courses, chiefly of the latter three subdivisions. Also, because the Western Himalayas, like the Eastern (to be discussed subsequently), belong mainly to India, this résumé will begin with the points-of-entry into India and will contain data on the various cities along these routes. Unlike Nepal, however, to trek in India, one must conform more strictly to the regulations. On the other hand, if one studies the section on **Customs and Manners,** on pages 47-48, and makes an effort to adjust to local conditions, there should be no reason why the trekking experience should not be pleasant and gratifying.

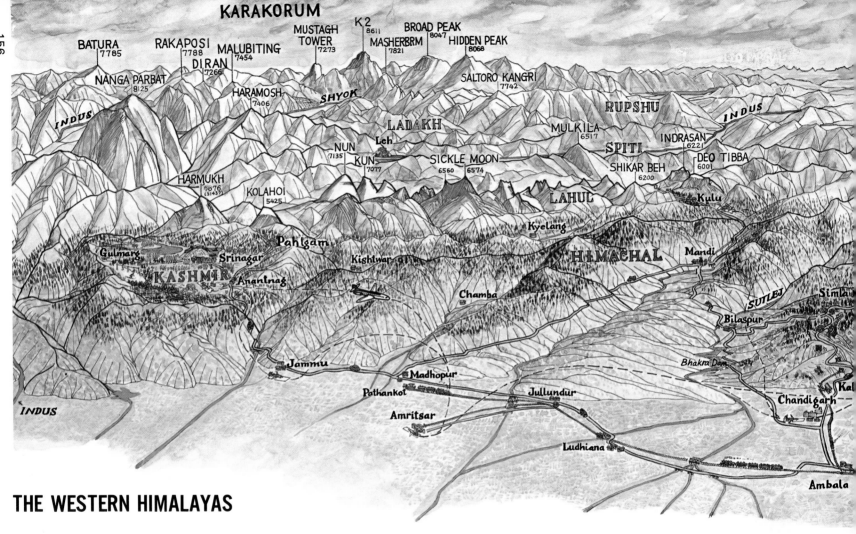

KARAKORUM

BATURA
7785

RAKAPOSI
7788

MALUBITING
7454

DIRAN
7266

NANGA PARBAT
8125

HARAMOSH
7406

SHYOK

MUSTAGH
TOWER
7273

K2
8611

MASHERBRM
7821

BROAD PEAK
8047

HIDDEN PEAK
8068

SALTORO KANGRI
7742

RUPSHU

INDUS

LADAKH

Leh

NUN
7135

KUN
7077

SICKLE MOON
6560   6574

MULKILA
6517

SPITI

INDRASAN
6221

DEO TIBBA
6001

SHIKAR BEH
6200

HARMUKH
%676
(5143?)

KOLAHOI
5425

LAHUL

Kulu

Gulmarg

Srinagar

Pahlgam

Kishtwar

Kyelang

Mandi

KASHMIR

Anantnag

HIMACHAL

SUTLEJ

Simla

Chamba

Bilaspur

Jammu

Madhopur

Bhakra Dam

Pathankot

Jullundur

Chandigarh

Kal

Amritsar

INDUS

Ludhiana

Ambala

THE WESTERN HIMALAYAS

1. The Principal Mountains

The four components of the Western Himalayas, are 1) the **Northern Kashmir Himalayas**, including the basin of the main stream of the **Indus River**, as well as arms of the Karakorum and Zaskar Ranges, as mentioned above.

Here are two towering peaks, **K-2** (8,611 meters), and **Gasherbrum** (8,068 meters), as well as **Siachen** (1,150 km^2 X 75 km in length), and numerous other giant valley glaciers of the compound accumulation area type; 2) the **Southern Kashmir Himalayas**, including the **Vale of Kashmir** and **Jammu**. Actually, the

entire territory, from the main stream of the Indus eastward to the west bank of the **Sutlej** at this latitude, was formerly within the Punjab Himalayas, but the Indian Government has since drawn a line from the **Ravi River** northeastward, dividing this region into the Southern Kashmir and Southeast Punjab Himalayas.

The highest peaks of this #2 region, are **Nanga Parbat** (8,126 meters) in the north, and in the south, **Nun** (7,135 meters) and **Kun** (7,077 meters). Other mountains here are only within the 5,000 to 6,000 meter class, but unlike Nepal, where there were only two echelons of rugged arcs, here there may be more than ten, making up a whole broad assemblage of jagged mountain peaks, farther than the eye can reach.

The 3rd sub-division, the **Punjab Himalayas**, are also called **Himachal Pradesh** — a popular region for trekking and mountain-climbing (based on the **Kulu River** Valley), although the mountains here are generally rather low in elevation, as for example, **Leo Pargial** (6,770 meters).

The 4th and last sub-division, the **Kumaun Himalayas**, lie between the Sutlej River and the border of Nepal — an area which has attracted many mountain-climbers in the past. High mountains include **Nanda Devi** (7,817 meters), and **Kamet** (7,756 meters), and south of these, the famous hill-stations, **Nainital, Almora,** and **Mussorie.**

2. Access

The approach to the Western Himalayas must begin with a flight arrival in Delhi, India's capital city. This is necessary because all forms of transportation, whether domestic airline (India Airlines, or I.C.), rail, or long-distance bus, all radiate from the capital. Regardless of one's destination in the region, or of which direction one is going, it is best to return to Delhi before proceeding. The journey may seem considerably shorter as the crow flies, but the use of Delhi as the hub of any trip is more efficient.

One can enter Kashmir either by air, by a combination of train and bus, or directly by long-distance bus, although this last is a trip of one night and two days, with the traveller providing his own accommodations. By train, one should take the line from the main station in Delhi to **Jammu.** Buses leave Delhi from the Inter-state Bus Terminus located in the northern part of the city behind the railroad station, near the **Kashmiri Gate** to the old fort.

The **Himachal** mountain area is reached by airplane, though flights terminate in **Bhuntar** in the **Kulu** Valley, and are rather limited in that these are centered on the months of September and October, while at other seasons, one must travel by bus from **Chandigarh. Simla,** on the other hand, is accessible directly from Delhi by bus, or by regular train as far as **Kalka,** and then by diesel rail-car for the remainder of the trip.

The **Kumaun-Garhwal** district of Uttar Pradesh is easily reached by bus from Delhi, so if one is blessed with two or three extra days in the capital, this can be a pleasant sojourn of sight-seeing in the mountains. Here, since the hotels are designed for summer holiday use, one can also take advantage of off-season rates, which cut costs, and the views are splendid.

DELHI

Delhi can be divided into two sections which contrast widely. The first is old Delhi, the archaic citadel and center of all northern India in olden times, from which ancient rulers administered their dynasties, whose fortunes rose and fell intermittantly. The second is **New Delhi**, a park-like, planned city, and the node around which radiates the main transportation network of the country.

With a population of about 4 million (1971 Census), the Delhi metropolitan area is India's third-largest, after Calcutta and Bombay. Following the Muslim invasion of northern India in the 13th century, Delhi was utilized as the capital of five successive dynasties, beginning in the 13th century with the so-called 'Slave' dynasty, and from then to the 16th century by the **Khiliji, Tughlak, Sayyid,** and **Lodi** dynasties, respectively. And since all were flavored strongly by Turkish culture, these are also known as the **Delhi Sultinate** (1206-1526), the last of which was ultimately over-run by Tamerlane's forces, under **Zahir ud-Din Muhammed** (1483-1530 [also known as **Babar** or **Baber]**), founder of the Mughal Empire of India, whose capital was later moved to Agra. However, in 1931, a new capital city (**New Delhi**), which had long been planned and in construction, was finally completed. The two cities are connected, of course, and one must be alert to realize when he is crossing the line into a traditional and far-different world.

1. Arrival

It goes without saying that since temperatures in Delhi are apt to be on the high side, one should be prepared with a quick change to lighter clothing. Customs officials may differ, but it can be anticipated that, in general, the inspection here will be strict, and that all luggage will be examined. Under the circumstances, the traveller would do well to inquire beforehand at travel agencies, airline offices, or at Indian diplomatic outlets, as to the restrictions and allowances in this regard, upon entering the country. Also, in order to create a favorable impression, it is always best during the customs inspection, to lean over backwards to cooperate in following the rules.

As in Nepal, one should list on the declaration form the amounts and denominations of all currency, the kinds of jewelry and precious metals being carried, the serial numbers and names of all cameras and other valuable equipment. And, since one is required to present this form upon departing the country, at which time the declarations may be compared to the currency, appointments, and equipment that one is carrying at the time, one should always know the whereabouts of this document and be ready to vouch for the accuracy of its statements.

When, at the exit, the final official has examined the already authorized customs certificate and has verified the baggage count, the traveller is free to begin the journey. While still inside, however, one should have visited the money-exchange window to procure a sufficient supply of Indian Rupees. From this moment forward, the traveller is on his own. Therefore, one should have checked all currency transactions to see that the bills are in good condition and in the proper denominations, that the totals are correct, and that one has not (only by dint of unbroken concentration during the counting process) been the victim of any sleight-of-hand. Although coins always seem in short supply, as noted, it is well worth the effort at this point, to try and procure an extra quantity.

Upon departure from the airport, it is customary to have the assistance of a porter, who will charge two Rupees for the service. If a cab-driver requests more than 12 Rupees for the trip into the city, the charge is excessive. One should also know that many taxis have either inoperative meters, or no meters at all. On the other hand, for four Rupees, one can travel to central Delhi in a motor coach which departs from outside the domestic airline terminal.

2. Life and Living

The Indian Government Tourist Bureau maintains a desk at the airport at which, if necessary, the traveller can request assistance in procuring hotel reservations. Since this facility is closed late at night, however, one would have to negotiate directly with a place of lodging at such times, so the traveller is wise to have made previous arrangements through the airline. Indian-style hotels are inexpensive and quite comparable to other places, though there are one or two differences worth mentioning. Toilets, for example, are the simple, slit-trench type that one used to find in Japan, though equipped with a flushing mechanism. And since doors are secured by padlocks, the traveller is safest if he uses his own lock, especially as this is well in keeping with local practise. Once, when the writer attempted to return his key to the front desk, the hotel clerk became imme-

Hotel Names	Addresses	Telephone	# Rooms	Air Conditioning		No Air Cond.	
				Twin	Single	Twin	Single
Ashoka Hotel	50-B Chanakyapuri New Delhi 110021.	370101	486	250 ($30)	175 ($20)	—	—
Akbar Hotel	Chanakyapuri, New Delhi 110021.	370251	163	225 ($26)	150 ($18)	—	—
Hotel Oberoi Intercontinental	Dr. Zakir Hussain Rd., New Delhi 110003.	386161	350	350 ($41)	250 ($30)	—	—
Claridges Hotel	12 Aurangzeb Rd., New Delhi 110011.	370211	130	205 ($24)	125 ($15)	—	—
Hotel Imperial	Janpath, New Delhi 110001.	311511	160	215 ($25)	135 ($16)	—	—
Hotel Janpath	Janpath, New Delhi 110001.	383961	202	180 ($21)	95 ($11)	—	—
Hotel Ambassador	Sujan Singh Park New Delhi 110003.	385431	89	115 ($14)	70 ($ 8)	—	—
Hotel Diplomat	9 Sardar Patel Marg (Diplomatic Enclave) New Delhi.	372003	25	160 ($19)	85 ($10)	—	—
Hotel Rajdoot	Mathura Rd., New Delhi 110014.	79583 (10 lines)	55	140 ($16)	95 ($11)	—	—
New Delhi YMCA Tourist Hotel	Jai Singh Rd., New Delhi 110001.	311915	117	135 ($16)	80 ($ 9)	75 ($ 9)	40 ($ 5)
Hotel Ranjit	Maharaja Ranjit Singh Rd., New Delhi 110001.	275021	195	120 ($14)	775 ($ 9)	90 ($11)	55 ($ 6)
Hotel Vikram	Ring Rd., New Delhi 110004.	625639	72	120 ($14)	75 ($ 9)	—	—
Lodhi Hotel	Lala Lajpat Rai Marg New Delhi 110003.	619422	200	120 ($14)	75 ($ 9)	—	—

Date on hotel charges in Delhi. (1976)　　　Rates in Indian Rupees ($1=8.5 Rupees)

(right)
Back street, Delhi, with a view of **Jama Masjid**, the largest mosque in India in the background.

(left)
Attractive Indian wares, lavishly displayed in an open-front store.

In Old Delhi, such relics as ancient gates and walls are frequently seen, as exemplified in this picture of **Delhi Gate**, located in the southeast quadrant of the city.

←

In the heat of the day, the shade provided by the trees that line the avenues is more than welcome.

diately suspicious that the room was adjudged unsatisfactory and that the guest was really attempting to leave. One is expected to carry his room key.

Hotel gratuities are something of a nuisance. In large hotels, for example, each task, whether it be shoe-shining, cleaning, carrying luggage, serving food, is handled by a boy belonging to a separate caste, and each, in turn, anticipates a tip.

Meal times are very specific, not only in hotels but generally in restaurants, even in less-trafficked places in the suburbs. At other than the specified times, therefore, one can find only snacks and such fare, as anything more would be at odds with local custom. One's schedule should thus be plotted well ahead of time with such things in mind. Breakfast hours are between 8 and 11; lunch, from 12:00 to 14:00, dinner, from 20:00 to 23:00 hours, and teatime, between 14:00 and 20:00 hours.

3. One-Day Treks in Delhi

(see the large-scale map on p. 164, and illustrations 1 - 10, of prominent sights, on pps. 162 - 166).

Tourist buses on regular schedules afford ample opportunity to visit notable scenic spots and places of historical interest. However, it may be more diverting to make individual walking tours which allow the traveller more insight into the tenor of Indian life. For such expeditions, although one should proceed according

Shops on Connaught Place, New Delhi.

to his own design, perhaps with map in hand, the following course is offered as an example.

Beginning at an arbitrary point, the grassy plot inside the circle marking **Connaught Place,** the hub of New Delhi's street network, one may be immediately confused when gazing about, to note the sameness of the Greek-style, white, columned buildings and shops which surround the circle. Upon closer scrutiny, however, one should discover that each street is separately identified by sign and number, and that the general layout from here can be oriented to the tall buildings in the distance, which can be made to serve as landmarks.

From this initial vantage point, then, one should locate between two of the columned

buildings, an Indian coffee house, with attached, partly outdoor restaurant, and behind this the white figure of the Baroda Bank building looming up, and finally, to the left of this, beyond a shopping facility called the Delhi Emporium, **Jan Path,** a broad, main thoroughfare running directly south from the circle. The first half of this walking tour, however, will be a visit to Old Delhi.-

The shortest route to Old Delhi is northward from the circle and under the railroad tracks, but as this is rather mundane, a somewhat more diverse route is suggested. On the west, at this juncture, one should note a tall, white, Greek-style building with a British Airways sign displayed prominently, to the north of which are the post office and more high structures sporting advertisement signs for such airlines as SAS and KLM. North of this, at the sign of the letter 'B', one should enter **Panchkuin Street.**

The first large intersection is the crossing of Connaught Circus, the avenue which surrounds

from New Delhi to Old Delhi

the starting point at Connaught Place, and along which are a number of shops, hotels, and restaurants. Beyond this, as we proceed along Panchkuin Street's left sidewalk, are a series of barrack-style eating places which gradually are superseded by shops dealing in lamp shades, then by furniture stores. Meanwhile, the street traffic, made up of ox and horse carts, scooters,

① 19:10 26 March '73
A. Jojima   New delhi (Connaught place)

trucks, bicycles, and such, passes busily on its way, while in the trees that line the thoroughfare squirrels play about, and flocks of **Gray Starlings,** parrots, and crows, add to the general clamor. Turning right at the next busy intersection, one walks along a sidewalk flanked by bustling stalls that openly attest to the vigor of urban pursuits, and after passing several alleys which run out to this artery, the street bears somewhat left and some concrete buildings come into view. It is here, in early morning, that stands are erected to sell vegetables, bananas, and the like. Nearby are shops dealing in crockery and ceramics. The trek bears right again and at the next rotary, where scooter-taxis assemble, one should enter an area crowded with shoppers and hawkers, whose voices are accompanied by the jangle of bicycle bells. When a triangular square is reached, with a gate to the New Delhi Station on the right, the trekking course turns once more to the left, but one may note that in front of the gate, taxis, scooter-cabs and carriages, hauled either by two white oxen or one rather emaciated horse, are awaiting potential riders.

Left of, and beyond the station, one turns

right again and mounts the stairs leading up to the bridge across the railway right-of-way and, on the opposite side, the road descends into Old Delhi. One turns left at the next intersection and when a parking area surrounded by an iron fence is seen, beyond this is the **Ajmeri**

③

Gate, the southwest entrance into the old fortress city, and through which the trek continues. It is well, however, to proceed cautiously along the narrow street beyond the gate, as in this area there are numerous, old-fashioned wells with hand-pumps, and all kinds of goods displayed directly in one's path. At the open space marking the next intersection, one can either turn left and proceed along **Larknan Bazar**, or if one is tired or out of time, by bear-

ing slightly to the right and taking a shorter route, proceed to **Jama Masjid.** Here, one sees numerous Muslims, whose women are recognizable by their veiled faces, and one hears either voices crying out for pedicabs or the entreaties of the drivers for passengers. One should again take care here to avoid being struck in the legs by the many hand carts, as the pushers are not accustomed to stopping for pedestrians. The path alternately narrows and widens in this area, and when a sign reading 'Hotel' written laterally, and 'Eagle' displayed vertically beneath, is seen, one should proceed to the next corner and turn right at a sign advertising 'DR. B.N. KANNA'. Here, one sees various individuals all working at such tasks as laundering around a

well, repairing shoes (with tools and equipment scattered about on the pavement), or unloading sacks of grain from ox-drawn trucks. The course bears left again and almost at once comes to another large street, **Chandni Chauk**, the main throughfare of Old Delhi,

Inside New Delhi Station.

ONE DAY TREKKING IN DELHI

Course follows numbers, 1 – 10

④

Red fort の門 – LAHORE GATE

Turkeman Gate の 南側.

10:00
27 March '93
A. Igawa

⑤

165

⑥

⑦

⑧

⑨

Jan Path
28 Mar.
a. Ogawa

New Delhi

New Delhi

INDIA GATE

Jama Masjid, Old Delhi.

Specialized shopping area, Old Delhi. →

⑩ Rashtrapit Bhawan

ous palace by **Shah Jahan**, the fifth emperor of the Mughal Dynasty, and beginning in 1639, construction took eight years. The famous, white **Tai Mahal** was also built under his tutelage, as will be mentioned subsequently. One should pause here and purchase a ticket at a booth near **Lahore Gate**, the entrance to the fort from Chandni Chauk, and after passing through, turn left and walk by a line of souvenir shops, after which is an enclosed space and a second gate, where an attendant will receive your ticket.

at the eastern end of which is the famous Red Fort, **Lal Qila. Chandni Chauk** is two to three times wider than the streets already experienced and has a center strip. To reach Lal Qila, one must push through throngs of unemployed artisans who are standing about in this area.

Lal Qila was built as a fort around a sumptu-

After observing the fort, the trek can proceed to Jama Masjid, where there is another

entrance fee, plus a charge for the privilege of taking pictures and another for checking foot-gear. Around this temple area, the northwestern sector is noted for metallurgy and one will see drills, cog-wheels and other apparatus; the western sector has an agglomeration of shops specializing in bedding, and in the south are a variety of establishments dispensing food and drink. Taking the street leading directly south, the course proceeds past eating, drinking and other commercial places, then descends slightly, narrows, and gradually approaches an intersection in the form of a mis-shapen 'T'.

Here, since this is a section of the old city devoted to such ornaments as necklaces and bracelets, members of the party may wish to disperse and amble through the streets individually — meeting again perhaps at **Turkman Gate**, which provides access to the fort from the south. Adjacent, is an open, park-like area called **Ramlila Ground**, across which a road approaches from the west, so that by taking this, the course eventually passes under the railroad tracks and links up with Connaught Place, from whence the trek began.

One day is appropriate for such a tour, although it can be accomplished in half this, in which case, the afternoon could be spent visiting New Delhi, which can be seen comfortably in that amount of time. One may wish to see the governmental office area and Parliament House, before pressing on through **India Gate** to the tomb of **Emperor Humayun**. Perhaps the reader can gain some visual impression of these places by examining the attached map, sketches, and photographs.

Ancient fort (**Purana Qila**), New Delhi.

4. Agra

The state of **Uttar Pradesh**, as mentioned, includes a part of the Greater Himalayas, the **Kumaun-Garhwal** Ranges, which spread over a vast area and envelop the western border of Nepal. With an area of 290,000 square kilometers, and a population of roughly 73 million, this capacious state contains not only the headwaters of the **Ganges River system**, but virtually the entire northern reaches of the **Plain of Hindustan**.

Agra, a medium-sized city of around 500,000 population, is located in a western sector of Uttar Pradesh, a little more than 200 kilometers directly southeast of Delhi. The city, being a repository of the glorious remains of ancient Mughal empires, attracts a constant stream of visitors from everywhere in the world, and at the same time, its surroundings have an unmistakably charming rural flavor. Despite what one may feel about visiting such historic places, which may prompt some, for example, to postpone this trip, and even though a visit to South Asia for this purpose alone may be inadvisable, once there, it would be foolhardy indeed not to make special effort to experience these sights.

Following the death of Humayun, shortly after he had assumed power in Delhi, **Akbar, the Great**, the third Mughal emperor, moved the capital to Agra. Here, he attempted to amalgamate Hinduism and Islam and, by employing many imaginative and brilliant reforms, especially of the governmental and tax structure, he helped greatly to consolidate the power of the empire. However, the apex of the prosperity of the Mughals came during the reigns of **Jahangir** and **Shah Jahan**, the fourth and fifth emperors, respectively. The **Taj Mahal**, built by Shah Jahan as a mausoleum for his favorite wife (and himself), is still so exquisite as to be known throughout the world as the 'Pearl of the Orient'.

The most pleasant way to sight-see in Agra is by departing Delhi in early morning on the 'Taj Express', which connects with a tour bus and returns you at the end of the day, by another express, to Delhi. Otherwise, one can take a round-trip tour bus directly from Delhi.

Sight-seeing in Agra should be oriented around three places, the tomb of **Sikandra, Fort Agra**, and the **Taj Mahal**, and, if time allows, to such mosques as **Itimad ud Daulah**, the city of **Fatehpur Sikri**, and various other historic relics of the Mughal Empire.

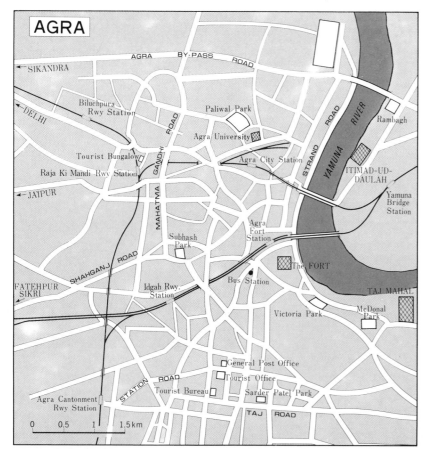

AGRA

SIKANDRA

DELHI

JAIPUR

FATEHPUR
SIKRI

AGRA BY-PASS ROAD

Biluchpura Rwy Station

Paliwal Park

Agra University

Tourist Bungalow

Raja Ki Mandi Rwy Station

MAHATMA GANDHI ROAD

STRAND ROAD

Agra City Station

YAMUNA RIVER

Rambagh

ITIMAD-UD-DAULAH

Yamuna Bridge Station

Subhash Park

SHAHGANJ ROAD

Agra Fort Station

Idgah Rwy. Station

Bus Station

The FORT

Victoria Park

McDonal Park

TAJ MAHAL

General Post Office

STATION ROAD

Tourist Office

Tourist Bureau

Sarder Patel Park

Agra Cantonment Rwy Station

TAJ ROAD

0   0.5   1   1.5 km

From a 'GUIDE PLAN OF AGRA' Agra City Office.

Akbar's Tomb, although here a mausoleum, represents a style of architecture begun during his lifetime, and features grand buildings arranged symmetrically over a broad area.

(left)
The **Taj Mahal**, built of pure white slabs of marble by Shah Jahan of the Mughal Dynasty in honor of his wife, was constructed between 1631 and 1654, and remains a favorite of visitors from far and wide.

As with **Lal Qila** in Delhi, the walls of the fort at Agra are constructed of red sandstone.

→ Page 169

Inside the walls stand magnificent buildings, including the fort, temples, both Muslim and Hindu, and harems.

Agra

THE KASHMIR HIMALAYAS

Kashmir paper craft

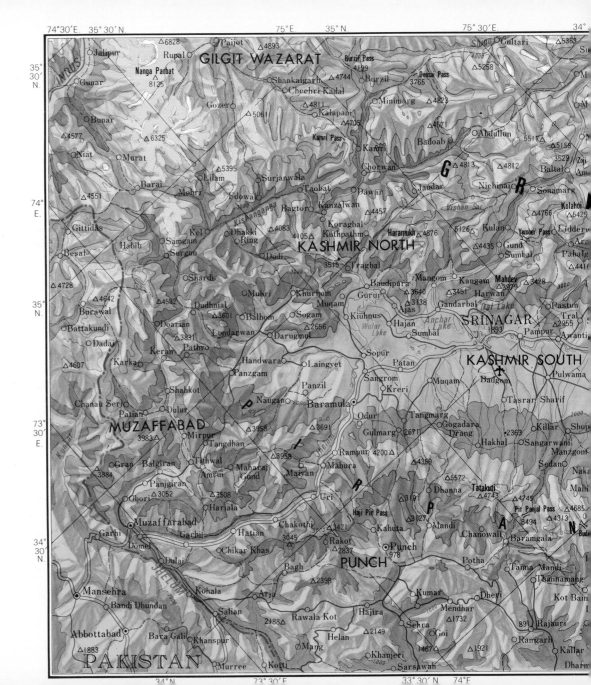

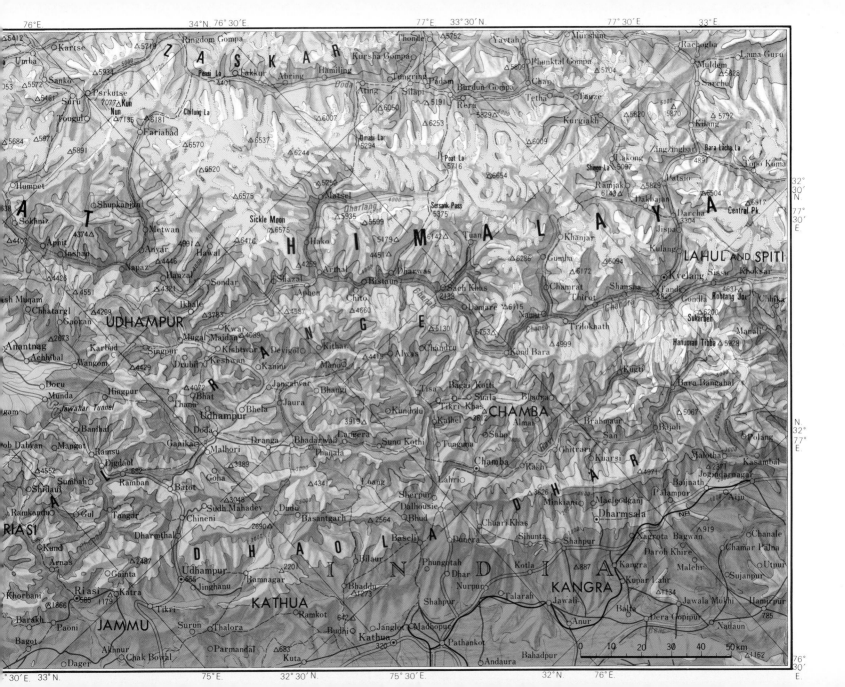

Cheese Vendor.

A fruit vendor.

Shish-kebab and a curry dish.

Vegetable-sellers of Srinagar arrive in boats.

Muslim woman in **purdah**.

(right)

Children of Srinagar.

Panorama of Srinagar showing houseboats lined up across the middle of the picture and the fort, **Hari Parbhat**, looming in the background.

← page 172
Multi-storied houses in the old city of Srinagar.

Srinagar

↑ A sandal-maker, and...
→ A sandal-wearer.

The village of Pahlgam.

←page 174
Stores, Tangmarg.

Tangmarg
and
Pahlgam

Gujar houses, made of lumber and earth, are often half-embedded in the ground.

THE HIMALAYAS
OF
HIMACHAL
PRADESH
AND
UTTAR
PRADESH

Krishna, as depicted in an 18th century Rajput drawing.

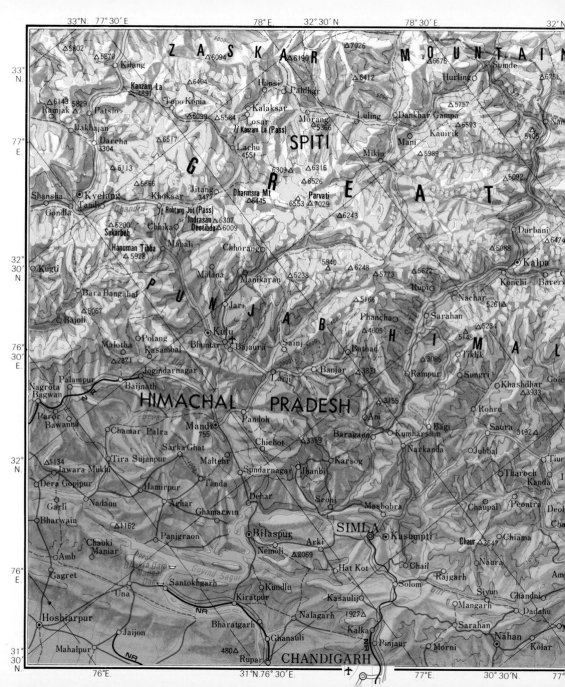

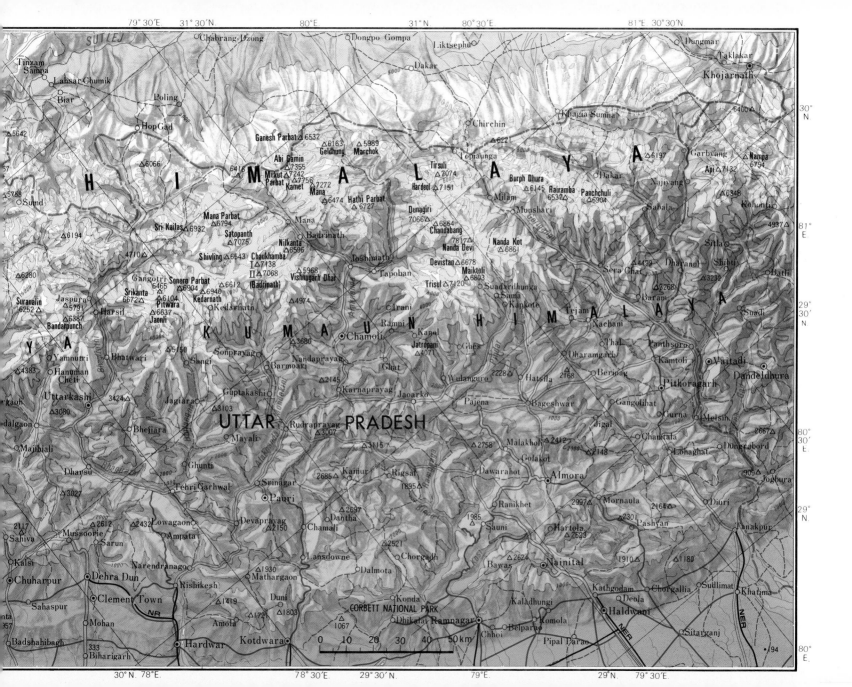

SUTLEJ

HIMALAYA

KUMAUN HIMALAYA

YA

UTTAR PRADESH

CORBETT NATIONAL PARK

Tinzam Sampa
Lahsar Chumik
Biar
Poling
HopGad
△5642
△6066
Chabrang-Dzong
Dongpo Gompa
Liktsephu
Dakar
Dungmar
Taklakar
Khojarnath
Chirchin
△6400
△6197
Garbyang
Api △7132
Nampa 6754
Najiyang
△6348
Kohonti
Sitla
△4937△
△81° E.
Dharamuli
Shibtu
Batli
△3232
△3268
Baram
Suadi
Tejam
Nachani
HIMALAYA
Thal
Panthsoro
Kamtoli
Vaitadi
Dandeldhura
Berinag
Pithoragarh
Gangolihat
Gurna
Melsin
Jigal
△2667△
Chanitala
Lohaghat
Dungrabord
△909
Yogbura
Diuri
Mornaula
△2164
Pashyan
Janakpur
Sullimat
Khatima
Sitarganj
Haldwani
Deola
Chorgallia
Kathgodam
Kaladhungi
Komola
Belparao
Pipal Parao
△94
△80° E.

HIMALAYA

Y A

Ganesh Parbat △6532
Abi Gamin
Mukut Parbat △7242
Kamet
Mana
Hathi Parbat △6727
Mana Parbat
Sri Kailas △6932
Satopanth △7075
Nilkanta △6596
Shivling △6543
Chaukhamba I △7138 II △7068
Vishnugarh Dhar
Gangotri Sonero Parbat
Srikanta △6104
Pitwara
Jaonli
Kedarnath
Bandarpunch
Yamnuri
Hanuman Cheti
Harsil
Bhatwari
Gangabagh
Geldhung Marchok △5989
Tirsuli △7074
Hardeol △7151
Dunagiri 7066△
Chandabang
Nanda Devi 7817△
Devistan △6678
Maiktoli △6803
Trisul △7120
Mana
Badrinath
Joshimath
Tapoban
Trani
Rampni
Chamoli
Jatropani △4071
Ghes
Topaunga
Burph Dhura
△6145 Rairamba
Panchchuli △6904
Milam
Munshari
Nanda Kot △6861
Suadarihunga
Sama
Kankote
Wulanguro
Hatsila
△2228
△2168

Surandin
Jaspura
Uttarkashi
Dhansu
Mussoorie
Sarun
Kalsi
Chuharpur
Clement Town
Sahaspur
Mohan
Badshahibagh
Biharigarh
Hardwar
Kotdwara
Amola
Matimargaon
Narendranago
Rishikesh
Dehra Dun
Tehri Garhwal
Ghunti
Srinagar
Pauri
Devaprayag
Lowagaon
Ampata
Chamali
Dantha
Lansdowne
Chorgadh
Dalmota
Konda
Dhikala
Ramnagar
Chhoi
1067
Sonprayag
Barmoari
Nandaprayag
Ghat
Karnaprayag
Jaoarko
Pajena
Bageshwar
Dharamgarh
Malakhoti △2412
Golakot
Dawarahot
Almora
Ranikhet
Sauni
Hartola △2523
Bawas △2624
Nainital
Kamur
Rigsal
Kanol
Guptakashi
Jagiara
Bhejiara
Mayali

0 10 20 30 40 50 km

Winter view of Simla when, in the morning, the weather may be ideal, only to turn blustery in the afternoon, with snow and perhaps thunder and lightning.

Winter scene,
Village of **Malana**.

People of Manali crossing a footbridge.

Simla
Manali
Mussoorie
Nainital

People of **Manali**.

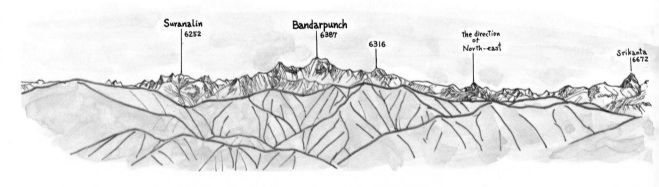

Himalayan panorama from **Mussoorie** (Lal Tibba)

The western side of the town of Mussoorie.

Panorama of **Nainital**, from Naini Peak.

Srikanta 6672　Jaonli 6637　Pitwara 6904　Sonero Parbat 6904　Kedarnath 6612　Satopanth 7075　Chaukhamba 7138　Badrinath 6974　Nilkanta 6596

10:34
24, March, '73
at LAL TIBBA
in Mussoorie

THE EASTERN HIMALAYAS

A statue of Yaksani, 2 BC.

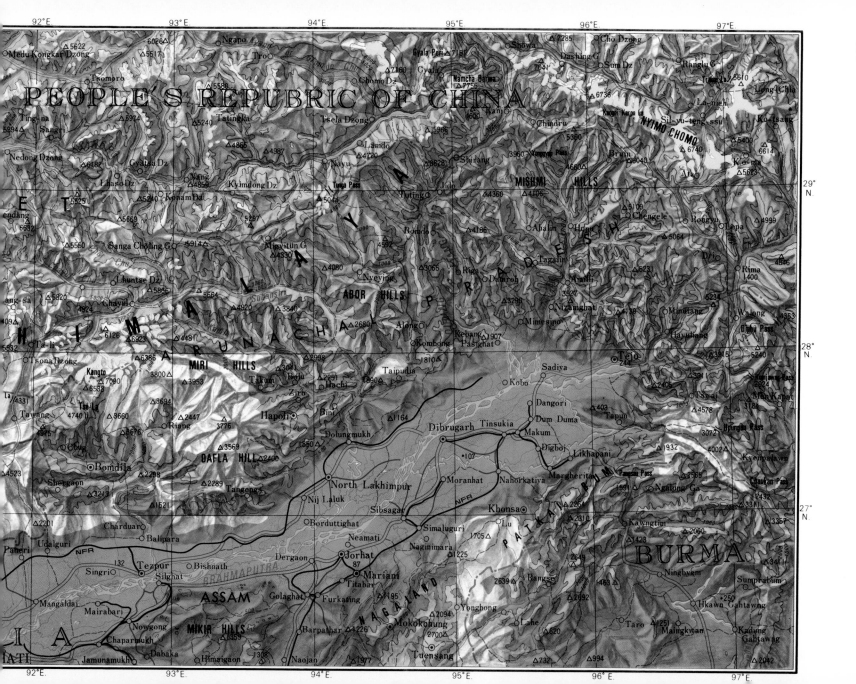

Temples, Tenzing Norgay Road, Darjeeling.

Darjeeling terminal station.

Panorama of Darjeeling, with **cryptomeria** trees, imported from Japan, in the right foreground.

From the tourist lodge of Tiger Hill, Darjeeling.

The famous Darjeeling tea.

Amarylis growing in the Universal Nursery, Kalimpong.

The Brahmaputra River in **Gauhati**.

Wild elephant, **Kaziranga**.

Houses of Assam.

Assam tea estates, utilizing the shade from the upper forest story.

KASHMIR

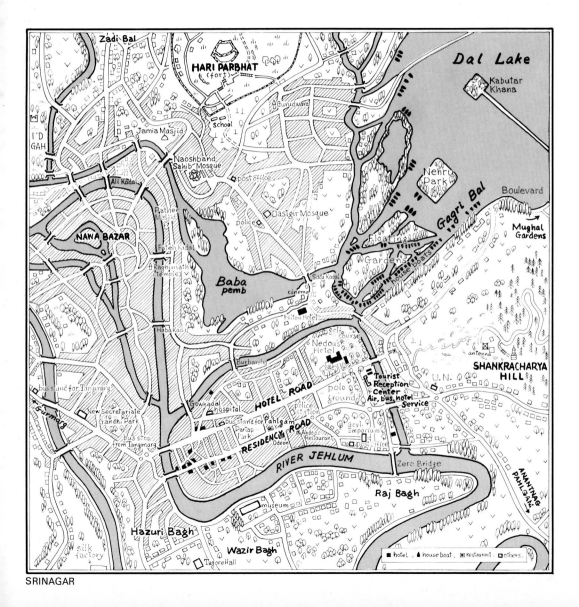

Map labels: Zadi Bal, HARI PARBHAT (fort), Dal Lake, Kabutar Khana, Gurudwara, I'D GAH, School, Jamia Masjid, Naoshband Sahib Mosque, Ali Kadal, Pather Masjid, post office, Dastgir Mosque, Nehru Park, Boulevard, NAWA BAZAR, police, Fateh Kadal, Ragunnath temple, Baba pemb, Gagri Bal, Floating Gardens, Mughal Gardens, house boats, Sada Kadal, cinema, Habakadal, Hilton Hotel, bus stand for Tanmarg, Gulmarg, Nedous Hotel, golf course, New Secretariate & Gandhi Park, Burbarshy, SHANKRACHARYA HILL, Tourist Reception Center Air, bus, hotel Service, Gowkadal, hospital, polo ground, U.N., antenna, police station, Paraap Park, HOTEL ROAD, bus stop from Tanmarg, bus stand for Pahlgam, Govt. emporium, Andoo Restaurant, post office, RESIDENCY ROAD, Odeon, RIVER JEHLUM, Zero Bridge, ANANTNAG PAHLGAM, Raj Bagh, museum, silk factory, Hazuri Bagh, Wazir Bagh, TagoreHall

Legend: ■ hotel, ▲ house boat, ▣ restaurant, □ others

1. Physical and Cultural Features

The **Northern** and **Southern Kashimir Himalayas** of northwestern India, belong to the state of Kashmir and Jammu. As noted, the former covers a vast area and includes the **Karakorum** (the Indian Government prefers the spelling, **Karakoram**, but here the customary transliteration is used, according to the original meaning, 'Black Stone Pass'), the **Ladakh**, and **Zaskar Ranges**, the **Soda Plain**, and **Ladakh Plateau**. The latter, on the other hand, has part of the main range, from **Nanga Parbat** to **Nun** and **Kun**, and in the south, the **Pir Panjal Range**, the **Siwalik Hills**, and the basin known as the **'Vale of Kashmir'**.

The Kashmir Basin (known as an 'Earthly Paradise') is occupied by lacustrine sediments in the form of terraces, heavily dissected by the **Jhelum River**, which has deposited a broad band of alluvium across its center portion. Running through the basin, furthermore, is a pearl-like strand of swamps and lakes of various sizes, so that the site of **Srinagar**, the capital, is spectacularly punctuated by water features, which are really the remains of a much larger lake which once completely filled the basin.

The populace, mostly Muslim but with a few Hindus, are mainly peaceful farmers, many of whom actually live in boats. In winter, these folk attempt to support themselves by such crafts as rug and jewelry-making, wood-carving, precious metal-working, and the production of artistic paper and textiles — the output of which industry then becomes the substance of summer trade, especially involving regular resort clientele and tourists. Meanwhile, in high mountain areas live the semi-nomadic **Gujars**, as well as the **Ladakhis**, followers of Lamaism.

The most pleasant time of the year to visit Kashmir is during June and July when the flowers are in full bloom.

2. Arrival at Srinagar

When the flight from Delhi approaches the airport at Srinagar in good weather, one should note the virile form of gigantic **Mt. Nanga Parbat** to the north, and contrast this with the rather sensuous figures to the east of the two peaks, **Nun** and **Kun**, which seem to project like the billowing breasts of a lovely woman. Unhappily, air-photography is forbidden in India.

Before one realizes, the plane has landed in the basin, whose roads, lined with stately poplars, look forth on an incomparably beautiful landscape. On alighting, one may be struck by a feeling of elation such as might accompany the final ascent of an alpine peak, and one wonders whether this euphoria is produced by the sudden opportunity to stretch the legs at high altitude. However, the elevation is only 1,590 meters.

The traveller now proceeds from the airplane through the gate and into the airport building where, as usual, the passport will be checked at the foreign arrivals desk. One is then urged to arrange lodgings by visiting the Tourist Bureau agency counter, and finally, to the right outside the main gate, luggage claim checks can be exchanged for the articles. From this location, after purchasing a 5 Rp. ticket, one can then be transported by motor coach to the Reception Center in Srinagar.

As the bus moves along over an asphalted road and up over a hill on its way to the city, it can be noticed that the scenery is particularly marked by three kinds of trees, the **chinar** (similar to the sycamore of America or the London Plane Tree, of Britain), the white-bark **poplar**, and the **willow** (resembling the pussy-willow). It can also be seen that under the high peaked roofs of the local residences, there is simply an open space, which suggests that the shape is merely to avoid damage by heavy winter snow. Upon entering the city,

one may be struck by the rather uniquely interesting atmosphere of the bustling bazar.

When the bus reaches the terminal on the grounds of the Reception Center, passengers are again asked about lodging reservations, which can also be made here. And, at this point, one should be prepared to fend off summarily, a persistent horde of ragged, would-be attendants, who are bound to rush forward, clamoring for the right to serve. One is constantly implored by such people, and by vendors and peddlers, even within the hotels. Their usual ploy is to inquire about the prices of the travellers belongings, prior to making an offer to purchase, so one is wise to be ready with an effective counter-remark.

3. Life and Living

In 1976, representative hotels in Srinagar were:

Name and Address	# Rooms	Twin Rates	Single Rates
Hotel Broadway, Maulana Azad Rd., Srinagar 190001 Tel. 5611	103	180 Rs ($21)	120 Rs ($14)
Nedou's Hotel, Maulana Azad Rd. Tel 2848~9	79	110—180 Rs ($13—21)	65—95 Rs ($9—11)
Hotel Oberoi Palace Srinagar, Tel. 2231~4	73	165—190 Rs ($19—22)	115—140 Rs ($14—16)

The Tourist Bureau accommodations include both regular hotel rooms, at 17 Rupees a night, twin, and so-called 'Retiring Rooms', at 12 Rp., twin.

Srinagar also boasts a unique form of accomodation, the house-boat, of which there are four classes, de-luxe, a, b, and c. These differ in price, according to the quality, size of boat, and the kinds of meals served. The practise resulted from a 19th century ruling by the local maharajah which, despite heavy demand by British colonial civilians and military personnel, for summer residences here, prohibited the building of resort structures. Consequently, in 1888, an M.T. Kenhard designed the first house-

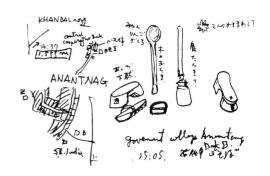

boat, and others quickly followed, so that the city was rapidly given a series of floating hostelries which, if unoccupied, usually carry a prominent sign reading, 'To Let'.

Inside these boats, the standard arrangement is for the living room, dining room, bedroom, toilet, bath, and kitchen to be built in a line, in that order. Meanwhile, the boats, and the landbound tourists are served by a fleet of 'shikara', or water-taxis, each with an attendant at the tiller to row you about on sight-seeing expeditions for a minimum charge of **10 paisa**.

Meals in Kashmir are similar to those of India, but the street-corner stalls dispense rather tasty fare in the **shish-kebab** (meat-paste broiled on a skewer) which, eaten together with unleavened bread, is both satisfying and inexpensive. Fruit is also most abundant. Other than the first-class hotels, reputable restaurants include **Ahadoes**, the **Grand**, the **Hollywood**, and the Capri.

By using the 'shikara' and sight-seeing buses, it is enjoyable to visit the lovely suburban gardens, the floating flower-beds, and other examples of the artistic imagination and former splendor of ancient Mughal princes, as well as to travel about the city and visit the impressive forts on the surrounding heights.

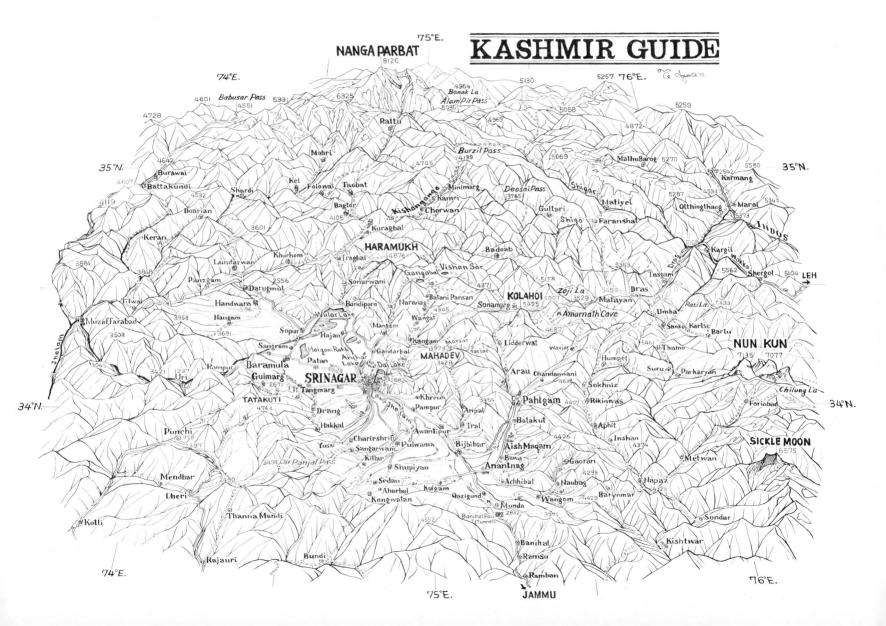

KASHMIR GUIDE

NANGA PARBAT
8126

75°E.

74°E.

5257 76°E.

4601 *Babusar Pass*
4551 533
6325
4964
Banak La
Alam Pit Pass
5030
5130
5259

4728
Rattu
4969
5058
4872

4642
Mohri
Burzil Pass
4199
5069
MathuBarog 5270

35°N.
35°N.

Burawai
4607
Kel *Folowal* *Taobat*
4705
Minimarg
Deosai Pass
3765
Shigar
2542
Karmang
5550

Battakundi
Shardi
4532
Bagtor
Kamri
Guttari
5287
Matiyel
4533

4119
Doarian
4105
Chorwan
Shigo
Faranshat
Olthingthang
Marol 5343
5373

Keran
3601
Kuragbal
Kishanganaa
5158
Indus

3884
Khurhom
HARAMUKH
4876
Badoab
5353
Kargil *Wakka*
Shergol 5104

3848
Lundarwan
2556
Tragbal
Gangabal
Vishan Sar
4371
Zoji La
5450
Dras
5562
LEH

Tilwal
Panzgam
Darugmul
Sonarwani
Balani Parisan
5007 3529
Matayan
Tassgam
RasiLa 5493

Muzaffarabad
3958
Handwara
1596
Bandipora
Narang
4345
KOLAHOI
5425
Sonamarg
Amarnath Cave
Umba
Sanko *Karlse*
Bartu

3508
Naugam
WularLake
Wangat
4687
Liderwat
5461
Thamo

3045
3421 1237
Rampur
3691
Sopur
Hajan
Sangrom
Haigam Rakh
Gandarbal
Kangam
Morsar
Tarsar
Wavjar
Humpet
NUN KUN
7135 7077

Uri
Baramula
Patan
Anchar Lake
Dal Lake
MAHADEV
3428
Arau
Chandanwani
4638
Suru
Parkaryan
Chilung La

34°N.
Gulmarg
2671
SRINAGAR
2682
Tangmarg
Khreuh
3454
Pahlgam
4407
Rikinwas
Sokhniz
Faribad
34°N.

TATAKUTI
4743
Drang
Pampur
Aripal
Batakut
4426
4374
Aphit
Inshan

Punchi
978
3127
Hakkal
Awantipur
Tral
SICKLE MOON
6575

Mendhar
3397
Yuse
Charirshrif
Pulwama
Bijbihar
AishMaqam
Bawa
Met wan

Sangarwan
Killar
Anantnag
Gaoran
4299
Napaz
4321

3494 *Pir Panjal Pass*
Shupiyan
Achhibal
Naubag
Barynmar
4429

Dheri
2490
Sedau
Aharbal
Kulgam
Qazigund
Wangom
Sondar

Kotli
Thanna Mandi
Kongwatan
Munda
2832
3971
Kishtwar

4552
Banihal Pass
(tunnel)

Banihal
Ramsu

Rajauri
Bundi
Ramban

74°E.
75°E.
JAMMU
76°E.

The tourist season in Kashmir is customarily between April 15th and December 10th, and in the 'off-season', offices and hotels are closed. And since all locations at over 2,000 meters are snow-bound at that time, these are inaccessible to both automobiles and animal-drawn vehicles. Only the **Gulmarg** ski area, as mentioned early in this volume, is open and frequented. Trekking, therefore, must be done between May and November, and preferably in June and July, when flowers are in blossom. When one considers the yearly snow time-table, September and October are probably safe enough, but the days grow rapidly shorter and temperatures are apt to be too low for comfort.

Trekking objectives may range from short to long-term, or from expeditions which employ ponies, to those which involve arduous climbing of rock faces and glaciers; but the kinds of freedom in trekking noted in Nepal, are simply a rarity elsewhere. Here, by discussing the objectives thoroughly beforehand with travel agents and guides, one must decide on the means most suitable to the intended purposes. If one wishes to include climbing and camping out in tents. with sleeping gear, a small expedition seems to be in order, complete with utensils and equipment. Moreover, locally available tents are often large and heavy, so that the entourage may take on a kind of military air.

Sample trekking courses in this area are:

1) Lake Gangabal (3,566 meters) and Mt. **Marmukh** (4,876 meters) — a 5-day expedition.

Lake Gangabal (2 x 1.5 kilometers), a glacial feature, is a residual form from the time when the glacier of Mt. Harmukh was considerably larger. The latter is a sacred mountain for

Pahlgam — Aran から南の山を見る.
Cirque glacier Valley と広葉亜高木－針葉の分布の関係.　　11:45, 22 Feb. '73. E. Ogawa.

Hindus, who gather here each September, so one must obtain permission from the Indian Military authorities to visit the area.

Since the automobile road through the **Sind Valley** is open from Srinagar to **Kangam**, it is wise to charter a car for the first leg of the trek. From Kangam, one should advance northward along the left bank of the **Wangat River**, to the village of **Wangat** (at about 2,100 meters), from which **Naranag** is only 5 kilometers distant. Here, there is a rest-house, and nearby, the remains of two ancient temples.

The second day, one must climb a steep slope to the summit at 3,300 meters, and since the trail is wet and slippery, caution is again in order. Lake Gangabal is 7 kilometers north of this summit, making up a total of 19 kilometers for the second leg. Other than Gangabal, there are many lakes in this area — all of them beautiful.

From the third day to the completion of the trek, one can hike around this area or climb Mt. Harmukh, and if one wishes a different return route, it is possible to follow the ridges eastward to the **Bramsar Pass** and descend the rugged path to **Chhatargul**. Another course, which is long but most attractive, traverses

many beautiful lakes and ends in **Sonamarg**, northeast of the capital.

2) Amarnath Cave — 7 to 8 days.

Another Hindu holy place, Amarnath Cave, lies in the corner of a deep valley, in the midst of a field of snow and ice, and within is a stalactite grotto which has been designated as a shrine. Although this sacred spot is a kind of barren place, devoid of vegetation, the course itself is through variegated territory, marked by torrential mountain streams, grasslands, and forests, and unless one waits until after July, the going is made even more difficult by snow. On the other hand, in August, when pilgrims are assembling here, there is no possibility of a quiet, peaceful trek. The length of this entire course is about 45 kilometers, for which one should allow at least one-week.

The first day one should proceed by bus to **Pahlgam**, and from there, either on foot or by hired car, 16 kilometers more over an unpaved road, to **Thanin**.

The second day begins with an 8-kilometer stretch from Thanin to **Zolpal** over a difficult trail, locally referred to as 'pisu' (grassy-slithery), from which, deep in the abyss below, the river remains in view. Zolpal lies in a pasture between two rivers and one may cross by snow patch bridge before proceeding east another 6 kilometers, where the trail meets a rocky path up the mountain to **Sheshnag** (3,600 meters). The third day, Sheshnag to Panchtarni, the fourth day to Amarnath Cave.

The famous caves are gigantic, measuring about 45 meters in height, width, and length.

Usually, however, pilgrims supplement the above course by turning right at Panchtarni and trekking for 18 kilometers to **Astanmarg**; thence to Thanin and back to Pahlgam.

3) Kolahoi Glacier and Mt. Kolahoi
—5 to 6 days.

On the first day, as in the previous course, one can use the bus from Srinagar to Pahlgam. From here, one proceeds to **Aru**, an 11-kilometer, one-day trip by mule or pony, though it is also possible to accomplish this in an automobile. In the Aru area it is advisable to camp in the pine forest that surrounds the village which, at 2,700 meters, has the atmosphere not only of a high but of a glacial valley.

The second day covers the 10 kilometers between Aru and **Lidderwat** (also **Lidrwat**) and the trail proceeds along a stream of cold, cloudy water (known as 'glacial milk') which rushes through a typical U-shaped glacial valley. A good camp site is to be had where a stream from **Tar Sar** in the southwest, joins the trail (although if one is early enough in reaching this spot, it may be better to proceed a bit farther upstream), where there is a broad meadow — a pleasant site for camping.

Day three concerns the approximately 15-kilometer trek from Lidderwat to **Kolahoi**, but after about 6 kilometers a road will be seen to emerge from the forest and to run eastward across the grassy surface. And after the disappearance of the final homestead of **Gujar Kotas**, on the opposite bank of the stream, the trail enters an area marked by frequent stream courses, as is indicated by its local name,

'Land of the 7 Streams'. So discomforting are the crossings here that the animals may become reluctant to continue, but gradually, as one follows more deeply into the valley, Mt. Kolahoi and its glacier will come into view. When reached, camping is best in a location slightly below the end of the glacier.

From here, it may be best to confine climbing activity to those with experience at ascending glaciers or steep, rock-strewn terrain. In any case, constraint is in order, with individuals cautioned to follow as secure and comfortable a course as is possible.

Travel and Trekking Agencies, Srinagar-based

A] Travel Agencies which handle all-India Tours.

1) Kai Travels (Oberoi Palace Hotel).
2) Mercury Travels ('')
3) Sita Travels (Nedou's Hotel)
4) Travel Corporation of India (Maulaua Azad Road).

B] Local excursion agencies.

1) Shirez Travels (Laubert Lane).
2) Sky Lark Travel Agents (Laubert Lane).
3) Trade & Tour (Bund). Tel. 2447
4) Kashmir Tours (Residency Road). Tel. 4852, 2833
5) Khagis Travel Service (Khuwaga Yerbal).
6) Kashmir Trekking and Hiking (Sonwar Begh).

カギがたてにかかって
あった。

—field note

5. Gulmarg

The **Pir Panjal Range**, which extends southward from the western side of the (Kashmir) basin, acts as a barrier to the super-heated air over the great Indian Plain, to its south, so that the Vale of Kashmir remains comfortably cool. **Gulmarg** lies on a beautiful, grass-covered

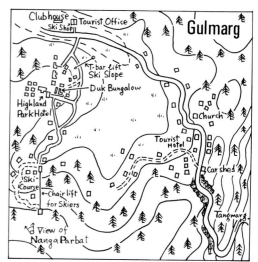

tableland, as though in the bosom of the mountain range.

In season, buses for Gulmarg leave from within the Tourist Reception Center in Srinagar, but in winter the departure point is in the western suburbs. The scene from the bus is generally pastoral but there are glimpses of horse-drawn vehicles travelling along the poplar-lined roads. However, since the road through the forest beyond **Tangmarg** is narrow and winding, it is necessary to change the mode of travel from bus to station-wagon. In winter, furthermore, this stretch of the road is snow-covered. But when you pass through **Gulmarg Gap** the landscape suddenly opens up and it is as though you were entering the portals of heaven.

Although unusual in South Asia, this area during the winter months becomes a foremost skiing center. Accommodations, however, are to be had only at the **Highland Park Hotel** or at the Government-operated 'Duk' bungalows in the same area, and since these are in heavy demand at this season, it is wise to have a reservation.

6. Pahlgam

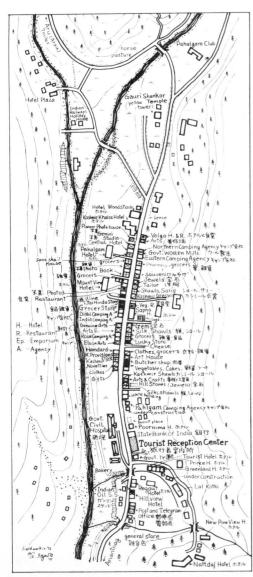

City Map of Pahlgam

The road to pahlgam

Pahlgam (or Pahalgam), situated about one-half-day's travel south of Srinagar, is a tourist center in the mountains of the basin's eastern sector.

By bus (which in winter leaves from a terminus on Hotel Road, northwest and opposite Partap Park) you travel southward to **Anantnag,** the main city of the south, and then north-northeast up the **Lidder River** to a point where the valley has been widened by glacial activity, the location of the site of the city of Pahlgam.

Until recently, Pahlgam was merely a pastoral village inhabited by Gujar shepherds, and as such, was a place of little, perhaps declining activity. However, with the advent of more modern conditions and because of the scenic charm of its surroundings, it has become a place of attraction to tourists. There is one main street (reminiscent of that in a 'Western' movie), lined with shops, information agencies, and souvenir stands, and around the periphery and in the suburbs to the rear of the town are large-scale hotels. Hence, Pahlgam is a trekking base mainly for the aforementioned Kolahoi Glacier, located deep in the valley, as well as for the peak, Harbhagwan, and for the pilgrimage course to Amarnath Cave.

14:23, 21 Feb. '73

field note

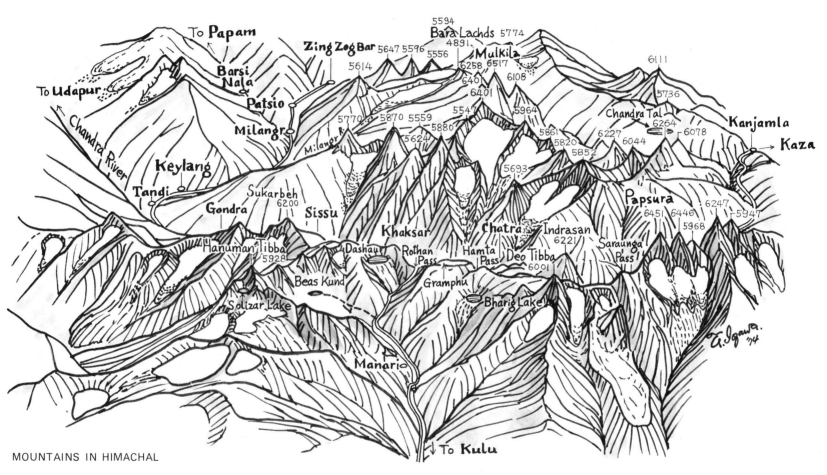

To Papam
Barsi Nala
To Udapur
Patsio
Chandra River
Milangr
Zing Zog Bar
5614
5647 5596
5556
5594
Bara Lachds 5774
4891
6258 6517
Mulkila
6401
6108
6401
6111
5736
Keylang
Tandi
5770
5870 5559
5547
5964
5880
5624
Chandra Tal
6264
6227 6044
6078
Kanjamla
Kaza
Sukarbeh
6200
Milangr R
5861
5820
5852
Papsura
6247
Gondra
Sissu
5693
6451 6446
5947
5968
Khaksar
Chatra
Indrasan
Hanuman Tibba
5928
Dashaur
Rothan Pass
Hamta Pass
Deo Tibba
6001
6221
Saraunga Pass
Beas Kund
Gramphu
Solizar Lake
Bharig Lake
Manario
To Kulu

MOUNTAINS IN HIMACHAL

1. Physical and Cultural Features

These mountains were once known as the Punjab Himalayas because they lay in what was then the Punjab District, or the 'Land of the 5 Rivers', its official title. However, when the district was partitioned upon the birth of Pakistan, this part was renamed **Himachal Pradesh** — a title which has come into greater and greater usage by local people, as well as in published materials, even though the name **Punjab** is still recognized by the Indian Government's Division of Natural Boundaries.

Three roughly parallel ranges are recognized to comprise the mountains of Himachal. The northernmost, the already-mentioned **Zaskar**, is a barrier between Ladakh and Himachal; south of this is the **Pir Panjal**, running from Kashmir, which, especially from the **Rohtang Pass** eastward, in height and extent, takes on the appearance and nature of the Greater Himalayas, of which it is an important part. Further east, this range becomes the **Nanda Devi**, of Uttar Pradesh, and the **Api**, of Nepal, both of which are catchment basins for the **Beas** and **Ravi** river systems. The southernmost and lowest is the **Dhauladhar** Range, at whose base lie such well-known hill stations as **Dalhousie**, **Dharmsala** (Dharamsala), and **Palampur**. Here also live the half-nomadic **Gaddis**, who practise a form of **transhumance**, and it may be interesting to tourists, as it was to our party, that among these folk, women are held in higher esteem than men.

2. Chandigarh

In 1947 when the western Punjab, including its capital, **Lahore**, became part of Pakistan, a new capital was contemplated in the eastern part of the province. Hence, since it was thought more expedient and economical, and though such projects are uncommon in India, rather than to refurbish a former community, an entirely new place — the model city of Chandigarh — was planned and constructed. Later, however, because of various circumstances, the state capital was shifted to **Simla**, and Chandigarh was designated a special, independent district, and one of which the Indians are intensely proud. If, for example, an Indian learns you have visited the city, his reaction will probably be one of praise and wonder.

Chandigarh was built from plans drawn up by two New Yorkers, **Albert Mayer** and **Mathew Novicki**, but following the accidental death of the latter, it was brought to completion by the famous Swiss architect, **Le Corbusier**, assisted by three younger technicians and planners.

The design is fundamentally in the grid pattern, with broad, intersecting thoroughfares, and the whole feature is laid out on a gently sloping surface, running northeast-southwest, at the foot of the Himalayas. The city is divided into various discrete sectors, according to function. For example, the administrative function is in the northern sector, the university and educational function in the northeastern, the commercial and business function is in the center, and the residential is in the southern. The plan, however, allows each sector to be rendered independent of the whole by the addition of such essential public facilities as shops, schools, clinics, banks, and means of transport and communication. The basic intention was obviously to locate residents and commercial facilities in wooded, attractively landscaped areas and, in the long run, to create a place of lasting beauty and utility, but of course, there is still much to be done. Nonetheless, the writer was moved to feelings of envy mainly because in his own culture, under these conditions, the physical attractions of an urban site are all too quickly eradicated — so eager are the builders to fashion what may very well become the slums of the future.

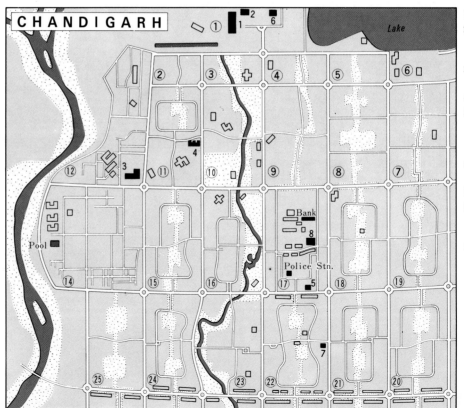

1. Secretariat.
2. Assembly Punjab & Haryana.
3. Nehru Hospital.
4. Y. M. C. A.
5. Bus Terminus & Tourist Bureau & Taxi Stand.
6. University Library.
7. Aroma Hotel.
8. Indian Airlines and Air India Office.
①~㉕ The Number of Sector.

from a guide map, City of Chandigarh.

3. Simla

Simla, capital of Himachal Pradesh, is the foremost hill station of India, and one of the chief mountain towns of the world. Furthermore, since the main governmental operations move here during the heat of summer, along with the personnel involved, it is almost as though Simla replaces Delhi at this season as the national capital.

The city is spread over a succession of ridges and reaches a linear extent of 12 kilometers. Its generally high buildings, which are attached to the sides of the ridges, rise symmetrically over this extent, creating a spectacular scene. Moreover, these structures are inter-connected by an intricate maze of steps and tunnels which, in effect, form the basic town plan.

Since, in addition to those who come here to combine business and pleasure, there are those who view Simla as a health and convalescent center, the city is well-equipped with such resort facilities as skating rinks, golf courses, skiing areas, and theaters, for both stage show and movies.

Perhaps because this was originally planned and utilized by the British, the shops and stores of the city are built to lend an atmosphere of Old World charm, which is in striking contrast to the usual Indian town center, with its vital hub-bub and restless air.

The most efficient means of transport to Simla is by airplane from Delhi to Chandigarh and then by taxi or bus. But if a slower method is desired, there is a direct bus route from Delhi, or if one has a nostalgic longing for a return to another age, there is a standard-gauge train from Delhi to Kalka and thence, by narrow-gauge, British-style mountain train, directly to Simla. This tiny, fascinating railway with its quaint stations, tunnels, and double-arched bridges — all of brick — is like a beautiful model.

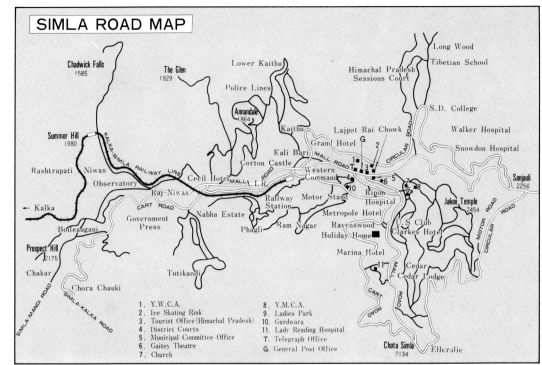

SIMLA ROAD MAP

1. Y.W.C.A.
2. Ice Skating Rink
3. Tourist Office (Himachal Pradesh)
4. District Courts
5. Municipal Committee Office
6. Gaitey Theatre
7. Church
8. Y.M.C.A.
9. Ladies Park
10. Gurdwara
11. Lady Reading Hospital
T. Telegraph Office
G. General Post Office

from a guide pamphlet, City of Simla

Hotels and Longings, Simla 1973			
Western Style Hotels	**Tel.**	**Lodging Cost, Indian Rupees**	
Baljees Grand Hotel	2347	Single	50~55
		Twin	80~90
Himland Hotel	3595	Single	20~25
		Twin	35~65
Oberoi Cecil Hotel	2073	Single	60~75
		Twin	100~135
Oberoi Clerke's Hotel	2941	Single	66~75
		Twin	100~125
Indian Style Hotels			
Aroma Hotel	3833	Single	4~10
		Twin	12~30
Ashoka Hotel	2166	Single	5~15
		Twin	10~25
Basant Hotel	3641	Twin	20~45
Bridge View Hotel	2037	Single	8~15
		Twin	15~45
Brightland Hotel	2659	Single	16~35
		Twin	35~75
Continent Hotel	3060	Single	15~35
		Twin	22~45
Flora Hotel	2027	Single	5~20
		Twin	10~35
Fountainable Hotel	3549	Single	15~35
		Twin	30~75
Gaylot Hotel	3150	Single	3~12
		Twin	5~20
Gulmarg Hotel	2109	Single	15~20
		Twin	15~55
Marina Hotel	3557	Single	8~20
		Twin	20~45

Masovic Guest House	3159	Single	8~20
		Twin	10~30
Nagson's Tourist Hotel	3399	Single	6~15
		Twin	8~25
Park View Hotel	3094	Single	5.50~10
		Twin	13~20
Pine View Hotel	3342	Single	5~15
	2715	Twin	8~30
Prestige Hotel	3601	Single	20~50
		Twin	35~60
Rocksea Hotel	2748	Single	15~20
		Twin	25~35
Simla Hotel	3218	Single	5~17
		Twin	15~35
Tashkent Hotel	2482	Single	6~12
		Twin	8~25
Thakur Hotel	2528	Single	10~20
		Twin	25~40
White Hotel	3476	Single	6~25
		Twin	10~45
Willows Hotel	2036	Single	15~30
		Twin	18~40
YMCA Hotel	3341	Single	20/head
		Twin	15/head
Government-Owned & Operated			
Wild Flower Hall	8212	Single	12
		Twin	20
Grand Hotel	2121	Single	3~13
	2587	Twin	5~20
Himachal State Operated			
Holiday Home	3971	Twin	10

Places of Interest Around Simla

1] **Jakoo Hill** (2,455 meters). This, the highest part of the city, and located in the eastern reaches, makes an ideal vantage point from which to observe the entire urban milieu.

2] **Glen** (1,830 meters). Located at the base of the northern slope, this is a prominent picnic ground in a forest setting.

3] **Chadwick Falls** (1,586 meters). Reached by descending northwestward into the forest, this waterfall of 67 meters, is especially striking in the monsoon season.

4] **Summer Hill** (1,983 meters). Identifiable by a school, Summer Hill stands west of the railway line in the western outskirts of the city.

5] **Kufri** (2,501 meters). Situated 13 kilometers from the city, this is a skiing resort area, the chief center of winter sports in India.

6] **Narkanda** (2,708 meters). Although a rather distant 64 kilometers from Simla, this location has excellent views of the Himalayas, from Southern Himachal to the northern part of Garhwal. By proceeding beyond here to the peak, **Hatu** (3,143 meters), however, the view is even better. Nearby are the town of **Kangra**, famous for miniature paintings, and **Dharmsala** (or Dharamsala), to which the Dalai Lama fled from Tibet in 1959. A bus leaves Simla daily in early morning and arrives at **Manali** in the **Kulu** Valley in early evening.

4. Trekking Courses in Himachal

In its highland catchment area on the northeastern fringe of the Pir Panjal Range, the headwaters of the **Beas River** system, which lie in the southwest portion of this area, are divided into a number of tributaries. Of these, the **Kulu Valley** trends north-south, while the **Parbati** describes an arc eastward and then southeastward from **Bhuntar**. South of this, two more valleys, both trending eastward, are the **Sainj** and **Tirthan**.

This region, which is rather a terminal one to

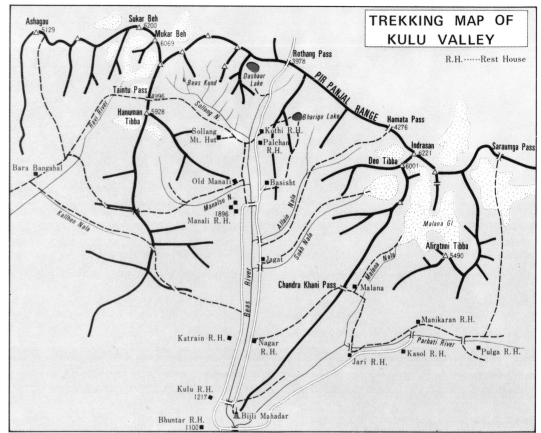

from a guide map of the Manali Mountain Climbing School.

feel the effects of the humid atmosphere of the south, nurtures not only beautiful grasslands and coniferous forests but glaciers as well. Compared to this, in the upper course of the **Chenab** River, which flows along the northern slopes of the Pir Panjal Range in the **Lahul** (Lauhul) District, or east of here, in the **Spiti** area, there are arid and semi-arid patches such as might be seen in the **Manang** and **Mustang** Districts of Nepal.

Trekking in this region is conducted from

the aforementioned town of **Manali** in the Kulu Basin, where the government maintains a school of mountaineering for the western Himalayas. This institution trains alpinists and assists programs for climbing and trekking, and in recent years, since the Indian government has favored this area in the granting of permits, the clientele for trekking and peak exploration has tended to increase. Furthermore, since 1974 when regulations were eased, allowing greater access to the **Lahul** and **Chamba** districts, the possibilities for trekking in Himachal were considerably enlarged.

The representative courses shown below are centered on the Kulu and Parbati Valleys, where the two most appropriate seasons for trekking are May to June, when flowers are in bloom, and September to October, following the monsoon. The latter is preferable perhaps because of the abundance at this season of local chestnuts and fruits. These courses are:

1] The glacial lakes of the Pir Panjal Range (about 5 days: $45 for a single person, $70 double, $120 for a party of 4, $200 for 8).

The first day trek is from Manali to **Bhrighu**, a distance of 13 kilometers, proceeding northeastward to the hot-spring of **Basisht** and continuing around this along the ridge, thence northward to glacial lake Bhrighu.

This feature is the source of the western tributary of the **Allain Nara**, and from here are excellent views of two high peaks, **Indrasan** (6,221 meters) and **Deo Tibba** (6,001 meters). Also, since the lake lies at 4,240 meters, there may be fine views over the ridges of the peaks of Lahul and Spiti.

Day two calls for a trek from Lake Bhrighi to **Rohtang Pass.**

The third day is a 6-kilometer course from Rohtang Pass to **Murrhi**, beginning with a climb to **Lake Shela Sar**, at 4,200 meters. From here, it crosses a grassland filled with alpine plants, and finally arrives at Murrhi, at 3,380 meters.

Day 4 is from Murrhi back to **Kothi**, a distance of some 6 kilometers. This begins with a descent to **Rahla**, at 2,600 meters, and then passes along the course of the Beas, where lovely water-falls are seen. Kothi, lying between a cliff on one side and a forested slope on the other, is at the apex of a road running between Kulu and Lahul, and is the site of rest house.

Day 5, from Kothi to Manali, covers the final 13 kilometers and en route it passes through the village of **Palchan**. The valley again gives

Bus Stop, Kulu.

ample evidence of glaciation, and in its characteristic U-shape would be an ideal study area for those interested in such phenomena.

2] Beas Kund to Manali Pass (about 10 days. $134 single, $210 double, $360 for a party of 4, $600 for 8).

This course has continuous, spectacular views of glacial valleys but, as in the above, certain difficulties must be anticipated. For example, there are many wild creatures here, particularly bears.

Day 1 — **Manali** to **Solang Nallah** (2,480 meters) — about 8 kilometers.

Day 2 — Solang Nallah to **Dhundi** (2,840 meters) — about 8 kilometers.

Day 3 — Dhundi to **Beas Kund** (3,540 meters) — about 6 kilometers.

Day 4 — Beas Kund to **Tentu Pass** (4,996 meters) — about 3.5 kilometers.

Day 5 — Tentu Pass to **Camping Ground** (3,856 meters) — about 10 kilometers. As in the Lahul District, this is an arid region.

Day 6 — Camping Ground to **Phulangot** (4,000 meters).

Day 7 — Phulangot to **Manali Pass** (4,988 meters) — about 6 kilometers.

Day 8 — Manali Pass to **Rani Sui** (4,200 meters) — about 6 kilometers.

Day 9 — Rani Sui to **Bhogi Thatch** (2,800 meters) — about 6 kilometers.

Day 10 — Bhogi Thatch to **Kalath** and **Manali** — 12 kilometers. The former is a hot-spring and is accessible by automobile.

3] Via Chandarkhani Pass to **Malana** and the sacred hot-spring of **Manikaran** (9 — days. $80 single, $125 double, $215, a party of 4; $360, party of 8).

Day 1 — Manali to **Naggar** — 21 kilometers along an auto road. Naggar is the traditional capital of this region.

Day 2 — Naggar to the foot of **Chandarkhani Pass** — 6 kilometers.

Day 3 — Chandarkhani Pass to Malana (2,100 meters). To go through the pass it is necessary briefly to climb a rocky surface, but from the pass there are views in all directions, and on clear days it is even possible to see Simla. Malana is rather in a world of its own, and features a temple housing the statue of an elephant which is said to have been a gift from Akbar. The village is divided into two parts and, according to custom, prospective spouses must be chosen from the opposite district.

Day 4 - Malana to **Manikaran** (1,500 meters). The latter is a sacred place on the northern bank of the Parbati River, and has hot-spring geysers whose discharges flow as falls into the river, at temperatures hot enough to cook rice. The hot-springs are also considered therapeutic for skin diseases and rheumatism. An ancient temple here has a statue of **Ram Chandra**, as well as carvings in archaic script.

Day 5 - Manikaran to **Jari**.

THE MOUNTAINS OF UTTAR PRADESH

1. Physical and Cultural Features

Upon entering Uttar Pradesh, the Himalayan mountain system becomes the upper basin of the **Ganges** (Ganga) River and its principal tributaries. And since the Ganges is considered particularly divine in Hinduism, the entire headwaters region is worshipped. Hence, it contains four such temples as, **Yamunotri, Gangotri, Kedarnath,** and **Badrinath,** where countless pilgrims regularly gather.

In this section, the main range of the Himalayas (here, remarkably regular in appearance) is arranged from northeast to southwest, close to the international boundary. **Nanda Devi** (7,817 meters), the highest peak of this segment, is located slightly east of the center of the state. These mountains, from the earliest days of Himalayan climbing, were a place of particular activity, but because of restrictions since World War II, their popularity has tended to lapse.

An outline of the main components of the mountain system of this region show that the westernmost group centers around Mt. **Bandarpunch** (6,389 meters), and makes up the headwaters of the **Yamuna (Jumna)** and **Tons** River systems. East of this are the glaciers, **Gangotri** and its tributary, **Chaturangi,** from which the **Bhagirathi** River flows, joining the **Jadh Ganga** (Janhavi) 27 kilometers downstream. **Kedarnath** (6,940 meters), to the south of Gangotri glacier, and Mt. **Chaukhamba** or **Badrinath** (7,138 meters), to its southeast, are two towering peaks of this cluster. Beneath Mt. Kedarnath

lies the glacier, Chorabari, from which the Mandakini (Mondakini) River flows. Moreover, the glaciers, **Bhagirath-Kharak** and **Satopant,** located on the eastern slopes of Mt. Chaukhamba, above, form the source of the river, **Alakananda,** along whose banks stands the temple of Badrinath. East of the **Saraswati Valley,** a northern tributary of the Alakananda, is another group of high peaks, headed by Mt. **Kamet** (7,747 meters).

The aforementioned mountain cluster is separated from the Nanda Devi cluster, to its southeast, by the **Dhauli Ganga Gorge,** with the **Pindari Glacier** and **Pindar River** in its eastern portion. East of this, as mentioned, are the mountains around Nanda Devi and **Nanda Kot** (6,861 meters), and in the extreme east are such mountains as those around **Trisul** (7,120 meters), and **Panchchuli** (6,904 meters). On the eastern side of the peak, Nanda Kot, is the glacier, **Milam,** from whose eastern extremity at the border of Nepal flows the **Kali** (or **Sarda**) River.

A particular feature of the Himalayas of Uttar Pradesh is the immense gorge through the center of the state, which creates special difficulties for the traveller. However, once this is crossed and the gently sloping grassland (or **Bugiyals**) is reached, a virtual paradise is presented, lying as it does against the great peaks, all glittering with ice and snow.

Within the gorge are U-shaped valleys fashioned during the advance of the Pleistocene ice sheet. Hence, there are dazzling views of such glacial landforms as truncated mountain spurs,

sheer rock walls, and hanging valleys, from which gush spectacular water-falls.

On the slopes below the glaciated portion are pine forests interspersed with stands of oak, and as one descends to the river terrace at about 1,000 to 2,000 meters, the first signs of human activity become apparent.

Nomadic mountain peoples here include the **Kinnauras** of the **Sutlej River** basin; the **Jedhs,** shepherds of the area around **Nilang,** a village at about 3,500 meters; the **Marchas,** who in summer only, live around **Mana,** north of the town of Badrinath; the **Anwals** of the Pindar, and the **Johris** of the Milam Valleys. In these parts, if one is not a nomad, and without the commercial stimulation provided by tourists or pilgrims, it would be almost impossible to make a living.

2. Hill Stations

Even in the height of summer when the people of the plains are gasping in extremes of heat and humidity, there are comfortable breezes blowing at higher elevations. Consequently, as a result of such favorable temperature differentials, certain hill stations and resorts were early established on ridges and near lakes, by military folk and business people from England, who at the time were the governors of India. These places thus became not only recreational sites but functioned also as centers of administration during the summer months. All such towns thus had military posts nearby, as well as a variety of inns, shops, churches, cemetaries, schools, and hospitals, and while their main purpose was to provide a comfortable atmosphere, with captivating views of the mountains as a background for routine duty, these communities were essentially places of **consumption.** As such, they were dependent largely on local sources of supply, but in locations too elevated or inaccessible, these were supplemented by such modern technology as electricity and modern water systems. Meanwhile, and in great contrast, there were also older agglomerations of traditional Indian structures, oriented around such places of **production** as pastures and cultivated fields.

Though the hill stations are called modern resorts, their architectural style seems more in keeping with a kind of classical Western tradition. Representative examples of such towns are, **Simla, Kasauli, Solon, Dagshai, Sabatha, Dalhousie, Nainital, Dharmsala** (Dharamsala),

Ranikhet, Mussoorie, Darjeeling, and Shillong, all of which are excellent viewing places for the Himalayas and the plains lying below. All are well-equipped, furthermore, with recreational facilities.

3. Mussoorie

Mussoorie can be reached by direct bus service from Delhi, although only one or two runs are made each day. On the other hand, the schedules are more liberal, both by bus and

train from Delhi to **Dehra Dun** and thence by bus to Mussoorie, so if one is willing to transfer, the trip can be made without undue regard to time. In winter, or in off-season, when views of the Himalayan Range are optimal, and when guests are few, accommodations are readily and cheaply available, but in summer, one must contend with huge throngs, anxious to savor the delights of the town, which was constructed in 1827 according to an idea attributed to a Captain Young of the Royal Navy.

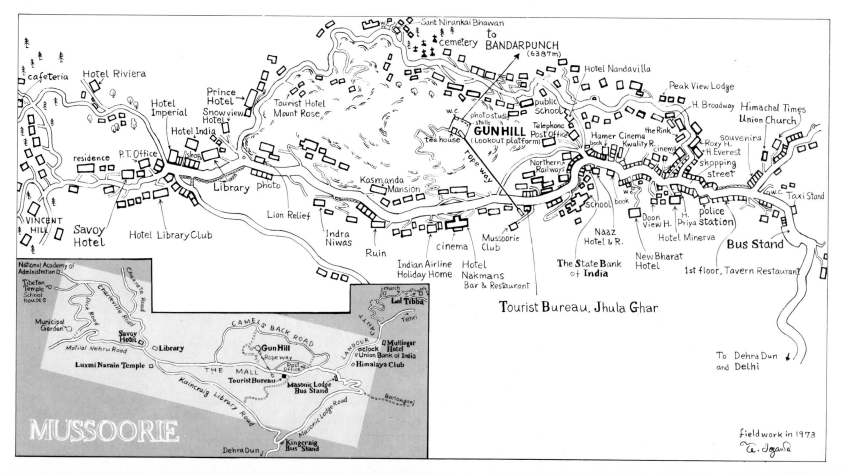

MUSSOORIE

fieldwork in 1973

The ropeway to Gun Hill in the geographical center of the town, provides access to a lookout platform and a souvenir stand run by a photographer, who also rents 'native' costumes. From here, one can see the western Garhwal cluster around Mt. Bandarpunch (6,382 meters), but such others as those around Kedarnath (6,612 meters) or Badrinath (7,068 meters) or Chaukhamba (7,138 meters), are visible only by climbing **Lal Tibba** (2,612 meters), in the eastern suburbs, near the military post.

From Mussoorie there are roads leading, among other places, to **Chakrata** in the Jumna Valley, and to **Chamba** in Garhwal, with the latter passing by a large Government-operated orchard.

The central business district lies in the southeast, between the bus terminal and Gun Hill and part way along the road toward Lal Tibba, but a circular road around the town, running north-south, links this section with the summer houses and hotels on the slopes round about.

4. Nainital

Nainital, with a current population of around 15,000, grew from a summer house built in 1841 by a British merchant named P. Barron.

Here, around a lovely high mountain lake, is a first-class resort, accessible by an excellent highway running north from the rail hub of **Kathgodam**, and which veers northward near Nainital and continues on to such places as **Almora** (1,676 meters). Prosperous apple, pear, plum, and peach orchards are seen along this road (which connects with the main highway), as it meanders along the mountain periphery and the southern lake shore and eventually reaches the bus terminal. Another road, tree-lined and peaceful, traverses the eastern lake shore and twists by a succession of hotels and shops that are arranged along it and on neighboring slopes, while theaters and movie houses occupy a broad stretch of level ground built by alluvial deposits from streams along the northern shore. From here, one can wander through hotels and a shopping area (bazar) before coming upon the city office in its calm setting in the midst of a stand of Himalayan **cryptomerias.**

Views of Nanda Devi are to be had only by circling around to the right side of the city office and then by bearing left toward **Naini Peak.** This is a walk of about two-hours from the bus stop, although it can also be reached by pony or on muleback. A rest hut at the summit serves light meals and teas.

Around Lake Nainital are numerous summer houses and sanitoriums, and nearby is an observatory, recently built, for satellite tracking. From 1975, the entire deep mountain holy region as far as such places as **Badrinath**, was made accessible. Hence, the number of foreign trekkers in this area has noticeably increased.

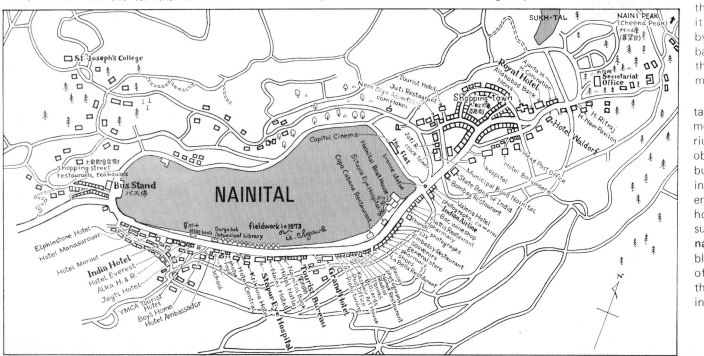

4

THE EASTERN HIMALAYAS

A Girl of Ghoom.

The Eastern Himalayas are bounded in the west by the **Kanchenjunga Himal** (mountain group), which lies along the borders of Nepal and Sikkim. The entire region can be sub-divided into two smaller sections, the **western,** made up of the Sikkim, Bhutan, and Darjeeling Himalayas, respectively, whose main mountains include **Kanchenjunga** (8,598 meters) and **Pauhunri** (7,128 meters), along the Sikkim-Bhutan border; **Chomo Lhari** (7,314 meters), on the Bhutan boundary at the border of the Peoples Republic of China; **Kula Kangri** (7,539 meters), east of this, and one more of obscure designation directly south, at 7,541 meters.

The eastern portion of this region, occupying the entire eastern part of Bhutan, and also known as the **Assam Himalayas,** is a bone of contention between India and the Peoples Republic of China. The former claims jurisdiction over the whole chain, from the Bhutan-Tibet border all the way eastward to the **Brahmaputra Valley,** including its stupendous gorge in the vicinity of **Namcha Barwa.** Consequently, the region was designated the **Northeast Frontier Agency** (NEFA) by the Indian Government, which attempted to strengthen its presence here, and more recently the name has been changed to **Arunachal Pradesh.**

This impressive mountain region lies between Mt. **Kangto** (7,090 meters) on the border of Tibet, north-northwest of the town of Riang, and **Namcha Barwa** (7,756 meters), the final eastern manifestation of the Himalayas, and the peaks it contains all measure up to Himalayan proportions, reaching such heights as 6,923, 4,920, 5,735, 5,044, and 5,966 meters, respectively, from west to east. Lying north of this rampart is the winding course of the Brahmaputra River (here known as the **Tsangpo**), along whose banks lies the peak, **Gyala Peri** (7,151 meters), whose presence forces the river into its characteristic comma-like meander bend in this sector.

Since to visit the entire region described above requires special Governmental permission, it would be well either to have obtained this beforehand at an Indian embassy, or, if not, to have made application at the appropriate agency in New Delhi or at the branch office in Calcutta. However, since this latter course might be a slow process, one should be prepared to exercise patience.

1. Arrival

As one alights and pushes his way into the steaming atmosphere of Calcutta, it is first necessary to ascend the gentle ramp to the second floor of the airport building, and during this interval if the arrival is at night, leaf-hoppers and moths will be seen in clouds around the flourescent lamps. When the quarantine and visa check are completed, one then descends the stair to the baggage claim area.

Some time later, when customs officials have been satisfied (see the section on Delhi), one will perhaps be free to depart the compound and to be met by the familiar horde of adults and children imploring for permission to assist in carrying baggage. Taxi and bus services are similar to those in Delhi, but since the bus (coach) departs **Dum Dum Airport** for Calcutta from the Domestic terminal and this is separated by some distance, there is some incovenience on this score. Certain airlines, however, provide free shuttle service, so the traveller should have ascertained this earlier.

The taxi trip, at 10-15 Rupees, takes about 30 minutes; the bus fare is 5 Rupees. And as one travels through the suburbs, noting such views as those of people casting nets into fish-cultivation ponds, or of trains being hauled by electric engines, the city is gradually entered. Calcutta has a rather seedy Western appearance, punctuated by densely crowded high-rise apartments, shops, and such, almost as though these were a kind of motif.

Calcutta is nonetheless a place of great vigor. Whereas most of us would soon wilt in such heat and humidity, the local people seem tireless. At the same time, there are those among them who dwell simply on porches or directly on the pavement, and one becomes quickly aware of their penetrating expressions.

Hotels can be had for as little as 10 Rupees, single, and prices range from this up to about 180 Rupees, but in the hot season, from April until September, and especially from April to June, it is much too uncomfortable to consider being without air-conditioning.

2. Life and Living

Before registering at a hotel desk, one should make sure of such matters at the nature of the accommodations and the time for morning call.

If the purpose here is merely to transfer flights, obviously almost any hotel will do. However, if one wishes to obtain clearances for climbing or even if the object is sight-seeing, since especially the uninitiated should follow a program that calls for the least expenditure of effort, a hotel should be chosen with one's purposes in mind.

Permission to visit places such as **Siliguri**, **Darjeeling** and **Kalimpong**, can be obtained from the **Foreigners Regional Registration Officer** at **Ran Jan 237 Lower Circular Road** in southern Calcutta. And to enter such areas of Assam as **Gauhati, Jorhat, Manas,** or **Kaziranga,** one ahould visit **Assam House, 8 Russel Street, Calcutta 71,** or for **Shillong** in the state of Meghalaya, **Meghalaya House, 9-10 Russel Street, Calcutta 71.**

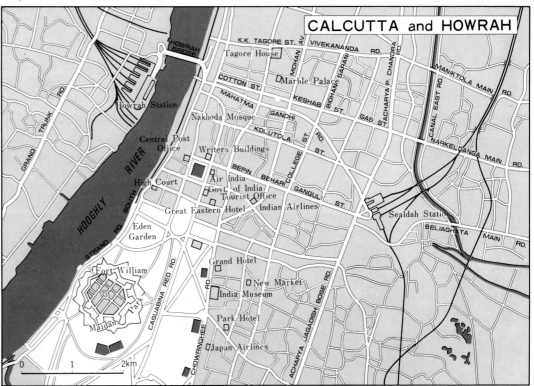

from a guide pamphlet.

If one is on a simple tour by air from Calcutta to **Gauhati**; thence by bus or taxi to **Shillong**, and if the period of stay is to be brief, no special permission is needed. But if the mode of travel is by train or any other overland means, clearance is necessary for both Assam and Meghalaya. And if one wishes to get off at **Siliguri** or other particular places in West Bengal, official sanction is also required.

DARJEELING AND THE SIKKIM HIMALAYAS

1. Physical and Cultural Features

Parallel north-south aligned ranges are a special feature of the Himalayas of this area. Here also is the basin of the **Tista River**, flowing south from Tibet, and which formerly was used by climbers headed for the Everest region.

From **Kanchenjunga** (8,598 meters), the highest peak of the **western part** of this sector, the **Singalila Range** runs southward as it declines in elevation and forms the border with Nepal, and in its northern portion, present and Pleistocene glaciers have formed a series of tablelands, from which rise such peaks as **Kangchengyao** (6,889 meters) and **Chomo Yummo** (6,829 meters), while in the **eastern part** is the **Dongkya Range**, containing Mt. **Pauhunri** (7,128 meters), **Mt. Chugalung** (5,759 meters), and **Mt. Dopendikang** (5,359 meters).

South of the above is the Darjeeling area of West Bengal, with such peaks as **Singalila** (3,679 meters), at the borders of Nepal, Sikkim, and Darjeeling; **Phalut** (3,596 meters), to its south, and finally, **Sandakphu** (3,323 meters). All these areas have trekking courses.

The capital of Sikkim is **Gangtok** (1,770

meters), which is linked to **Siliguri** by a fine automobile road, and which, from ancient times was a center of trade, commerce, and religion for the then independent kingdom of Sikkim, but its status was changed in 1974 when the country came under the jurisdiction of India, and it is now a local administrative center.

The people of the area were originally Lepchas and Tibetans but tribes from Nepal and the lowlands of Bengal were added in the course of time. These latter adhere to Hinduism while the former are generally Lamaists.

2. Darjeeling

Darjeeling, a hill-station with a present population of about 42,000, is situated at about 2,100 meters, and is 90 kilometers north of the Bagdogra airport.

The flight by turbo-prop aircraft from Calcutta to **Bagdogra** takes only about 1½ hours, but another 3-hours are needed for the motor trip from here to Darjeeling. Otherwise, one can make the trip by regular train from Calcutta to Siliguri in 16-hours, with another 7½ hours to Darjeeling by narrow-gauge railway. For 25-45 Rupees, there is also a night bus which runs from Calcutta to Siliguri in

12-hours, if one is interested in such alternatives.

Lodging costs for first-class tourist hotels in Darjeeling are 30-80 Rupees, single, and in Indian-style or less-expensive places, beds and rooms are available for 5-20 Rupees. Travellers should consult reputable West Bengali travel agents, who are known for their kindness to tourists.

It is customary in Darjeeling to go by jeep to observe **Kanchenjunga**, and to see the sunrise from **Tiger Hill**. However, it is also charming to relax in a lodge near the viewing places and spend a whole day enjoying the scenery.

As suggested, since the town of Darjeeling features not only fine views of Kanchenjunga, a famous narrow-gauge railway, and a cryptomeria forest, but also such interesting local folk as the **Lepchas** and **Nepalese**, when one approaches here from the west, there may be the sudden feeling that one has entered the world

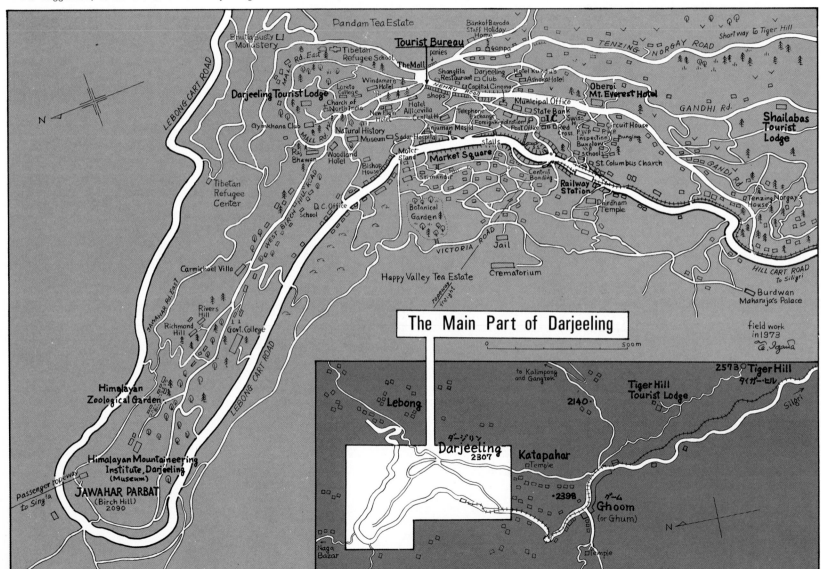

The Main Part of Darjeeling

field work in 1973

of Asia.

Although the scene around Darjeeling contains sporadic stands of the **giant cryptomeria** which are generally regarded as a natural peculiarity of the site, these trees were originally imported from Japan during the **Meiji Period** (1868-1912) and, probably because of the similarity in the bio-geographical setting, they have since become like native forms.

Place of Interest Around Darjeeling

1) Himalayan views from **Tiger Hill** (2,590 meters).
2) **Lake Senchal** — Situated about 10 kilometers from Darjeeling, this is actually a reservoir for the town's water system.
3) **Batasia Loop** — Located along the narrow-gauge line, about 5 kilometers from Darjeeling.
4) **Ghoom (Lamaist) Monastery**
5) **The Himalayan Mountaineering Institute** and **Zoological Park**.
6) **The Natural History Museum**.
7) **Lloyds Botanical Garden**
8) **The Tibetan Refugee Self-Help Center**.
9) **Happy Valley Tea Estate**.

3. Kalimpong

The course from Darjeeling to Kalimpong begins with a return to **Ghoom** and then turns eastward and down along the ridge until the **Tista River** is seen below. It then zig-zags down the slope and across the bridge, from which the river will appear cloudy and grayish-green, as is typical of water that flows from a pool at the end of a glacial train. From here, the road ascends an incline through cultivated fields and reaches the summit area, or the rim of a **col**, along which, from north to south, lies the town of **Kalimpong** (1,200 meters).

As Kalimpong is known as a gateway to Sikkim and Bhutan, it is also the site of a local market, held each Wednesday and Saturday, so

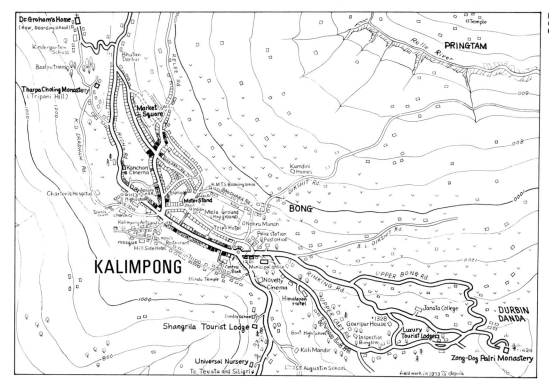

on these days particularly the town atmosphere is enlivened by visitors from these and other distant places. Connections from Darjeeling are usually by public jeep, at 9 Rupees for a front seat. There are also regular buses running from Kalimpong to Siliguri and **New Jalpaiguri**. In Kalimpong, there are at least two tourist lodges and three regular hotels, but it is best to have procured reservations at state-run tourist agencies in either Calcutta or Darjeeling.

Places of Interest Around Kalimpong

1. **Dr. Graham's House** — This is really a boarding school, located half-way up the gentle slope of Mt. **Deolo** (1,696 meters), northeast of the town. The compound includes a dormitory capable of housing 18 persons, and a large church.
2. **The Tharpa Choiling Monastery (Tripani Hill)** — A (Yellow-Hat) Lamaist temple and school near Dr. Graham's House, where groups of juvenile acolytes can always be seen in attitudes of prayer and meditation.
3. **The Arts and Crafts Center** — Near the **Col**, opposite the girl's senior high school.
4. **The Zong-Dog Palri Monastery** — Located on **Durbin Danda**, a low hill in the southern part of the town, where a new concrete Lamaist temple is presently under construction.
5. **The Universal Nursery** — Reached by taking the road leading down to the Tista River to a point where there are a series of terraces buttressed by rock walls. Here, in green-

houses, various kinds of orchids and cacti are cultivated, and surrounding these are **amaryllis** gardens, whose blossoms are seen to best advantage in the month of April.

6. **Gouripur House.**
7. **The Swiss Welfare Dairy.**

ASSAM

1. Physical and Cultural Features.

The **Himalayas of Bhutan** (or the **Easternmost Himalayas**) are currently closed to foreign visitors by Government order. The local people here maintain a rather primitive life-style which was virtually untouched by outside influences, even during the long British colonial period — a situation which continued under the Indian government after independence in 1947. More recently, however, in order to bolster its own presence and to oppose efforts toward expansion by the Chinese, the Indian government has been building roads and installing more modern facilities. The name has also been changed to **Arunachal Pradesh,** although the mountain ranges, as in the past, are still known as the **Assam Himalayas.**

The western portion of this area, as mentioned, is dominated by a high cluster of peaks around Mt. **Kangto** (7,090 meters), but there are at least three other clusters, whose glimmering cover of ice and snow is an additional attraction in this area. All belong to the **Bharali River Basin**, a tributary of the Brahmaputra, into whose waters the Bharali rushes headlong.

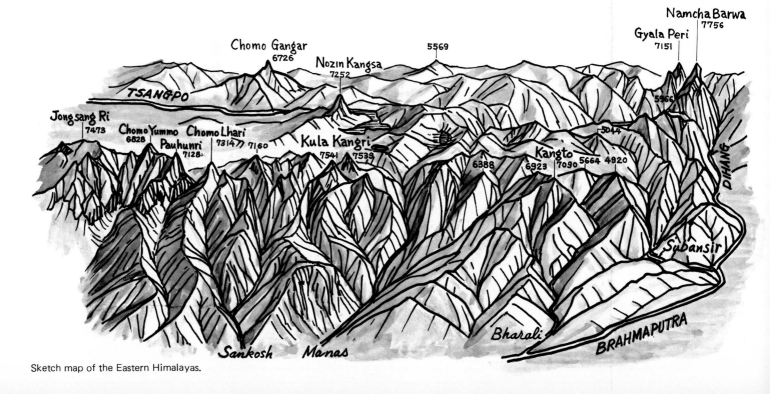

Sketch map of the Eastern Himalayas.

East of this is the basin of the **Subansir River**, surrounded by mountains in the 5,000 meter class. And finally in the extreme east is **Namcha Barwa**.

Assam, in northeastern India, is also, as stated early in this volume, representative of the so-called 'Laurel Forest Cultural Complex', which spreads eastward from here through South China and even to Japan. Here one finds silkworm cultivation and the production of material, the making of lacquer-ware, the growing of tea, **milpa** or slash-and-burn agriculture, the cultivation of **paddy** (irrigated rice) and the brewing of rice liquor.

Tea gardens occupy the lowest stratum of the forest canopy, at least where trees have been planted. Tea factories also dot the scene and houses are constructed amost entirely of bamboo, from the roofs to the walls and ridge poles. However, since this is also India's primary area for petroleum production, one also sees forests of petroleum derricks.

Since travel is permitted in the lowlands of the gently-flowing Brahmaputra, one should apply, as noted, for a visitor's permit at Assam House in Calcutta.

2. Gauhati and Shillong

Shillong, a hill-top city and Assam's capital, is located in the center of the Meghalaya District, and is accessible by taxi or bus from the large city of **Gauhati**, on the southern bank of the Brahmaputra. The latter, which was once the capital of an ancient emperor, **Pragjotishpur**,

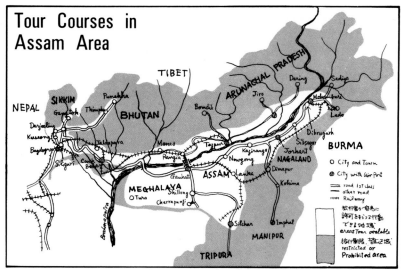

known as the 'Light of the East', has been modernized to become a node of land, sea, and air transport, and is the gateway to Assam. Here also, since there are numerous schools, research institutes, and a university, one can see why Gauhati is the educational center of the district.

An iron bridge, as though it were connecting India with eastern Asia, spans the broad Brahmaputra at this point, linking Gauhati with its northern suburbs. Buses run from here to Shillong six times each day from the bus terminal located south of the station at the foot of an over-pass, although it can be reached as well by a five-minute walk north from the office of Indian Airlines, where airport limousines deposit passenger arrivals. Tickets for the 3-hour, 103 kilometer journey by de luxe bus to Shillong, are purchasable here for 6 Rupees 50 Paisa. The mimeographed thickets of about post-card size, contain the prices and destinations written in pencil. And since during the trip, the bus stops for a long rest, it is pleasant to have tea during this interval or to frequent the stalls near the rest-stop which dispense

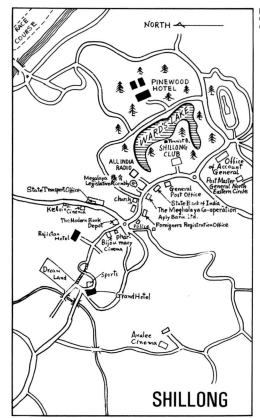

pineapples, bananas, and various local varieties of squash. One may also note with interest the many ways the local people have of weaving bamboo into the sides of their houses.

Shillong, at about 1,500 meters, features a park and pond in the center, surrounded by a pine forest, bounded, in turn, by a labyrinth of roads. Places of interest hereabouts include **Burra Bazar**, **Shillong Peak** (with views of the Himalayas of Bhutan and Assam), and **Cherrapunji**, 58 kilometers south, which is famous as the place with the highest rainfall (about 11,630 mm/year) on earth. Lodgings include the comfortable **Pinewood Hotel** (Phone 3116), the **Peak Hotel** (Phone 3145), and the **Shillong Tourist Bungalow** (Phone 4933).

3. Jorhat and Kaziranga

The town of **Jorhat**, located on the south bank of the Brahmaputra, is situated slightly east of the center of Assam. Around the town, fields of Assam tea are laid out in all directions, but since many rather tall (20 meter) trees have been planted at irregular intervals, the view from the air is one of a sparse woodland. It is diverting to fly to Jorhat and to visit an ancient meander bend on the southern bank of the river where there is now a large tropical swamp containing such interesting fauna as the one-horned rhinocerous and the wild buffalo. However, if one wishes to visit a wild animal refuge, the **Kaziranga Sanctuary** is located 97 kilometers west of Jorhat — a trip made to best advantage in the months of February and March when there is the least fog and the vegetation is thinnest. Since the number of lodging places and available rooms, not to mention the elephants which provide transport, are all in limited supply, however, one should make reservations by calling the **Tourist Information Officer,** at **Kaziranga 3,** or by visiting the **Government Tourist Offices** in Calcutta.

Upon flight arrival in Jorhat, before continuing to Kaziranga, one should stop immediately at the Indian Arilines office and confirm the return reservation. Charges, single, for round-trip taxi fare to Kaziranga, one night's lodging and meals, and a guided tour by elephant transport to and from the animal refuge, are about 300-400 Rupees, but only 200 Rupees per person in parties of 2 or 3.

Since animals are plentiful here, one is almost certain to see rhinocerouses, wild elephants, various deer, wild boars, buffaloes, and water birds. Occasionally, the experience is enlivened by the retrieval of a stray deer horn by a transporting elephant, some lucky passenger thus receiving a prized souvenir.

Another pleasant place to visit when in operation, is the market located nearby in **Deling**, where it is amusing to see such items on display as fresh limes, small fish, arrow and spear heads, and vegetables that appear to be the prototypes of eggplant and cucumbers. Here, one can also encounter people who represent certain tribes not otherwise seen in India.

Assam also has the **Manas Animal Sanctuary** and three hot-spring resorts, but if one is planning to visit here in the first place, it would be a pity to omit side-trips to **Mohanbari** and **Lirabari**, the most remote locations that are officially open to tourists. The **Assam Frontier Travel Service** in Jorhat (Phone Jorhat 664, or cable AFONTRAVEL) can arrange all guide and tour services and accommodations.

Kaziranga Tourist Life

Author's Postscript and Acknowledgements

While travel guides are normally compiled from the recorded experiences of many, this volume has tried to center its presentation around data accumulated by the writer himself in his travels in the area. This work is thus a kind of distillation of personal experiences, illuminated most importantly by maps which, in the writer's opinion, are the ultimate means of geographic expression. Therefore, the cartographic, photographic, and other illustrations in this volume — the vast majority of which have been created by the writer — are presented as additional evidence of the author's feelings and reactions to these places. The business of compiling data by means of field surveys entailing numerous visits, and of writing the text and preparing the illustrations took nearly five years to complete — from 1972 to 1976. During this period some five months (November 20, 1972 — April 21, 1973) were spent in on-the-spot field surveys, but previously, for nearly three months (September to November, 1970), the writer was a member of the Makalu Expedition of the Tokai Branch of the Japan Alpine Club, followed by two more months in the area (December 1971 to January 1972) at the Nepal Explorers Academy (AMKAS). Finally, from November 1974 to February 1975, the writer was included in the Glaciological Expedition Team to Nepal 1974 (GEN-'74). Thus, this work is based mainly on the information and experiences accumulated as a result of these various undertakings.

Although my original purpose was to offer a pleasant and colorful volume at a reasonable price, and one that might be found not only on study desks but also on coffee tables in living rooms, no sooner had the field work begun in earnest than prices rose to the point of frustrating most of these initial hopes. Originally also, I had intended to personally draw all the maps, but after completing half the section on Kashmir I realized that this was a challenge — similar to that of climbing the length of the Himalayas — which might, in itself, take 10 years to complete. The book, therefore, contains five comprehensive maps, and certain others that were mechanically transcribable from my field sketches or from my collection of illustrated pamphlets, that have been produced through the courtesy of the Senshu Drafting Company.

However, despite the difficulties entailed, that the book was finally completed is due in great measure to the cooperation and assistance of many individuals, some of whom I wish to mention here.

First, are those responsible for the basic planning, editing, and publication — the members of the Yama-Kei Publishers Company, particularly its former president, Mr. Kichizo Kawasaki, and its executive director, Mr. Yoshitake Murakami, director of the First Publications Section, and Mr. Masatsune Abe, Head of the Drafting Department.

During the field surveys I was accompanied by Mr. Shuji Okazawa, and I wish also to thank Yasumasa Tsuji of Air India, also Mr. Pran Nath Seth, Director, and Ms Noriko Toyoshima, of the Government of India Tourist Office's Tokyo branch, as well as Ms Asha K. Malhotra, Director of this agency's office in New Delhi. I am grateful as well to various persons at the Tourist Reception Center, Srinagar; to Mr. Harnam Singh, Director of the Manali Mountaineering Institute; to Mr. P.R. Mahajau of Simla; Mr. Gangli and Mrs. Shanta Banerjee of the Government of India Tourist Office, Calcutta; to Ms M. Ghalay of the West Bengal State Tourist Office, Darjeeling, and to Mr. Mukhia of Kalimpong. Among those who offered particular assistance in Nepal are Dr. H. Gurung of the H.M.G. (Government) Planning Committee; various members of the Japanese Embassy in Kathmandu; Mr. Takeshi Miyahara and Mr. and Mrs. Ohgawara of the Everest View Hotel; Mr. Saburo Suzuki of Nippon Koei; the manager of the Kathmandu office of Tiger Tops Jungle Lodge and to Mr. J. Edwards and many others at the lodge itself; to Mr. James Roberts of Mountain Travel; Mr. Yuji Maruo, currently on the staff of Tribhuvan University and to such other staff members there as Krishna Kumal Pradhan, Subaruna Krishna Shrestha, and Dharma Ratna Silikpar; to the **Sirdar**, Karma Sherpa, and Jambu Sherpa, later appointed a **Sirdar**, and to Nimanorbu Sherpa who trekked with us; also to Mr. Goswamy of AIR TV, Srinagar; Mr. C.L. Sah Thulghara of Nainital.

Further, I wish to acknowledge the work of Mr. Yugo Ono, currently of Tsukuba University, of Shoichi Aoyagi and Nobuko Hongo of the Japan Tourist Cultural Institute, and of Mitsuru Hirose a Design Director of Sogo Kobo, in structuring and editing the volume and in arranging the field notes, pictures, maps, and photographs. Mr. Hirose was responsible for editing the basic format, and Mr. Aoyagi for the text, and the final layout was arranged by Mr. Toshio Inoue — to all of whom I express my warmest thanks. In conclusion, I wish to reiterate my feeling of gratitude to Mr. Yoshitake Murakami of the Yama-Kei Publishers Company for overseeing the entire operation.

Lastly, let me add a word of thanks, in no sense less-earnestly felt than those expressed above, to my wife, Yoshiko, and to other members of my family, for their forebearance and understanding while I was constrained to devote my time and energy to the task of completing this volume.

For the English edition of this book, the author wishes to publicly acknowledge his sincere thanks to Mrs. Michiko U. Kornhauser and Professor David H. Kornhauser for their admirable translation.

208 Sincere thanks are also due to Mr. H.C. Sarin, President of the Indian Mountaineering Association, who has provided the foreward.

Tomoya Iozawa

January 13, 1980

Résumé:

Tomoya Iozawa, born 1933, Yamagata Prefecture, Japan.

- 1954-63 As a member of the Doppyo Tokokai (Alpine Club), climbed variation routes of Mt. Yatsugatake, the buttress of Mt. Kitadake, Kashima-Yari, and participated in survey of Uonuma Sanzan and the Okutadami Mountain Region of Japan.

- 1957 Graduated from Tokyo University of Education, Department of Geography, Faculty of Science.
  Thesis: Landforms of Kashima Yari, and the Ice Block of the Kakunezato Area.

- 1957-70 Cartographer, Geographical Survey Institute, Tokyo, participating in experimental program to interpret the fallen snow by means of aerial photographs.

- 1970 Resigned from Geographical Survey Institute, joined Makalu Research Team and studied glacial landforms in the Himalayas and Japan.

- Main Publications:
  'Tozansha no tameno Chikeizu Tokuhon' (Map Reading and Landform Analysis. A Handbook for Mountain Climbers.) 1967, revised in 1972.

Translators:

Michiko Usui Kornhauser, born Japan, 1936, Graduated Okayama University, 1959; Grantee, East-West Center, Honolulu, Hawaii, 1961–1963. Married, 1965.

David H. Kornhauser, born Philadelphia, 1918, Professor of Geography, University of Hawaii; Graduate of University of Michigan; Special Interest, Japanese cities and city life.

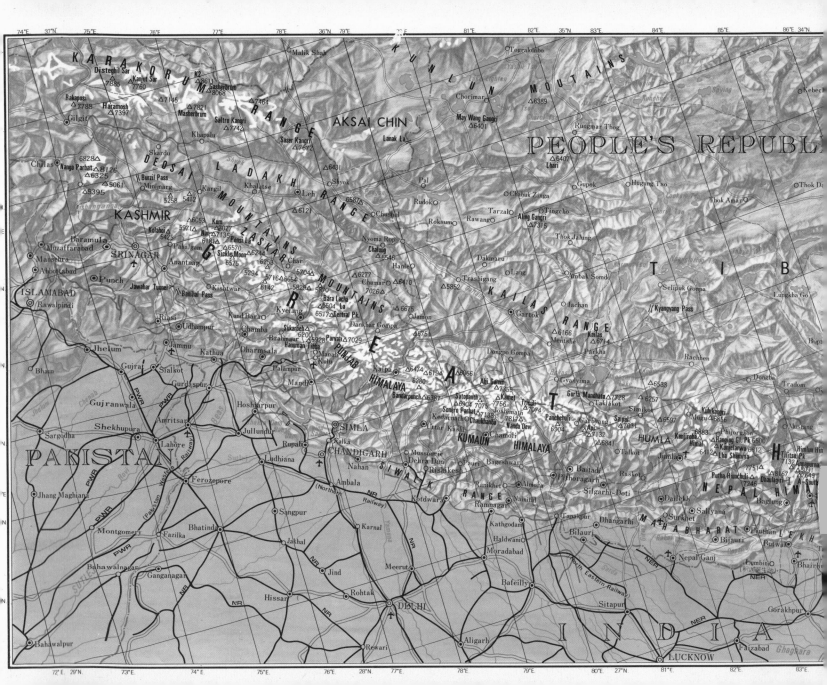